Routledge Revivals

Defence Science and Technology

Defence Science and Technology (1993) discusses the key questions surrounding defence and civil industry, highlighting the complex nature of this relationship and the equally complex determinants of corporate government policy in this area. Defence-related industries are central to the economies of most of the advanced nations, with defence and civil industrial bases often inextricably linked.

Defence Science and Technology

Adjusting to Change

Edited by
Richard Coopey, Matthew R.H. Uttley and Graham Spinardi

Routledge
Taylor & Francis Group

First published in 1993]
by Harwood Academic Publishers

This edition first published in 2026 by Routledge
4 Park Square, Milton Park, Abingdon, Oxon, OX14 4RN

and by Routledge
605 Third Avenue, New York, NY 10017

Routledge is an imprint of the Taylor & Francis Group, an informa business

Publisher's Note
The publisher has gone to great lengths to ensure the quality of this reprint but points out that some imperfections in the original copies may be apparent.

Disclaimer
The publisher has made every effort to trace copyright holders and welcomes correspondence from those they have been unable to contact.

A Library of Congress record exists under LCCN: 93001362

ISBN: 978-1-041-25601-4 (hbk)
ISBN: 978-1-003-74743-7 (ebk)
ISBN: 978-1-041-25606-9 (pbk)

Book DOI 10.4324/9781003747437

DEFENCE SCIENCE AND TECHNOLOGY

Adjusting to Change

Edited by

Richard Coopey
Business History Unit
London School of Economics and Political Science, UK

Matthew R. H. Uttley
Centre for Defence Economics
University of York, UK

and

Graham Spinardi
Research Centre for Social Science
University of Edinburgh, UK

harwood academic publishers
Switzerland • Australia • Belgium • France • Germany • Great Britain • India • Japan • Malaysia • Netherlands • Russia • Singapore • USA

Harwood Academic Publishers

Private Bag 8
Camberwell, Victoria 3124
Australia

58, rue Lhomond
75005 Paris
France

Glinkastrasse 13-15
O-1086 Berlin
Germany

Post Office Box 90
Reading, Berkshire RG1 8JL
Great Britain

3-14-9, Okubo
Shinjuku-ku, Tokyo 169
Japan

Emmaplein 5
1075 AW Amsterdam
Netherlands

820 Town Center Drive
Langhorne, Pennsylvania 19047
United States of America

Library of Congress Cataloging-in-Publication Data

Defence science and technology : adjusting to change / edited by
Richard Coopey, Graham Spinardi, Matthew Uttley.
p. cm. -- (Studies in defence economics ; v. 3)
Includes index.
ISBN 3-7186-5400-8
1. Military research. 2. Defense industries. I. Coopey, R. (Richard) II. Spinardi, Graham. III. Uttley, Matthew. IV. Series : Studies in defence economics (Chur, Switzerland) ; v. 3.
U390.D44 1993
355'.07--dc20 93-1362
CIP

 Printed in Singapore.

Contents

Acknowledgements

This research was conducted with funding from the Economic and Social Research Council (ESRC) and administered by the Science Policy Support Group (SPSG). Discussions with Peter Healey (SPSG) helped to formulate collaboration between the various contributors, and eventually to the present structure of the book. Despite the pivotal role of both ESRC and SPSG in making this edition possible, the opinions expressed herein do not necessarily reflect the view of either institution.

Thanks are extended to Professor Keith Hartley who made the facilities of the Centre for Defence Economics available for preparation of the final manuscript. The editors are also indebted to Nicholas Hooper, the deputy director of the Centre for Defence Economics, who meticulously read the entire manuscript and submitted helpful comments and constructive criticisms. In addition, Philip Gummett and Donald Mackenzie provided invaluable advice on the preparation of Chapter 1. Any deficiencies are, of course, the responsibility of the editors themselves.

Last but not least, the editors express thanks to Margaret Cafferky, Roberta Blackburn and Barbara Butler who bore the brunt of secretarial and editorial assistance in the final stages of publication.

Contributors

David Buck is a research fellow in the Centre for Defence Economics at the University of York. His research interests include defence economics and military research and development. Recent publications include *Defence Industries and Equipment Procurement Options* with N. Hooper, in S. Kirby and N. Hooper, and *The Cost of Peace* (Harwood Academic Publishers, Chur, 1991).

Dr Richard Coopey is currently a research officer in the Business History Unit at the London School of Economics. He has previously held research posts at the University of Wisconsin, Madison, and the University of Manchester. He is joint editor with S. Fielding and N. Tiratsoo of *The Wilson Years* (Pinter, London, 1992).

Dr Martin Edmonds is director of the Centre for Defence and International Security Studies (CDISS) at Lancaster University, and editor-in-chief of *Defense Analysis*. His research interests include civil-military relations and defence analysis. Recent publications include *Armed Forces and Society* (Westview, Boulder, 1990).

Dr Philip Gummett is reader in Government and Technology Policy at the University of Manchester. He has numerous publications in defence technology policy including (with J. Reppy, ed.) *The Relations between Defence and Civil Technologies* (Kluwer, Dordrecht, 1988).

Professor Keith Hartley is director of IRISS and the Centre for Defence Economics at the University of York, and editor of *Defence Economics*. His research interests include defence economics, procurement and collaboration. Recent publications include *The Economics of Defence Policy* (Brassey's, London, 1991).

Professor Donald MacKenzie is in the Department of Sociology at the University of Edinburgh. His primary research interests is the sociology of the social history of science and technology. Recent publications include *Inventing Accuracy: A Historical Sociology of Nuclear Missile Guidance* (MIT, 1990).

Dr Stephen Martin is a research fellow in the Centre for Defence Economics at the University of York. His research interests include international collaboration in industry and all aspects of government-mandated counter-trade. Recent publications include "European Collaboration in Aerospace: Recent Trends and Future Prospects", *European Research*, Vol. 2, Pt. 6, November 1991.

Dr Stephen Schofield is a research fellow in the Department of Science and Technology Policy at the University of Manchester. His research interests include arms conversion and he is currently involved in preparing a report on defence science and technology for the Parliamentary Office of Science and Technology (POST).

Dr Graham Spinardi is a research fellow in the Research Centre for Social Sciences at the University of Edinburgh. His primary research interest is the social study of technology. Recent publications include *Polaris to Trident: The Development of US Fleet Ballistic Missile Technology* (Cambridge University Press, Cambridge, 1993).

Matthew Uttley is a research fellow in the Centre for Defence Economics at the University of York, and an honorary research associate of CDISS, Lancaster University. His research interests include weapons acquisition and competition policy in the UK defence sector. Recent publications include ''Contracting-out and Market Testing in the UK Defence Sector: Theory, Evidence and Issues,'' *Public Money and Management*, January–March 1993.

William Walker is a senior fellow in the Science Policy Research Unit at the University of Sussex. He is currently researching defence technology policy towards nuclear proliferation. He is joint editor, with C. Freeman and M. Sharp, of *Technology and the Future of Europe* (Macmillan, London, 1992).

Chapter 1

Defence Science and Technology: Setting the Scene

Richard Coopey, Graham Spinardi and Matthew Uttley

The Changing Defence Environment

The late 1980s and early 1990s have witnessed profound change in the international security environment. For over forty years after the Second World War the security perceptions of Western industrialised states were defined in terms of bipolar East-West conflict; a system predicated upon a clearly identifiable adversary in the Soviet Union, which necessitated high and predictably incremental levels of expenditure on equipment and manpower[1]. The demise of the Soviet Union and the fragmentation of the Warsaw Pact has forced a fundamental reevaluation of defence policies, weapons procurement strategies and research and development (R&D) agendas throughout the NATO Alliance. The process of reexamination, however, is further complicated by new risks and uncertainties both within Europe and elsewhere in the world: regional instabilities in the Gulf, former Yugoslavia, and the political and economic restructuring of Eastern Europe.

Events in the international milieu have had immediate effects on defence policy in the United Kingdom which are mirrored throughout Western Europe. First, the downgrading of the military threat posed by the Warsaw Pact is reflected in declining defence budgets: as a share of national output, UK defence expenditure is currently expected to fall from 3.9% of GDP in 1990-91 to 3.2% in 1995-96[2]. Second, the process of adjustment is taking place under popular anticipation of a 'peace dividend'. At issue here is the mechanism by which national defence research, development and production capacity will respond to declining military demand.

The prospect of long-term declines in defence expenditure raises two central issues for UK defence science and technology. Planners are confronted with the task of identifying potential conflict scenarios, and formulating appropriate defence science and technology policy responses to meet future equipment requirements. Not only is the assessment of these requirements problematic, but there are other complicating factors. Under new budgetary regimes, defence ministries and armed forces face an increasingly difficult range of choices including manpower versus equipment; quantity versus the quality of equipment; nuclear versus conventional forces; and army versus naval versus air forces. Furthermore, being self-reliant in defence technology is no longer an option for the UK. Consequently, questions emerge over the implications of technological dependence on overseas suppliers if the UK seeks to offset defence cuts by importing defence equipment and materiel from abroad. Similarly, budgetary constraints raise questions of the opportunities and costs associated with both international collaboration in the development and production of future defence systems, and of the role defence science and technology will have in the process of European integration.

Changing threat perceptions have also raised questions of economic, rather than military, threats to national security. In the USA, in particular, the growth of national indebtedness during the 1980s provoked fears about economic competitiveness, and a feeling that federal R&D funding (of which an increasing proportion was devoted to defence R&D) could be exploited more fully in generating economically beneficial innovations[3]. Albeit from a different starting point, declining defence budgets brought about by the end of the Cold War, and the anticipation of a substantial restructuring of defence industries has focused attention on the relationship of defence R&D and production to economic performance throughout Western Europe.

Defence Science and Technology

Problems with both definition and data arise in attempting to say what defence science and technology comprises. The delineation between science and technology is by no means obvious, especially in many of the high technology areas which characterise much modern military R&D. Science and technology are indeed such interrelated disciplines, and ones involving such similar practices, that they can be considered together as, in Latour's term, 'technoscience'[4].

Attempts to distinguish science and technology are possible. However, they may not only suggest a false dichotomy, but also a misleading relationship between the two. Thus some see technology as simply "the appliance of science". For example, John Garnett states that: "The genesis of a weapon system ... begins with a piece of theoretical science"[5]. This unidirectional and deterministic view finds little support in historical and sociological studies of science and technology[6]. What emerges instead is a picture of two related disciplines, often with many interactions by which one can stimulate developments in the other.

In the changed world situation, with reduced defence budgets and anxieties over economic performance, a number of key questions arise concerning defence science and technology:-

- What influence does the specifically military origins of funding have on the content of technological development?
- Have high levels of defence research and development (R&D) represented a wasteful use of resources, or do defence technologies generate useful spin-offs?
- What is the potential for conversion of defence industries and what role should government play in this process?
- With declining defence budgets incentives may be created to seek cheaper military equipment and components from overseas sources. Under these circumstances, how will the UK economy be affected if aspects of advanced R&D

cease to be conducted indigenously?

Collaborative weapons development offers a mechanism for pooling defence research, development and production resources. What role is collaboration likely to play in the post-Cold War defence procurement process?

. What role is the Single European Market (SEM) likely to play in the future of defence and civil science and technology?

Answering these questions requires the analysis of a range of relationships and processes, both historical and contemporary. Thus the chapters in this book draw upon a number of disciplines and differing analytical methods. The primary focus is on the UK, but the conclusions are intended to provide a basis for international comparison. Each chapter in the book is self-contained and presents the authors view on one aspect of UK or overseas defence science and technology. The editors have not sought to impose a view, and as a result the chapters reflect both the differences in approach between the disciplines and the various sides of the debate over the future of UK defence science and technology. For consistency of presentation, the chapters have been divided into three sections.

Section 1: Defence R&D and National Capability

In Chapter 2, David Buck and Keith Hartley provide an overview of the data on defence R&D and their limitations. Despite the problems with the data there is still little doubt that defence R&D spending as a proportion of national income has been higher in the UK than almost any other nations except the USA, France and the former Soviet Union. It is this central characteristic of high UK defence R&D levels, relative both to other nations and to civil R&D, that is our main interest here. Britain's high level of R&D expenditure has fuelled the controversial `crowding-out' versus `spin-off' debate. Critics of UK defence policy have argued that high levels of defence R&D expenditure diverts scarce resources away from potentially valuable civil applications. In contrast, supporters of defence R&D have stressed its contribution to advancing technology and maintaining the civil economy at the frontiers of the technological state-of-the-art. In the chapter, Buck and Hartley subject the `burden' or `benefit' arguments over defence R&D to critical scrutiny and produce a number of interesting conclusions. First, under closer investigation, the existing literature on the crowding-out/spin-off debate has largely been anecdotal. After assessing a range of alternative methodologies to approach the issue, the authors' findings, based on analysis of comparative civil and military qualified scientists and engineers' (QSEs) wage rates, tentatively refute the crowding-out effect. Second, the authors identify the roles that public policy can play in in the reallocation of manpower resources from military to civilian activity.

Government policy must address two main issues as regards defence science and technology. First, what policy should be pursued to meet the requirements that have been set for defence science and technology? Second, and less consensually, what role should defence science and technology play in overall national science and technology policy, particularly with regard to civil innovation?

The primary function of government spending on defence science and technology is, of course, to meet the defence technology requirements of the armed services. Here, the trend has been for less and less defence technology to be researched, developed and produced indigenously. Increasingly, the UK has bought components or complete weapons systems overseas or entered into collaborative arrangements to develop and produce defence systems. The issues surrounding the consequent reduction of national defence capability, and thus UK `technology dependence' on overseas sources, are explored by Martin Edmonds in Chapter 3. The analysis traces the rise of international interdependence in weapons technologies since the Second World War, and the issues this has created in terms of foreign dependence. Edmonds identifies two issues of contemporary significance: first, that current UK dependencies in defence technology extend throughout the supplier network; and second, that these dependencies may have serious long-term implications for the maintenance, development and ultimate international competitiveness of the UK national technological and manufacturing base. Like Chapter 2, the analysis points to a role for national government funding; in this case, to maintain a capacity in dual-use `enabling' and `keystone' technologies.

Section 2: Case Studies

One obvious contribution that the social sciences can make to the debate is to provide detailed historical accounts of the role played by the state in using defence science and technology as a tool of industrial policy. Indeed, analysis of such historical accounts can provide a better understanding of the virtues and shortcomings of state intervention. The second section of the book adopts the case study approach in considering three historical examples of government involvement: the performance of previous governments' attempts to enhance spin-off from defence R&D for civil outputs; the implications of government defence funding in research establishments for civil uptake on defence-sponsored R&D; and government attempts to foster particular indigenous defence and civil industries.

Throughout the 1980s, the government's approach has been to eschew state intervention in the form of an interventionist industrial policy. Indeed, in 1989 this view was made explicit: "The Government does not ... see the Defence Budget as having an industrial sponsorship role or a responsibility for technologies unrelated to defence needs; that would lead to muddled roles and inefficiency"[7]. Under the Wilson government of the 1960s, however, the Ministry of Technology (Mintech) was established with the explicit purpose of harnessing the expertise of the government's defence research establishments to benefit UK science and technology in general. In Chapter 4, Richard Coopey examines the effects of Mintech in redirecting the activities of its very large defence establishments towards civil projects. The analysis produces a number of lessons relevant to the `intervention versus laissez faire' debate. On the one hand, and perhaps surprisingly, Coopey's analysis reveals enthusiasm among defence scientists and engineers for programmes aimed at boosting the civil economy. On the other hand, this stands in marked contrast to the lack of sustained political willpower to carry programmes forward, and the bureaucratic resistance and inertia which characterises higher levels of governmental decision making structure.

Clearly, with high post-war defence expenditure, the military have played a large role in shaping the UK research agenda over a range of technologies. In Chapter 5, Donald MacKenzie and Graham Spinardi analyse, through selective case studies, how the predominantly military role of government research establishments has shaped the areas of research undertaken, and also the effects on subsequent technical developments in the relevant sectors of British industry. The chapter addresses a fundamental question: what influence does the specifically military origins of funding have on the content of technological development? This question is broken down into two parts. First, what is the influence of the military on research choices and priorities? Are certain directions of research prioritised and others neglected because of the large proportion of UK R&D directed towards the military? And second, even if the funding is from a military source, does it follow that the research must be military in essence or could it be `pure' research involving generic technologies. Does it, so to speak, make any difference to the behaviour of electrons in a semiconductor whether it was developed under the aegis of the MOD as opposed to that of a civil orientated company or a university? Or to the scope for application of the resulting technology in different contexts?

The Chapter develops a number of interesting conclusions. The government research establishments came into being in support of the military, and this has continued to be a major focus of their work and a major source of their funding. Within this general understanding of their mission, however, there has been considerable scope for a core technology Establishment like the Royal Signals and Radar Establishment (RSRE) to pursue long-term research that has no direct military applications. As the history of thermal imaging technology demonstrates, RSRE's scientists have had considerable discretion in the past to decide what they think is important, even if the armed services did not agree. The study also reveals the "delicate process of technology translation" necessary to successfully exploit commercial developments within the research establishments. In addition, however, the analysis highlights exogenous economic and cultural factors which can block successful translation.

In Chapter 6, Matthew Uttley continues the historical theme, focusing on a specific product area - helicopters in post-war Britain. In tracing the evolution of the industry, and government policy aimed at intervention to boost domestic capacity, Uttley demonstrates that the chosen strategy of one sector of government in attempting to foster innovative diversity met with limited success. He also shows, however, how Westland obtained domestic market dominance through a strategy of relying on licenced production of United States helicopter designs. He then assesses the impact of this *prima facie* dependence on United States know-how for the United kingdom, pointing to the scope that licenced production offers for the retention and enhancement of indigenous British design and development capacity.

Section 3: Industry, Procurement and Conversion

The third section of the book contains three chapters which investigate specific policy options confronting the UK, and other West European states: first, the impact of defence restructuring for European integration of science and technology; second, the scope and prospects of international civil and military equipment collaboration; and third, the issues of conversion and diversification.

The emerging international security paradigm has profound ramifications not only for the UK, but for procurement policies throughout European defence industries. With the opening of civil markets in the context of the Single European Market, and the restructuring of defence requirements, issues such as `dual-use' technologies and `spin-off' are being thrown into a Europe-wide focus. In Chapter 7, Philip Gummett and William Walker examine political and economic changes in Europe in the context of technology policies, and comment on the probable effects of new industrial configurations. They advocate the integration of the military and civil science and technology base, using the opportunity for change for governments to redirect military R&D and productive capacity towards new civil products and markets.

In the UK, reductions in military procurement budgets threaten many jobs and even the survival of companies. In some instances, such as VSEL at Barrow after the completion of the Trident submarine contract, the prospects for the company and for local employment are particularly bleak. Of course, for some companies exporting provides an alternative to supplying the MOD. Generally speaking exports have been encouraged by the Government as not only beneficial to the balance of trade, but also as a way of reducing R&D costs for expensive weapons system development. With budgetary constraints confining the MOD's purchases to roughly two hundred of a new fighter aircraft or tank, exports can provide a proportionally large increase in total production over which R&D costs can be amortised. However, the dangers of the weapons trade and the proliferation of technologies that could aid weapons development (especially of `weapons of mass destruction'), mean that the imperative for companies to export to survive must be balanced by the wider perspective of international security.

In any case, increasing exports is likely to be neither easy nor adequate to make up the shortfall from decreasing MOD procurement and R&D support mechanisms - collaboration in the development of future weapons systems, and the conversion and diversification of existing defence companies - have adopted centre stage in the debate over the future of UK defence science and technology policy.

One approach to reducing the costs of development and production is to enter into a collaborative project with one or more partner nations. In Chapter 8, Keith Hartley and Stephen Martin examine the history of such projects, in both defence and civil developments, and assess the factors which have accounted for previous successful and unsuccessful programmes. This analysis generates two distinct conclusions. First, collaborative weapons development can provide the UK with a mechanism to acquire defence equipment more cheaply than conducting a comparable indigenous programme. In this respect, a dynamic for increased collaborative activity may well be created as defence equipment planners face declining procurement resources. In formulating these observations a series of policy `guidelines' are formulated which may optimise the conduct of future collaborative arrangements. Second, and equally significant, the chapter identifies a number of impediments that increased collaboration may create to effective European-wide industrial conversion. As the European states increasingly develop weapons systems in partnership, an implication may be the creation of a multilateral pressure group of defence industries. This pressure group, and its potential influence of national governmental defence policies, may serve to divert attention from the core question of reducing overall defence outputs.

Conversion, wholly or partly, of companies from military to civil production is thus a key issue of major economic importance. Conversion has been heralded as essential for companies, and regions, which are heavily dependent on defence. The issues central to the conversion debate are in many respects the same as those for spin-off. Both are concerned with shifting technology from the military domain to civil production, but differ in the nature of technology. Whereas spin-off is typically focused on transferring bits of technology, usually from one organisation to another, conversion deals with *in situ* transformation of plant, organisation and skill. Therefore simply focusing on finding civil products as the goal of conversion may not be fruitful. Although in theory it may seem that a company can convert to making these new products, in practice it is `social' and not `technical' conversion which is the obstacle.

For this reason a more fruitful approach may be to make a distinction between conversion and diversification. A defence dependent region can adapt itself to reductions in the defence market, not through the conversion of particular factories, but rather by promoting the start-up and growth of civil production in general. Rather than attempting, often unsuccessfully, to graft commercial attitudes onto firms with traditions of cost-plus contracting with the MOD, this approach to diversification focuses its efforts on firms which are completely civil through and through. If successful the diversification efforts will lead to the creation of jobs in which former defence workers can utilise some of their existing technical skills, whilst also learning new social skills and adapting to a differing organisational approach.

In Chapter 9, Steven Schofield investigates these twin themes of conversion and diversification. While welcoming renewed study, the chapter argues that the concept of arms conversion requires a radical re-evaluation and overhaul if it is to be relevant to the conditions of the 1990s. The analysis points to the need to broaden the concept of conversion to embrace not only wider economic and political determinants of defence production, but also to understand the need to implement wider social and economic programmes, perhaps learning from the experience of `community conversion' themes in the United States.

Conclusion

The UK has a significant legacy in the field of military science and technology[8]. With so much invested in defence science and technology, and so much dependent employment (about ten percent of the manufacturing workforce), the prospect of sharp reductions in defence spending is politically unappealing. Hard choices lie ahead, with painful consequences for many. In the long run though, a reshaping of the defence sector, and a reformulation of the relations between military and civil science and technology, could be to the benefit of UK industry and the UK economy. The challenge is to find a way of moving beyond the rhetoric of `intervention' and `picking winners', on the one hand, and untrammelled liberation and market competition on the other, towards a new framework for policy in this most political and crucial of areas. This requires radical rethinking - of concepts as well as policies. It is to that process of rethinking that this book, the product of a set of studies by a multidisciplinary group of social scientists, is devoted.

Endnotes

1. For more details see, for example, Spanier, J., **Games Nations Play**, (New York: Holt, Rinehart and Winston), 1984, pp. 97-100.

2. **Autumn Statement 1992**, HM Treasury, (London: HMSO).

3. This concern led to congressional legislation, starting with the Stevenson-Wydler Technology Innovation Act of 1980, to enhance technology transfer out of government-funded agencies. See Schriesheim, A., **Towards a Golden Age for Technology Transfer**, *Issues in Science and Technology*, Vol. VII, No. 2, Winter 1990-1991, pp. 52-58; and Edmonds, M., Uttley, M.R.H. & Hayhurst, G., **UK and US Dependence on Foreign Technology on Defence Research and Development**, *Science and Public Policy*, Vol. 17, No. 3, June 1990, pp. 157-169.

4. Latour, B., **Science in Action**, (Cambridge: Harvard University Press), 1987, p. 174.

5. Garnett, J., Technology and Strategy, in Baylis, J., Booth, K., Garnett, J. & Williams, P., Contemporary Strategy, (New York: Holmes & Meier), 1987, Vol. I: Theories and Concepts, p. 92.

6. See Barnes, B. & Edge, D., **Science in Context**, (Milton Keynes: Open University), 1982, Part 3.

7. The government view was given in response to, and is included in, the Cabinet Office Advisory Council on Science and Technology, **Defence R&D: A National Resource**, (London: HMSO), 1989, p. 5.

8. See, for example, Kaldor, M., **The Baroque Arsenal**, (London: Andre Deutsch), 1982; and Edgerton, D, **Liberal Militarism and the British State**, *New Left Review*, No. 185, January-february 1991, pp. 138-169.

Part 1

Issues in Defence Science and Technology

Chapter 2

The Political Economy of Defence R&D: Burden or Benefit?

David Buck and Keith Hartley

Introduction

Defence research and development (R&D) continues to be controversial. Critics claim that Britain spends "too much" on both defence and on defence R&D. Excessive spending it is argued, diverts scarce resources, and scientific manpower from more highly valued civil uses, with adverse effects on the economy's growth rate and international competitiveness. In contrast, the supporters of defence R&D stress its contribution to the protection and independence of the UK; its contribution to maintaining the defence sector at the frontiers of technology (the `leading edge'); and through spin-off and technology transfer, its contribution to general technological progress throughout the economy.

This chapter subjects the various claims and counter-claims surrounding defence R&D to critical scrutiny. The economic logic of the different arguments are assessed and available evidence reviewed. Initially, UK defence policy is related to wider developments and trends following the 1990 Conventional Forces in Europe (CFE) Treaty, and the probable implications these issues have for future UK and Western defence R&D expenditure. There follows an overview which describes and presents the facts on the UK defence R&D market, placing it in international context and discussing some statistical caveats. The performance of the market is assessed and consideration is given to whether defence R&D is a benefit or a burden. The conclusion considers future prospects and policy options.

Future Trends and Implications for Defence R&D

With the 1990 CFE Treaty and subsequent unilateral arms limitation initiatives, there are prospects of substantial cuts in future defence spending throughout Europe, the USA and the former USSR. These developments provide the background against which UK defence policy and its R&D requirements need to be assessed. A framework is needed for thinking about these changes.

A starting point is the likely *future threat* facing the UK and Europe (risk assessment). Will the threat come from within Europe or from the rest of the world; what form will it take; and will it be viewed as major or minor? Policy-makers have to make difficult choices in a world of uncertainty which are made more complex by the long time-horizons required for the development and operation of modern equipment (eg a 40 year life-cycle for the UK Trident submarine force).

Defence planners also have to make assumptions about NATO's future and about likely developments in both technology and arms control agreements (including voluntary unilateral initiatives). Judgements are also required on a society's future willingness to pay for defence compared with, say, social welfare spending, and on the future ability to pay for defence as reflected in the economy's growth rate and its international competitiveness. Answers to these questions will lead to various *economic scenarios* affecting national defence policies, and hence the size and composition of defence budgets which, in turn, will affect its defence industrial base and economy (depending on whether defence spending is viewed as a burden or benefit to the economy).

Defence cuts will have an impact on the size, structure, composition and performance of defence industries. Reduced spending on equipment will mean fewer new projects, shorter production runs for projects, more international collaboration and probably a greater willingness to buy from abroad, all with implications for R&D. The result will be smaller defence industries, with likely changes in their composition reflecting modified demands for air, land and sea equipment. For example, it has been forecast that shipyards and producers of land systems (eg tanks, armoured vehicles) are especially vulnerable, whilst electronics and high technology firms might benefit (see Chapter 9).[1]

Defence contractors are adopting, and will continue to adopt, a variety of responses to these changes. Their options include job losses, plant closures, a search for new markets at home and overseas, national and international mergers and take-overs, and exit from the defence industry. Estimates suggest that between 1990 and 1995 there might be some 350,000 to 500,000 job losses in West European defence industries.[2] With such excess capacity in Europe and elsewhere, export markets for defence equipment are likely to become highly competitive. As a result, firms are likely to seek new growth markets in defence such as the Far East, and/or diversify into civil markets. In this context, it has been suggested that the real `Peace Dividend' may be the release of the `brightest and best' technical minds involved in defence R&D for revitalising the civil sector. This argument, however, needs careful analysis. There is only anecdotal evidence that the defence sector attracts the "brightest and best". Furthermore, defence R&D work may be sufficiently different and specialised so that personnel require highly expensive retraining. There is no guarantee that the workings of the labour market alone will lead to an optimal outcome. Manpower may simply be released and not re-absorbed into the economy.

The 1990 CFE Treaty will determine the broad parameters of future NATO defence spending and force structures. These are likely to be characterised by the following features:-

1. Cuts in defence budgets, the question being how much and how quickly?
2. Cuts in manpower, especially in conscript forces, with a greater emphasis on equipment and possibly on reserve forces (eg smaller but better equipped forces).

3. Arms control constraints on force structures. These constraints might provide incentives to substitute unregulated for regulated and constrained inputs. For example, outside the controlled regions forces and equipment not subject to arms control restrictions might be expanded (eg naval forces), and new technologies might be developed which increase the effectiveness of equipment.
4. Substitution effects. Within reduced defence budgets, substitution of defensive for offensive forces and equipment is likely. Examples include greater emphasis on surveillance and early warning systems, the monitoring of arms control agreements, the capability for rapid deployment and defensive missiles and air defence aircraft.
5. A lower state of readiness of the armed forces. This will reduce costs through running-on existing equipment (older weapons), less training and lower stocks of ammunition and equipment.
6. Smaller defence budgets are likely to increase emphasis on enhanced efficiency in armed forces and equipment procurement. For example, states will need to re-appraise their traditional procurement policies and are likely to be more willing to open their national markets to foreign suppliers. Here one possibility might be the creation of an EC Single Market for defence equipment.

What most of these features have in common is an expanded role, within a falling budget, for R&D. Whether this will result in an overall increase in real defence R&D is unclear, but R&D is likely to be insulated from the general trend of falling expenditure. Equipment at the expense of manpower and qualitative force multipliers to bypass arms controls measures rest on healthy R&D programmes. Surveillance and arms control validation technologies need to be greatly enhanced, and rapid deployment of flexible forces requires new equipment. Information technologies and software developments will continue to absorb a large proportion of funds.

Against this trend, in the short term, is the tendency towards running on existing equipment, retrofitting (eg mid-life updates for aircraft) and lower stocks of ammunition and equipment. However, retrofitting and running on require not only maintenance but also R&D. Large head-line programmes and projects could suffer, but there will be a multitude of necessary small-scale contracts. The residual threat from the former Soviet Union is still in the minds of defence planners. However, it is significantly down-graded, allowing a lower state of general readiness with the possible option to retain the capacity to rebuild forces should they be needed. This theory of "reconstitution" lies very much behind the US Administration's approach to defence policy.[3] With regards to the industrial mobilisation aspects, the former Deputy Secretary of Defense announced:-

"[We] must sustain the critical elements of America's defense industrial and technological base by maintaining a robust investment in defense research and development...The Department of Defense can and will do its share to strengthen the defense industrial and technological base."[4]

Whitt II takes this speech to imply that reconstitution really means greater emphasis on R&D at the expense of standby production capacity. However, such remarks could also be interpretted as concern over defence and civil dependence on foreign (chiefly Japanese) technology, stating the DoD's tacit industrial policy role in the absence of a similar civilian body in the US.[5] The convergence of purely military factors and wider industrial aspects are powerful forces for stability, and possibly an upsurge, in DoD support for R&D. United States defence R&D expenditure increased by 80 per cent in the ten years to 1990. Although Congress has authorised the first real cut in the defence R&D budget for twenty years this is somewhat of a surprise because:-

"...actual spending on R&D was not only expected to resist decline in FY 1991, but is even expected to increase in coming budgets."[6]

Predicting the path of defence R&D in the other Western countries is more difficult. Expenditure is dominated by the UK and France (accounting for 85 per cent of EC defence R&D expenditure) who, for largely historical reasons, made commitments to independent nuclear deterrents and comprehensive indigenous defence industries in the immediate post-war years. Defence absorbed a rising proportion of most EC government R&D budgets in the 1980s.[7] Whether the trend will continue is uncertain.

An explicit industrial role for the defence ministry is absent in most EC countries because equivalent civil institutions exist, though there are signs that in Italy and Spain at least, the defence ministries are drivers of broader-based technology policy.[8] In Germany the defence ministry has a statutory duty to assess all defence R&D for its civil applicability and the support of non-defence or `dual-use' work. In addition, other ministries (especially the Federal Ministry for Research and Technology (BMFT)) fund certain defence R&D. Though the situation in France is less institutionalised, government policy is to support firms who transfer technology successfully into commercial areas.[9] In contrast, the UK MoD has consistently claimed that its over-riding task is to procure cost-effective defence equipment, but that its remit does not extend into wider industrial policy issues.

It is apparent that most defence ministries are becoming more interested in wider industrial concerns as a means of securing their budgets, and because technological competitiveness is now seen as a key element of national security. We may therefore see more *non-defence* R&D (narrowly defined) channelled through defence budgets as a concession to the military, and because non-defence R&D is perceived as a cost-effective mechanism to sustain the indigenous technological base. This is particularly true of countries with less developed industries such as Spain, where international collaborative deals import foreign technology and expertise (see Chapter 8).

In conclusion, defence R&D is likely to remain stable or rise in the United States due to military and industrial pressures. In the rest of the Western Alliance the trend is less certain. If defence ministries do become more aware of wider industrial matters and technology is perceived as the key to competitiveness, funding for R&D from defence ministries may rise, though resources could also be channelled through industry, science or technology ministries. "True" defence R&D may also increase because of the future trends in NATO defence spending. The UK and France are the greatest defence R&D spenders in Europe. The CFE Treaty, further arms limitation negotiations, competitiveness worries and other eventualities are likely to have major impacts on the UK. In the next section we place the UK defence R&D sector into a clearer context in terms of markets, expenditure and manpower, before discussing `burdens' and `benefits'.

Overview

1. The UK Defence R&D Market

On the demand side, the UK defence R&D market is dominated by the Ministry of Defence (MoD). The Ministry purchases air, land and sea equipment on behalf of the Armed Forces and Ministry operational requirements specify technical needs (eg for a new combat aircraft, missile, tank or warship). When the operational requirements are determined, the Ministry has to decide whether to purchase the new equipment from the UK, from abroad, or through collaboration with international partners (see Chapter 8).

The supply side of the market comprises publicly- and privately-owned enterprises specialising in defence R&D, or undertaking R&D within a range of defence and civil activities. A distinction can be made between research work and development work, with much of the latter undertaken in private industry. Indeed, it has been MoD policy throughout the 1980s to devolve design, development and project support work to industry whilst the government's defence research establishments concentrate on longer-term innovative research.

The Government owns six major defence research establishments: the Royal Aerospace Establishment (RAE: aerospace); the Royal Armament Research and Development Establishment (RARDE: land systems); the Admiralty Research Establishment (ARE: sea systems); the Chemical Defence Establishment; the Royal Signals and Radar Establishment (RSRE: radar, electronics); and the Atomic Weapons Research Establishment (AWRE: nuclear systems). The research establishments enable MoD to act as an intelligent customer for defence equipment, advising the Services on the potential and limitations of new or emerging technologies, as well as technical and support services throughout the weapons acquisitions process.

In 1985, Defence Technology Enterprises (DTE) was created as a private company. Its primary aim was to promote diffusion and spin-off of technologies generated in the establishments which were potentially marketable in the civil sector. By 1989, DTE had arranged 42 licenses, which were expected to lead to at least £60m worth of sales over an eight year period.[10] The DTE ceased operations as an effective unit in 1990.

Further institutional changes were to occur. Under the Government's *Next Steps* policy, the four principal non-nuclear research establishments (ARE, RAE, RARDE, RSRE) form the core of a new Defence Research Agency (DRA), created in April 1991. The aim is to establish the DRA as a trading fund, selling its R&D services to MoD and to other customers.[11] Also in April 1991, the Chemical and Biological Defence Establishment (CBDE) was established as a Defence Support Agency, giving it greater management flexibility. For 1992-3, the planned expenditure of the DRA was £650m and the CBDE was some £33m. Since total intramural defence R&D was about £1bn, it can be assumed that expenditure on nuclear R&D at the AWRE was approximately £300m.[12]

In late 1992, the DRA announced plans to reduce its workforce of 11,700 by about 2,000. It also plans to close a number of sites, particularly in the south of England, dispensing with about 50 per cent of its buildings and 60 per cent of its land. The objective is to rationalise the DRAs extensive research activities, so concentrating on larger and more efficient units (eg Farnborough, Malvern), with the intention of reducing running costs by £90M per annnum. These changes reflect the DRA's aim of becoming a trading fund, as well as the UK's reductions in its Armed Forces (Options for Change) and a continued concern about defence absorbing scarce scientific resources.

Defence R&D work is also conducted in universities, further educational establishments and private industry. Major defence companies such as British Aerospace, Rolls-Royce and GEC undertake defence R&D (mostly Government-funded), as well as production, repair and maintenance work. They might specialise in specific types of defence equipment (eg helicopters: Westland; aero-engines: Rolls-Royce); in providing equipment to one Service (eg Navy submarines: Vickers Shipbuilding and Engineering; or Army tanks: Vickers Plc); in a range of defence equipment for different Services (eg aircraft, missiles and ordnance: British Aerospace); or there might be a diversified enterprise with both military and civil components (eg British Aerospace; GEC). Private sector companies vary in size: in 1990-91, there were 125 companies paid £5m or more by MoD (including foreign companies), with five of these each receiving over £250m.

British defence equipment projects follow a life-cycle which proceeds through a *development stage* involving feasibility study and project definition to a commitment to full development, followed by production, in-service support, mid-life up-dating and disposal. Typically, development work accounts for about one-third of total project costs whilst production accounts for the remaining two-thirds (Figure 2.1) On major projects the costs are substantial: the UK development costs for the EH101 helicopter, for example, are estimated at £1.37 billion, and £2.72 billion[13] on the European Fighter Aircraft programme.

Under current MoD competition policy, rivalry is promoted at the feasibility, project definition, development and production stages in a project's life cycle. As a result, a design contractor cannot assume a guarantee of a production order, enabling MoD to introduce rivalry and contestability into markets which were previously non-competitive. However, the possibility that development and production work can be undertaken by different contractors creates two problems. First, where production work is more profitable, firms might be less willing to undertake development work at existing profit rates. Second, problems arise in establishing and protecting property rights in new ideas, and transferring technology between contractors is not costless.

Figure 2.1: Development and Production Costs

Development Cost	34%
(Feasibility Study)	1%
(Project Definition)	7%
(Full Develoment)	92%
Production Cost	66%
Total Acquisition Cost	100%

Source: Ministry of Defence, **Learning from Experience**, HMSO, London, 1988

Competition for development work is usually based on price and non-price criteria (Figure 2.2). The Ministry has increasingly favoured fixed price or incentive contracts rather than cost-plus contracts. Indeed, the share of MoD contracts (development and non-development) by value priced on a cost-plus basis has declined from 22 per cent in 1979-80 to 1 per cent in 1991-92.[14] Non-price criteria are also used for project selection, especially in the early stages of development. Traditionally, MoD has defined its equipment requirements as detailed technical specifications, a practice which has changed with the introduction of Cardinal Points Specification. Under new arrangements the Ministry outlines its requirements in broad terms, leaving contractors to determine how best to meet them. As a result, it is claimed that "gold plating" of equipment has been reduced, whilst industry has been given flexibility in its use of available technologies.[15] Of course, if the market is restricted to UK suppliers then competition is not always possible. There are UK domestic monopolies in aerospace equipment (British Aerospace, Rolls-Royce, Westland), nuclear-powered submarines (VSEL), tanks (Vickers Plc) and torpedoes (GEC). However, a domestic monopoly can always be subjected to potential competition (contestability) by "opening-up" the UK market to foreign firms.

Figure 2.2: UK Defence R&D Market

Buyers	Form of competition	Suppliers of defence R&D	Rest of UK economy (spin-off)
MoD Overseas customers	1. Prices (fixed prices; incentive contracts)	Government DRA Universities Further education establishments	DTE (1985-1990) Publications Conferences
	2. Technical proposals	Private industry (UK and overseas)	New civil products Patents

2. UK Defence R&D Expenditure

Before reviewing the figures the limitations of R&D statistics should be acknowledged. The basic problem is one of measurement at both *conceptual* and *practical* levels. Although the conceptual problems have been alleviated with the introduction of the *Frascati* definitions, the concepts of 'research' and 'development' are open to wide and differing interpretations. For instance, the distinction between aeroplane development work and pre-flight testing and refinement is not immediately apparent. Furthermore, different countries use differing classifications: most US R&D statistics, for example, report Research, Development, *Testing and Evaluation* (R,D,T&E) expenditure, which complicates international comparisons.[16]

In the practical dimension, most firms and organisations use accounting systems which are not consistent with Frascati definitions. Consequently, Frascati R&D details have to be 'retrieved'[17], which inevitably leads to inaccuracies and approximations. Measurement problems clearly exist in the UK. For instance, MoD claimed to fund defence R&D in industry to the tune of £1516m in 1985, whereas industry reported receiving only £1012m. The MoD's figures represent a 50 per cent increase for the same work! The discrepancy is explained by the MoD's accounting system: essentially *all* pre-production work is classified as R&D whereas the firms involved use a narrower classification.[18]

For the UK and most OECD countries, the only reasonably reliable and consistent figures are those relating to government funding. Government-funded defence R&D has tended to be regarded as a proxy variable for *total* defence R&D performed or funded in, or by, a country. Despite these reservations, the information available does help to identify underlying trends and movements in UK defence R&D expenditure over time, and also allows reasonable comparisons with other countries.

Table 2.1 shows the evolution through time of government-funded UK defence R&D. Column 1 documents the rise in expenditure (current prices) from the 1960s to the recent past. The thirty years to 1990 have seen a greater than ten-fold increase in nominal expenditures. The second column shows the same data in constant prices to provide a guage of how patterns in real defence R&D expenditure have changed over the period. Real expenditure on defence R&D fell throughout the 1960s and rose to former levels by the late 1970s. Since 1985 there has been a dramatic fall in the level of defence R&D spending of 25 per cent in real terms to 1991. This may seem a direct consequence of the Government's announced policy to cut defence R&D in real terms over the decade 1987-98[19], as well as the end of NATO's 3 per cent directive. However, the fall may also reflect MoD's policy of shifting risks in production and development to industry (eg via competitive fixed-price contracts). Thus R&D may become internalised, and be reflected in higher procurement prices and company-funded R&D rather than MoD-funded R&D.

Table 2.1: U.K. Defence R&D Expenditure

	£million		Defence R&D as percentage:	
	Current Defence R&D	Constant Defence R&D	GDP	Military Spending
1960	224	1748	0.87	13.52
1965	263	1720	0.73	12.58
1970	257	1325	0.50	10.52
1975	664	1850	0.63	12.86
1980	1628	2272	0.71	14.90
1985	2116	2116	0.59	11.66
1986	2046	1976	0.53	11.01
1987	2015	1855	0.48	10.54
1988	1991	1720	0.43	10.24
1989	2161	1744	0.42	10.41
1990	2315	1756	0.43	10.62
1991	2250	1596	0.39	9.20

Notes: i. 1985 constant prices from applying the GDP deflator at a 1985 base
ii. 1990 and 1991 figures are estimates.

Source: CSO, **Economic Trends**; Cabinet Office, **Annual Review of Government Funded Research and Development**; Council on Scientific Policy - various reports; Select Committee on Science Session, **HC213** Session 1968-69; and CSO, **R&D Expenditure and Employment**, 1976. Military expenditure figures, except 1991 from MoD, **Defence Statistics 1992 Edition**; **SIPR Yearbook** - various issues.

The mid-eighties also saw the cancellation of the Nimrod Airborne Early Warning (AEW) system, which was a significant consumer of defence R&D resources. Nevertheless, the government's commitment to reducing the 'burden' of defence R&D seems to have been borne out by the figures (column 3): defence R&D expressed as a percentage of GDP is a proxy for the 'burden' that such expenditure places on the whole economy. In the ten years from 1980 there was a 40 per cent fall in the proportion of GDP devoted to government-funded defence R&D.

Table 2.2: Functional Distribution of UK Government-Funded Defence R&D

Percentage Shares of Defence R&D

	Ships and Underwater Warfare	Ordnance	Aircraft	Guided Weapons	Other Electronic	Other
1980	14.1	8.1	34.4	12.4	15.6	15.3
1981	17.8	8.9	29.7	13.3	15.5	14.8
1982	15.7	8.9	32.5	12.8	15.5	14.6
1983	17.3	9.3	29.3	12.9	14.9	16.2
1984	18.6	8.7	24.2	15.0	16.2	17.3
1985	18.4	8.2	22.7	15.7	17.2	17.8
1986	18.4	5.9	27.8	13.4	18.3	16.1
1987	16.1	6.1	28.5	14.6	13.9	20.8
1988	15.4	8.3	27.8	15.5	14.9	18.0
1989	16.1	8.0	26.9	15.7	14.9	18.5
1990	15.0	7.8	29.3	15.6	14.9	17.4
1991	15.0	7.8	29.3	15.6	14.9	17.4

Notes: i. All figures are percentages and may not add to 100 due to individual rounding.
ii. 1990 and 1991 figures are provisional.

Source: MoD, **Statement on the Defence Estimates** - various years.

Table 2.2 shows the functional distribution of MoD's defence R&D budget. Aircraft is the dominant category, reflecting the high costs of equipment and support for the UK aerospace industry. Another interesting feature is the ships and underwater warfare category which more than doubled its relative importance over the period 1977-84, but subsequently declined. The pattern is due to the Trident hull programme and various torpedo and sonobuoy projects which are now past their peak expenditures. The changing shares highlight the effect of procurement cycles on the allocation between major equipment headings.

Table 2.3 outlines the implications of the Levene Reforms introduced in 1983-84 - the government's commitment to increase the share of defence R&D performed in industry. Data are presented which illustrate the evolution of intramural and extramural defence R&D expenditure for the period from the mid-sixties to the present. Extramural expenditure has fluctuated between 50 per cent and some 75 per cent of total expenditure which peaked in 1980, but fell subsequently. Unsurprisingly, the vast majority of extramural expenditure is spent in private industry. However, for the 1980s, there is no evidence of a significant time-trend showing that private industry is obtaining an increasing share of the defence R&D budget.

Table 2.3: UK MoD Extramural and Intramural Defence R&D Expenditure

	Current Prices (£m)		Constant Prices (£m)		Extramural as a percentage of
	Intramural	Extramural	Intramural	Extramural	Total R&D
1966	110	169	689	1058	61
1970	108	159	557	820	60
1975	253	436	705	1215	63
1980	448	1261	625	1759	74
1985	693	1752	693	1752	72
1986	735	1637	710	1581	69
1987	740	1558	681	1434	68
1988	797	1468	687	1268	65
1989	932	1495	752	1207	62
1990	902	1551	684	1177	63
1991	925	1718	656	1219	65

Notes: i. 1991 figures are estimates
ii. Fiscal years, constant prices at a 1985 base

Sources: MoD, **Statement on the Defence Estimates** - various years; CSO, **R&D Expenditure** (1973); CSO, **R&D Expenditure and Employment** (1976); and MoD, **Defence Statistics 1992 Edition**.

Table 2.3 also presents data on the real cost of intramural and extramural expenditure over the period (1985 prices). The data indicate relatively constant intramural figures, but significant variations in the extramural component. One possible explanation is that this reflects procurement cycles, either across the board or of dominant projects such as Trident and Tornado, which are based in industry. In the short run therefore, it is unlikely that any commitment to increase extramural expenditure in relation to intramural expenditure will show up. Conversely, if procurement cycles *are* so dominant they could completely subjugate such a commitment and render it practically impossible to implement. Adjusting or detrending R&D data for major procurement cycles would seem a sensible approach to assessing variations in defence R&D spending.

Table 2.4: UK Government Funding of Defence and Civil R&D

	Current Prices (£m)		Constant Prices (£m)		
	Defence R&D	Civil R&D	Defence R&D	Civil R&D	Ratio of Defence to Civil R&D
1965	263	236	1720	1543	1.11
1970	257	347	1325	1790	0.74
1975	664	831	1850	2315	0.80
1980	1628	1556	2272	2171	1.05
1985	2116	2235	2116	2235	0.95
1986	2046	2321	1976	2242	0.88
1987	2015	2404	1855	2213	0.84
1988	1991	2512	1720	2170	0.79
1989	2161	2671	1744	2156	0.81
1990	2315	2838	1756	2153	0.82
1991	2250	2831	1596	2008	0.79

Notes: i. Figures for 1990 are provisional and 1991 estimates.
ii. Deflated by GDP deflator at 1985 base.

Sources: CSO, **Economic Trends** - various years; Cabinet Office, **Annual Review of Government Funded R&D** - various years.

A criticism of the UK is that compared with major competitors it spends a higher absolute and relative amount on defence, as opposed to civil, R&D. Table 2.4 suggests that the ratio of defence to civil R&D is determined by the variations in the defence sector. During 1985 it was almost one-for-one, declining to 0.79 and remaining stable since. What is certainly the case is that defence R&D does, on average, take an almost equal slice of the total government-funded R&D expenditure, though there seems to be little direct substitution between the two sectors in real terms: a cut in defence R&D does not imply an equivalent increase in civil R&D and vice-versa.

The next three tables present data of a comparative nature which illustrate the UK's position relative to its main competitors. Table 2.5 presents the ratio of government-funded defence to total public R&D for the years 1983-89. The USA and UK are clearly in a league of their own, spending (on average) more on defence than civil R&D. Next follows France, still a comparatively large spender (due to its policy of high self-sufficiency in defence equipment). The remaining nations, the former FRG, Italy and Japan devote a much smaller proportion of their public R&D resources to defence. Nevertheless, the UK is the only one amongst this sample that actually spent a smaller proportion of its R&D resources on defence in 1989 than in 1983, and this during a period when real civil R&D was also falling in the UK (see Table 2.4).

Table 2.5: Government Funded Defence R&D as a Percentage of Total Public R&D

Percentages

	France	FRG	Japan	Italy	UK	US
1983	33	10	n.a	6	50	64
1984	33	10	n.a.	8	51	66
1985	31	12	4	10	51	68
1986	32	12	4	9	49	69
1987	36	13	4	7	45	69
1988	37	12	5	10	44	67
1989	37	13	5	10	45	65

Source: Cabinet Office, **Annual Review of Government Funded R&D** - various years.

The best source of international comparative data are the **SIPRI Yearbooks**. However SIPRI ceased to report defence R&D expenditures in 1988 and for consistency between sources Table 2.6 terminates in 1986. Nevertheless, the general trends in the relative magnitude of the defence R&D 'burden' through time and across countries are clear. The USA devoted more than 1 per cent of its massive GDP in the 1960s to defence R&D, falling to 0.55 per cent by 1980. Subsequently, during the Reagan Administration, the 'burden' had climbed to almost 1 per cent again by 1986. In absolute terms the US commitment to defence R&D dwarfs that of any other nation, with the probable exception of the former USSR, but as a proportionate 'burden' on the economy the UK is not far behind devoting nearly 0.7 per cent in 1986. Indeed for the period 1974-81 the UK actually devoted *more* of its GDP to defence R&D than the US.

Table 2.6: Defence R&D as a Percentage of GDP

	Percentages					
	France	FRG	Japan	Italy	UK	US
1965	n.a.	0.16	0.01	0.01	0.81	1.25
1970	0.35	0.17	n.a.	0.02	0.50	0.79
1975	0.34	0.14	0.01	0.01	0.63	0.61
1980	0.40	0.12	0.01	0.01	0.73	0.55
1981	0.50	0.10	0.01	0.04	0.68	0.58
1982	0.46	0.10	0.01	0.03	0.63	0.70
1983	0.45	0.11	0.01	0.03	0.65	0.72
1984	0.48	0.11	0.02	0.05	0.67	0.75
1985	0.45	0.14	0.02	0.06	0.67	0.86
1986	n.a.	n.a.	n.a.	n.a.	0.66	0.98

Notes:
i. GDP is GDP or closest equivalent, given differences in national accounting methods and conventions.
ii. SIPRI data subject to qualifications detailed in the original sources.

Sources: GDP from OECD, **OECD Economic Indicators Historical Statistics** - various issues. Defence R&D from SIPRI, **SIPRI Yearbook** - various issues.

Table 2.7 outlines the proportion of selected total defence budgets which are absorbed by defence R&D. As well as having purely descriptive appeal this may provide an insight into the relative `self-sufficiency', in the broadest possible terms, of each nation's defence effort. Again, the familiar story unfolds: the USA and UK dominate, then France and finally the remaining three. However, for most of the period, the UK spent a greater proportion of its defence budget on R&D. France too spent more in this respect during the early 1980s than the USA.

To summarise, as a relative drain on national resources or defence budgets, defence R&D expenditures in the UK and France are approximately comparable to the US. This reflects the support for the defence industrial base in both countries, involving an effort to maintain an industrial capability in almost all areas of defence equipment.[20] Other European countries devoted much less government-funded expenditure in absolute and relative terms. It must be remembered however, that `government-funding' is only a proxy for total expenditure on defence R&D. Unfortunately little is known about industry's private venture defence R&D spending and further research in this area is vital. It is likely that a non-trivial proportion of the observed fall in real government-sponsored defence R&D in the UK has flowed from a shifting of risk from MoD to industry as part of the Levene reforms, as well as procurement cycles and cost reductions through efficiency gains.

Table 2.7: Percentage Share of Defence R&D in Military Expenditure

	Percentages					
	France	FRG	Japan	Italy	UK	US
1960	6.84	1.66	1.59	0.70	n.a.	n.a.
1965	10.83	3.71	1.50	0.63	12.53	13.85
1970	8.43	5.10	n.a.	0.72	10.56	10.25
1975	9.04	3.74	1.26	0.49	12.93	10.64
1980	10.16	3.57	1.31	0.51	15.41	10.47
1981	12.10	3.01	1.35	1.70	14.49	10.50
1982	11.28	3.04	1.41	1.16	12.38	11.25
1983	10.97	3.25	1.49	1.50	12.67	11.20
1984	11.80	3.38	1.57	2.36	12.68	11.88
1985	11.30	4.28	1.94	2.84	13.10	13.08
1986	n.a.	n.a.	n.a.	n.a.	13.51	14.73

Source: SIPRI, **SIPRI Yearbooks** - various years.

There are major problems in arriving at reliable estimates for privately-funded or performed defence R&D, especially in the UK. The **Statement on the Defence Estimates** have provided a consistent breakdown of the MoD's *funding of* R&D in industry since FY 1975/6. Before this date information was gathered infrequently and was often highly aggregated. The discrepancy between MoD and industry definitions, referred to earlier, is also cause for concern. Even if this were not the case however, the MoD's figures ignore defence R&D performed in industry but *not* funded by the MoD. The largest proportion of this `missing defence R&D' is company-funded R&D, but also includes work carried out on behalf of foreign organisations and governments, other domestic firms, research associations and government departments.

The most accessible and in-depth sources of information concerning UK industrial R&D is the **Business Monitor MO14 Industrial Research and Development Expenditure and Employment** released through the Central Statistical Office. These volumes provide benchmark surveys for the years 1975, 1978, 1981, 1984 and most recently 1989, and contain detailed aggregate and sectoral details of expenditure and employment. Although there have been small changes in definition in the survey, these are problems of `second-order' importance.[21] The Business Monitors disclose that for the fifteen years to 1980 the UK government provided some 30 per cent of all industry R&D funds. This figure has since dropped dramatically to about 15 per cent with industry providing 70 per cent and the remaining funds originating overseas. However, the pertinent question of whether the fall in government-funded R&D is a consequence of a run-down in defence or civil support, or indeed both, cannot be answered. Until 1991, the Business Monitors and all other intermittent government sources of data on private industrial R&D have simply ignored the distinction between defence and civil R&D.[22] The Business Monitor released in the Summer of 1991 distinguished between defence and civil for the first time. The summary in Tables 2.8 and 2.9 below provides details for product groups in industry.

Table 2.8: UK Industrial Defence and Civil R&D Expenditure 1989

	£ millions		
	Civil	Defence	Total
All Product Groups	5947	1653	7600
Chemicals	1674	19	1692
Mechanical Eng	175	30	206
Electronics	1539	721	2259
Other Electronic Eng	108	5	114
Motor Vehicles	496	8	504
Aerospace	335	735	1070
Other Manufactures	558	48	605
Non-manufactures	1063	87	1149

Note: i. Figures in £m.
Source: CSO, **Business Monitor MO14 1989: Industrial Research and Development Expenditure and Employment**, Table 2.8.

These provide us with the first reliable data, albeit a `snapshot', of the distribution of UK defence and civil R&D across broad industrial groupings. Of the total R&D spent in industry in 1989, defence took a comparatively modest 22 per cent. This average hides wide disparities across product groups: it is below average in six of the eight headings, implying a highly skewed distribution. It is aerospace and electronics, in both relative and absolute terms, which comprise the largest slice of the defence R&D cake, accounting for almost 90 per cent of all defence R&D carried out in industry in 1989. Aerospace is the largest defence R&D sector in absolute terms, its percentage reliance on defence R&D also being double that of electronics.

The government funded only 5 per cent of civil industrial R&D in 1989 but 60 per cent of defence R&D (in absolute terms three times as much). Industries' own funds cover 75 per cent of civil expenditure incurred, but only a quarter of defence R&D where funds from overseas contribute almost as much. Thus the defence industrial sector as a whole, and aerospace and electronics in particular, are far more dependent on government support than is civil industry. The contrasting information in Tables 2.3 and 2.9 highlights the disturbing inconsistency between the figures of the MoD and industry. Table 2.9 tells us that industry actually received £943m for defence R&D from government in 1989, yet Table 2.3 indicates the MoD's extramural expenditure was £1495m, of which £1285m went to private industry, a discrepancy of over 35%. Indeed, the MoD claims to give £36m more to industry than it reports received from government for defence *and* civil R&D. A discrepancy of this magnitude cannot be explained by recourse to small changes of definition or coverage, and relate instead to the substantial problems of classification identified at the beginning of this section.[23]

Table 2.9: Source of Funds for UK Industrial R&D 1989

			£ millions
	Civil	Defence	Total
Government Funds	306	943	1249
Overseas Funds	739	284	1023
Private Industry	473	62	535
Own Funds	4430	364	4794
Total	5947	1653	7600

Source: CSO, **Business Monitor MO14 1989: Industrial Research and Development Expenditure and Employment**, Table 2.9.

3. UK Defence R&D Manpower

Although there is less information available about R&D manpower than expenditure, there are fewer consistency problems across the industry-government interface because staff, as opposed to expenditure, rarely cross that interface. Each sector is distinctly separate from the other and disparities in definition as to what constitutes `working on R&D' rarely surface and to what extent they exist is unknown.[24]

Table 2.10 shows that total central government employment on defence R&D fell from 40,300 in 1975 to a projected 22,100 by 1993 - a drop of more than 45 per cent. Importantly, `Qualified Scientist and Engineer' (QSE) manpower levels fell from 7500 to 4700 or 37 per cent, indicating an absolute reduction in numbers but increases in the intensity of QSEs. It seems likely, that as part of the historical evolution of the MoD research establishments, changes in the size and distribution of employment can partially be explained by the emergence of the *intelligent customer* role and the down-grading of development as an intramural priority. Highly qualified evaluators (QSEs) would be expected to be retained at the expense of more routine staff engaged in development work. However, the evidence only partially supports this view.

Table 2.10: Central Government Employment on Defence R&D

			Thousands	
	Total	QSEs	Tech's	Others
1975	40.3	7.5	6.9	25.9
1980	34.7	7.1	5.7	21.9
1985	23.8	5.1	3.9	15.0
1986	23.3	5.0	3.9	14.4
1987	22.7	5.0	3.9	14.1
1988	22.8	4.9	3.8	14.0
1989	21.4	4.7	3.7	13.0
1990	22.2	4.9	3.7	13.7
1991	21.2	4.8	3.7	12.8
1992	21.1	4.7	3.7	12.7
1993	21.1	4.7	3.7	12.7

Notes:
i. There is a break in the series from 1985 when reporting method changed from `as at 31/12' to `average for the year.'
ii. 1990-93 are estimates.

Sources: CSO, **Economic Trends** - various years; Cabinet Office, **Annual Review of Government Funded R&D** - various years.

A breakdown of intramural R&D expenditure between research and development is only available from 1982-83 onwards. From 1982-83 to 1986-87 the ratio of research to development did rise to a high of 0.65. Since then it has fallen consistently, to a projected 0.47 in 1992-93.[25] This fall is probably a result of the MoD reforms and a pre-emptive increase in industry contract work before and after the creation of the DRA in April 1991. The Research Establishent's development facilities (for example, wind tunnels and test chambers) are likely to further increase the ratio of sub-contract development to research.

Measuring defence R&D employment in industry is subject to the same problems as industrial expenditure (eg lack of coverage, infrequent surveys, changes in definitions and sample sizes and no distinction between defence and civil employment). The MoD does not collect industrial defence R&D

employment statistics and although certain industries do survey their members (eg The Electronic Industries Association), this gives only a very partial picture of the underlying situation. Fortunately, the 1989 Business Monitor sheds some light, again for the first time, on the split between defence and civil employment on R&D. The crowding-out debate has focussed on the assertion that defence R&D absorbs *too many* skilled personnel (usually QSEs), to the detriment of the civil economy.

Table 2.11 shows that industrial defence R&D work *is* more QSE intensive than civil (QSEs account for 50 per cent and 48 per cent of all staff engaged on R&D respectively) but it is doubtful whether it is significantly so. Somewhat surprising is that on average, civil industry spent £90,106 per QSE compared to the defence industry's £87,000 in 1989. However, these statistics are very difficult to interpret: they could reflect the relative QSE intensities, the differences in efficiency between the two sectors, or even the value in terms of expenditure that firms place on their QSE staff. We shall return to the analysis of relative wage-rates as a means of testing the crowding-out hypothesis in a later section. Having described the market, questions arise as to how well it works.

Table 2.11: Employment on Defence and Civil R&D in UK Industry 1989

	Civil	Defence	Total
Scientists and Engineers	66	19	85
Technicians, draughtsmen and lab. assistants	37	9	46
Administrative, clerical and other	36	9	45
Total	138	1653	7600
Total Expenditure (£m)	5947	1653	7600
of which salaries and wages (£m)	2609	602	3211

Note: i. Employment figures are in thousands.

Source: CSO, **Business Monitor MO14 1989: Industrial Research and Development Expenditure and Employment**; Tables 20 and 21.

Economic Performance

1. The Defence R&D Market

The performance of the UK defence R&D market has been the focus of considerable controversy. Critics point to cost escalation, delays in delivery, the failure of equipment to meet operational requirements, unreliability, a lack of export sales, too little spin-off to the civil sector and project cancellations. An MoD study found that typically, projects increased in real costs by 66 per cent from their initial estimates and by almost 30 per cent after full development started.[26] By 1990 the EH101 Merlin helicopter was more than a year behind schedule with a real cost increase of almost 30 per cent. Moreover, the Merlin is estimated to have a development to production cost ratio of about 1.1:1 which is regarded as uneconomic.[27] Likewise, the Light Anti-Tank Weapon (LAW 80) entered service five years later than planned with an increase in real development costs of 40 per cent.[28]

Inevitably, questions arise about the causes of poor performance and the criteria to be used in assessing performance in defence R&D markets. Typically, economists assess markets in terms of how well they are working and whether they show signs of major market failures resulting from monopolies, other imperfections, and harmful or beneficial externalities. State intervention is then proposed as a means of correcting for major market failures. On this basis, it *might* be concluded that since they are state-owned, the Government's defence research establishments and the DRA are working properly (operating in the public interest) and that market failures are confined to the private sector. Certainly, before the introduction of a competitive procurement policy, UK defence markets were imperfect: they were protected and non-competitive with cost-plus contracts and a "cosy" relationship between MoD and its suppliers. All of this suggests that these market failures were policy-created and policy-preferred, with governments as the source of market failure! This changed in 1983 with the introduction of competition into procurement and MoD; adoption of a more commercial attitude by subjecting defence firms to competition, fixed price or incentive contracts, and to risk-taking. In contrast, the former defence research establishments and the DRA are state-owned enterprises which have been traditionally protected from competition. Since 1983, efforts have been made to shift or contract-out some of their work to private industry, and the creation of the DRA is designed to introduce more commercial criteria into the agency.

Can the market failure approach explain the observed features and typical criticisms of UK defence R&D markets? Cost escalation, delays, gold plating and unreliable equipment can theoretically be explained, at least in part, by non-competitive markets and cost-plus contracts. Of course, suppliers are not the sole explanation of market performance. On the buying side, MoD's performance as a procurement agency and project manager is a further explanatory variable.[29] By their very nature, defence R&D markets are characterised by uncertainty. On this basis, no one can accurately predict the future so that mistakes are likely and initial estimates about cost, time and performance for new equipment have to be taken for what they are, namely, estimates about an uncertain future. This suggests that a search for zero cost escalation on new high technology defence equipment projects will be fruitless, and not necessarily optimal. There are, though, policies which might reduce cost escalation, delays and performance failures. For example, proceeding on an incremental basis allows the procurement agency to acquire additional information about the technical feasibility of an operational requirement, so enabling more accurate estimates to be obtained before proceeding to full development.[30] Or, a nation can purchase foreign defence equipment "off-the-shelf", paying an appropriate levy to compensate the overseas supplier (or its government) for the risks and uncertainties of R&D.[31]

Cuts in future defence budgets are likely to force MoD to reconsider the costs and benefits of its R&D programme. Increasing emphasis is being given to technology, and where MoD decides to retain key strategic technologies in the UK it will face further difficult choices. Should it drive a hard bargain with greater chances of bankruptcy, or should it protect the UK defence R&D base so as to provide an industrial capability for future expansion to respond to new and unexpected threats (the reconstitution argument)? Moreover, which are the essential strategic technologies; what is their strategic contribution; how costly are they; and does a commitment to maintain such technologies in the UK signal the end of competition in those spheres? For example, the US Department of Defense has a Critical Technologies Plan which identifies 22 technologies regarded as essential to guarantee the long-term qualitative superiority of US weapons systems (see Chapter 3). The technologies include micro-electronics, software, sensitive radars, passive sensors, robotics and high temperature, high strength, and high weight composite materials.[32] Such a technology policy raises wider questions about the benefits of defence R&D: what are the benefits of defence R&D; what about spin-off; and what are the costs, especially in relation to claims that defence R&D crowds out valuable civil investment?

2. The Benefits of Defence R&D

Supporters of UK spending on defence R&D claim a variety of military and wider technological and economic benefits.[33] The purported military benefits include the maintenance of a domestic strategic capability to ensure independence and security of supply, together with the ability to develop equipment to meet the requirements of the Armed Forces. In the technology sphere, it is claimed that defence R&D ensures that a nation remains at the frontiers of technology enabling it to achieve a comparative advantage over its rivals. There are claimed to be further economic benefits: that UK defence R&D supports jobs, contributes to the balance of payments and provides a valuable source of new ideas and technology which can be applied to the civil sector. But achieving these benefits is not costless, and consideration needs to be given to alternative methods of achieving the same or similar results. Indeed, more fundamental questions needs to be asked about the objectives of UK defence R&D: is the ultimate end the protection of UK citizens; or is it concerned with a broader set of economic and social objectives, some of which might be more appropriately pursued by other government departments?

Defence R&D markets are particularly criticised for their failure to achieve more spin-off to the civil sector. The belief is that the technology created by defence R&D should be more relevant and transferrable to the civil sector. This argument suggests a market failure in that a pool of valuable defence knowledge is not being transferred and exploited by the civil sector.

The relevant market is concerned with the dissemination and trade in ideas and intellectual property. Such markets are characterised by information problems and by difficulties of specifying property rights in ways which are legally enforceable at reasonable cost. How do the creators of new ideas in the defence sector discover whether their knowledge has market value in the civil sector; and how do potential users in the civil sector discover what is available in the defence R&D sector, and whether it has potential value in the civil economy? Information is not a free good: buyers and sellers need incentives if they are to devote scarce resources to searching the market. This raises three issues. First, the definition of the market must embrace the potential civil application of defence R&D undertaken at the Government's DRA, educational establishments and private industry. Second, how well the market in technology transfer works will depend on the behaviour and motivation of buyers and sellers in the market. (Have staff in the defence R&D sector the incentive or authority to sell their ideas to the civil sector?) Third, are there any major organisational, institutional and contractual barriers to information flows about defence R&D? For example, to improve the institutional arrangements for providing spin-off the MoD supported the creation of Defence Technology Enterprises, whose aim was to search for promising ideas in the research establishments and to alert interested companies.[34]

The interesting policy question remains: is there enough technology transfer, and how do we begin to answer this question? There is the belief that there exists a massive pool of valuable ideas generated by defence R&D simply awaiting exploitation by the civil sector. This view ignores the economics of information markets and property rights in ideas; it also neglects the fact that applying defence R&D ideas to the civil sector might be too costly, and that much defence R&D is specific to defence. Here, it is also relevant to remember that a considerable amount of defence development work is undertaken in private industry. There may be major barriers to transferring defence technology *within* and *between* firms. Within firms, companies might separate their defence and civil work for reasons of security, procurement and accounting practices, and regulatory requirements (see Chapter 9). Between firms, barriers to technology transfer can arise because having established property rights in valuable ideas, a firm will be unwilling to transfer such knowledge to other firms free of charge.

Such behaviour is not unique to defence (eg patenting by pharmaceutical companies). More generally, the relatively limited technology transfer either within or between private firms could reflect the fact that transfer is not regarded as profitable, or firms are not profit-maximisers (eg they act as satisficers).

The defence spin-off debate has been neglected by economists. Yet the potential existence of spin-off is postulated as the major positive economic externality arising from defence R&D. Efforts to measure spin-off might start by focusing on its market value and contribution to raising national output. This is a complex exercise requiring appropriate data which isolates the contribution of other influences on output. In the absence of such data, the alternative requires the use of proxy indicators. Examples include the number and value of new civil products, new production techniques and civilian patents which can be attributed to defence R&D; the effects of spin-off on company profitability; and in terms of transferrability, staff turnover between the defence and civil sectors. Indeed, the scientific labour market might be central to technology transfer. In the absence of firms transferring technology within or between themselves, ideas and knowledge can flow through the mobility of labour.

Thus, evaluating the role and actual and potential importance of defence spin-off is no easy task. In order to assess the success or otherwise of such spin-off we need to know three things. First, how to define and measure technology. Second, how to assess its potential transferability between sectors and third, how to evaluate the impact that transfer has on the recipient sector (see Chapter 5). In relation to the first two points the MoD stated that:-

"The chances of DTE uncovering what one might call a large number of ripe plums, bits of our technology that can be put straight on the market...are probably quite small."[35]

Transferability depends on many variables, not just the applicability of the technology itself. The MoD's view about DTE seems to have been vindicated. By 1990, five years after its birth only a small staff remained and the DTE `ferrets', employed within the research establishments to locate and transfer technology, had stopped work. The reasons for the decline of this much heralded organisation warrants further study, but its demise demonstrates that the recognition and transferability of defence technology is a complex area. Transfer may be easier in private industry where it can be internalised through informal contacts, common R&D departments and the mobility of staff. However, again the evidence is anecdotal, although valuable. Rigorous studies need to be undertaken in this area. The third point is perhaps even thornier: it is virtually impossible to identify all the *potential* impacts of a spin-off product or process and to measure them. Is it more valid to measure at a point in time, or over time (how long)?[36]

A partial approach to this problem (not yet applied to the defence sector) is to measure the reduction in production cost to firms and consumers of a technological innovation.[37] However, it is often difficult to identify such spill-overs. It is unusual for a development, especially in a private firm, to be purely a military development or purely backed by company or government defence funds. Assessing spin-off at an aggregate level by summing the results of detailed case studies is impractical and potentially misleading. Another approach is the econometric study. Despite limitations, the *net* effects on the economy of defence R&D spending may be assessed with some confidence in a correctly specified and tested model. Econometric studies are however, sensitive to the quality of data, specification and lag structure of the model - problems which are all severe in the study of defence R&D. It is also difficult to derive a *testable* model which isolates the influence of spin-off: is there a proxy variable for spin-off given the problems of identification raised above? Even if we could assess the economic affects of actual spin-off, if potential spin-off is not occuring it is simply not possible to assess the harmful or beneficial affects to society which that spin-off might have had.

A rigorous economic evaluation of spin-off at the economy-wide level does not seem possible at the present time. Until major conceptual and measurement problems are resolved analysts have to rely on a growing body of qualitative case-study evidence. However, we still cannot make meaningful generalisations such as, `there is not enough spin-off' or `there is sufficient spin-off' to justify defence R&D on economic grounds. Fortunately, the burdens of defence R&D are easier to assess.

3. The Burdens of Defence R&D

In the UK, the Ministry of Defence has stated that:-

"...the Government shares the underlying concern of those who fear that necessary investment in defence R&D may crowd out valuable investment in the civil sector...Britain's resources of qualified scientists and engineers and the skilled manpower supporting them, are not inexhaustible..., and it would be regrettable if defence work became such an irresistible magnet for the manpower available that industry's ability to compete in the international market for civil high technology projects became seriously impaired."[38]

In fact since 1985 there have been reductions in the level of government-funded defence R&D spending, both in real terms and as a share of the defence budget. Table 2.1 shows in narrow terms that the defence R&D burden has declined precipitously, as approximated by its share of GDP. However, other studies have been critical of defence R&D for broader reasons. One concluded that civil research into high technology areas in Great Britain has been impeded by the:-

"...absorption of a large proportion of the pool of skilled manpower by military R&D and production"[39]

Similarly, the Council for Science and Society's report on UK military R&D noted that the central question concerns the opportunity cost of military R&D:-

"...would the resources currently employed in defence make a greater contribution to jobs, technology, the balance of payments, and, ultimately, to human welfare if they were used elsewhere in the economy?"[40]

In 1989 the Advisory Council on Science and Technology concluded an extensive investigation into the economic implications of defence R&D. It too was concerned about the:-

"...pre-emption of resources ... too large a part of industry's innovative management and financial capacity (is) being concentrated upon military technologies which have not provided companies with a competitive advantage, or the incentive to acquire one, in civil areas".[41]

The effects of defence R&D are:-

"...believed to be realised through market distortions which produce either an excessive allocation of resources (primarily qualified scientists and engineers [QSEs]) to defence, or else a lack of private sector incentives to exploit technologies to the maximum benefit of both defence and civil sectors"[42]

Clearly, this is a field dominated by myths and emotion which need to be subject to independent evaluation and empirical testing. Three questions need to be addressed. First, what is meant by crowding-out? Second, why and how does it occur? And third, what is the evidence?

At a general level, defence is not unique. Crowding-out occurs whenever an economy's resources are fully and efficiently employed. R&D expenditure on Trident and the European Fighter Aircraft may be at the expense of the NHS; expenditure on the NHS may be at the expense of education and transport. Thus, all activities involve the sacrifice of something else, and choices about the *desirable* level of UK defence R&D spending raise at least three issues. First, an assessment is required of society's preferences and its willingness to pay for domestic defence R&D: this involves an appraisal of the mechanisms for expressing such preferences (eg voting, elections, interest groups, lobbying, etc).[43] Second, to enable society to make informed choices, evidence is needed on the magnitude of any crowding-out effects or trade-offs. Third, any economic appraisal of UK defence R&D needs to include all its direct and indirect costs and benefits. For example, the wider economic consequences of defence R&D are likely to act with lengthy lag effects so that any impact on the civil economy might not appear until many years later.

The crowding-out hypothesis also needs to be clarified. What is being crowded-out: investment or civil R&D expenditure, or is it scarce scientific manpower? If manpower is the constraint, a distinction needs to be made between the short and long-run, or between stocks and flows. If the supply of scientists is perfectly inelastic, an increase in demand will raise their price. But over time, and in a properly-functioning market, a shortage of scientists will raise relative salaries and attract more manpower into the field. Failure of the labour market to respond to relative scarcities suggests the potential for public policy measures to improve the operation of the market. Nor does it follow that in the short run, a reduction in UK defence R&D will release manpower resources for civil R&D: released resources might move into administration and management, they might become unemployed, or even emigrate.

More generally, questions arise as to what *extent* defence R&D and civil R&D expenditure and employment are substitutes. It is also possible that the effects of crowding-out are more intangible, operating through corporate culture and management attitudes. Traditionally, managers might have become attracted by, and dependent on the special and unique technological, quality and contractual (cost-plus) requirements of defence R&D markets, so creating a culture of dependency rather than enterprise. In this context, crowding-out means that firms are diverting their resources to protected defence markets (the magnet effect), creating a harmful externality in which defence firms are not entrepreneurial. In turn, this would be reflected in adverse effects on their international competitiveness (a culture which might have changed with MoDs new competition policy).

However, the quotations above indicate that the prime concern about the UK defence sector is that it attracts an "excessive allocation" of highly qualified and scarce R&D manpower. Whilst it is difficult to determine what a non-excessive allocation of QSEs for defence would be, a proxy measure for the pressure that the defence sector exerts on the market for QSEs is the relative remuneration of defence and civil QSEs.

From Table 2.11, salaries and wages accounted for 44 per cent of total civil R&D but only 38 per cent of defence R&D. Since there is little or no concern in the literature about the supply of technicians, clerical or other R&D staff, except QSEs, there can cautiously assumed to be a reasonably elastic supply of such staff. Thus their wages and salaries should be approximately equalised across the civil-defence interface. This in turn implies that the discrepancy in wage shares is in large part due to the lower pay of defence R&D QSEs relative to their civil counterparts. Defence QSEs are probably at a larger proportionate disadvantage financially than is suggested by the average pay-differential of £3064 per annum between industrial civil and defence R&D workers in 1989.[44]

The implications of this finding are difficult to interpret. The defence industry, in aggregate, certainly does not appear to be attracting manpower through superior pay-rates. However, by the same token civil industry may have to offer higher salaries to entice QSEs from the greater status and challenge of defence work. Defence R&D expenditure is also heavily concentrated in the aerospace and electronics industries (Table 2.8). In contrast, civil R&D is widely dispersed, although especially concentrated in chemicals (chiefly pharmaceuticals). This asymmetry in the distribution of defence and civil R&D may also be an important factor in the differential average salary. Unfortunately, further disaggregation at the industry level is not possible for salaries and wages. Our aggregate comparison could be biased if salaries are generally higher in the chemical industry than in electronics and aerospace. What is needed, but not available, are data on relative defence and civil salaries in the *same* industries.

There is, therefore, some tentative evidence that crowding-out does not operate through pay inducements, but information at the industry level is necessary before we can be sure. However, staff may also be crowded out by the influence of other factors such as status, and salary may be a relatively minor consideration.

What is clear is that satisfactory tests of the crowding-out hypothesis require much more in-depth data about both civil and defence expenditure and employment. There is also a serious lack of clearly-specified models showing the relationship between all the relevant variables in the system. Such an approach is often ignored. Instead, emphasis is given to simple models which attribute all the UK's economic problems to a single cause, namely high levels of defence spending (particularly R&D), where correlation and causation are often confused. For example, the ACOST Report concluded that the evidence for the crowding-out or pre-emption of resources by the defence sector is often anecdotal and inconclusive.[45] Other studies have made contrary assertions and have found that not only does military spending crowd-out investment, but that it has a greater crowding-out effect on investment than welfare state expenditures.[46] However, these results are not universal. When they were subjected to further empirical tests, it was found that they were sensitive to the nations included in the sample, to the use of time-series analysis for each nation, and to distinguishing defence R&D from other components of military spending.[47]

Conclusion and Policy Options

The future trend in UK defence R&D expenditure is difficult to predict. On the one hand, radical changes in Europe's political and military environment might shift the focus from manpower to equipment and lighter, more mobile and rugged forces. All this suggests change, and the substitution of equipment for manpower requires R&D expenditure. On the other hand there is concurrent pressure on total military budgets, and a specific commitment in the UK to gradually reduce real defence R&D expenditure to 1997. The Overview section starkly illustrates the fact that defence R&D as a *direct* burden on the UK economy has fallen dramatically since the early 1980s. On balance the likelihood is that it will continue to do so.

However, defence R&D also has *indirect* economic consequences and it is important to address these issues in order to determine its net effects. The performance of the defence R&D market is one such indirect effect: internal efficiency needs to be improved. This chapter has also addressed the two main economic issues, spin-off (a positive externality) and crowding-out (a negative externality). Unfortunately, the actual and potential extent of spin-off is particularly difficult to identify. One approach may be to study the cost-reducing impact of defence innovations. However, aggregation to sector-wide levels is impausible at present. Crowding-out and the the diversion of scarce QSEs is postulated as the major indirect burden of defence R&D. However, recently available data does not support the view that the defence sector lures manpower by means of higher salaries. Instead, the status and technical challenge associated with defence work may be significant non-monetary attractions.

In terms of policy options, any future proposals to cut defence R&D will encounter opposition from those groups likely to lose from such a policy. Concern will be expressed about the losses of both jobs and the UK's `leading edge' technologies. The issues are likely to be reflected in some major procurement choices, such as the cancellation of a large on-going project (eg EFA; EH101 Merlin helicoptor), or a decision to import rather than `buy British'. Increasingly, pressures on defence budgets will require some difficult choices, with defence R&D as one element in the choice-set. Other options include cuts in manpower and equipment for each of the Armed Forces. There will also be economic and political pressures to increase European co-operation in defence procurement (see Chapter 8). The EUCLID programme is an example of future possibilities for co-operation (see Chapter 7). Similarly, it is unlikely that European nations will incur the duplications of costly R&D, reflected in the simultaneous development of three modern combat aircraft (EFA, Gripen and Rafale).

The prospect of cuts in defence R&D raise questions about the appropriate role for public policies. The search for a Peace Dividend requires a re-allocation of resources from military to civilian activities. Such an adjustment will take time and involve costs reflected in the unemployment of capital and labour. Public policy has a role in assisting the re-allocation through manpower and regional policies. On an optimistic note there is no shortage of challenging research problems within the civil sector for released QSEs. Examples include basic research in universities, a new generation of supersonic airliners, space exploration, environmental problems and health research. However, the danger is that QSEs may have defence-specific skills and in some instances retraining costs may have to be borne by government.

Endnotes

1. Anthony I., Allebeck A.C. and Wulf H., **West European Arms Production**, Stockholm International Peace Research Institute, 1990.

2. *Ibid.*

3. See Whitt II, D., **American Realignment of Defense Management Decision-Making**, Solicited Research Report 6, Centre for Studies in Defence Resources Management, National Defence College, Kingston, Canada, 1992. (For a broader discussion of the current evolution of US defence policy.)

4. Remarks prepared for delivery by J. Atwood in **Industrial Base Shares Inevitable Gulf Victory** to Washington DC Chapter of the National Security Industrial Association on 21/2/91, *Defence Issues*, Vol. 6, Number 9 (undated) p. 2. Quoted in Whitt II *op. cit.* p. 40.

5. For a good exposition of this controversial role see Yudken, J. and Black, M., **Towards a New National Needs Agenda for Science and Technology Policy: The Prospects for Democratic Science and Technology Policymaking**, in Bischak G. A. (ed), *Towards a Peace Economy in the United States*, Macmillan, London 1991; and **Defence Technology and Industrial/Technology Policy in the USA**, Appendix 6 in Science Policy Support Group, *Future Relations Between Defence and Civil Science and Technology*, London 1991.

6. Deger, S., **World military expenditure**, *SIPRI Yearbook 1991 World Armaments and Disarmament*, Oxford University Press, 1991, p. 119.

7. The increase has been particularly marked in Germany, Italy and Spain (rising from 9.6% to 13.3%, 5.7% to 10.3% and 6.4% to 19.1% respectively during 1983-1989). France has also seen a rise from 32.7% to 37%. The situation in the smaller EC states is more stable and the defence share of the total public R&D budget in the UK has actually fallen. Data from **Main Science and Technology Indicators**, Organisation for Economic Cooperation and Development, Paris, various issues.

8. See Graziola, G. and Nones, M., **Recent trends in R&D in Italy and in military R&D in particular** in Gummett, P. and Reppy, J. (eds), *The Relations between Defence and Civil Technologies*, Kluwer Academic Publishers, Dordrecht 1988; for Spain see and Molas-Gellart. J., **Spanish Participation in the International Development and Production of Arms Systems**, *Defense Analysis*, Vol. 6, No. 4, 1990.

9. Parliamentary Office of Science and Technology, **Relationships Between Defence and Civil Science and Technology**, POST, London 1991, pp. 20-21.

10. Ministry of Defence, **Statement on the Defence Estimates**, Vol. 1, HMSO, London, 1989, pp. 33.

11. Dunsire, A., Hartley, K. and Parker, D., **Organisational Status and Performance: Summary of the Findings**, *Public Administration*, 69, 1991, pp. 21-40.

12. Ministry of Defence, **Defence Statistics 1992 Edition**, HMSO, London, 1992.

13. *Ibid.*

14. *Ibid.*

15. HCP 431, **The Procurement of Major Defence Equipment**, Defence Committee, HMSO, London 1988.

16. However, in the US the distinction between development and the down-stream activities of routine testing and evaluation is at least made obvious.

17. See HL 44, **Definitions of R&D**, House of Lords Select Commitee on Science and Technology, HMSO, London, 1989-90, for a discussion of the interpretation and implementation of the Frascati definitions. In particular the UK MoD asserts that it has more trouble in fitting accounting data to the definitions than in interpreting the definitions themselves.

18. See HL 44, *op. cit.*; HL 47, **Classification of Defence R&D Expenditure**, House of Lords Select Committee on Science and Technology, HMSO, London, 1991-92; and HCP 105, **Classification of Defence Research and Development Expenditure**, National Audit Office, HMSO, London, 1991, for an in-depth discussion of the classification debate.

19. Ministry of Defence, **Statement on the Defence Estimates**, Vol. 1, HMSO, 1987, p.48.

20. See chapter by Gummett, P., **The Government of Military R&D in Britain**, in Mendelsohn, E., Smith, M,. and Weingart, P. (eds), *Science, Technology and the Military*, Kluwer Academic Press, Dorderecht, 1988.

21. A possible exception being the periodic reshuffling of certain corporations' public or private status as they are nationalised and privatised (eg the UKAEA became a private company in 1986 and was therefore surveyed as a *private concern* by the CSO. It was included in the annual survey of *government* departments in the previous year).

22. Such as the more regular, but less comprehensive, surveys reported in issues of **Trade and Industry**, **British Business** and the **Business Bulletins**.

23. See Buck, D., **Problems with UK defence R&D statistics**, *Science and Public Policy*, 1993 (forthcoming) for a detailed account of these problems.

24. HL 44, *op. cit.*, devotes only two paragraphs to R&D personnel.

25. Data from Ministry of Defence, **Statement on the Defence Estimates**, HMSO, London - various years.

26. Ministry of Defence, **Learning from Experience**, HMSO, London, 1988, p. 6.

27. HCP 145, **The Procurement of the EH101 Helicoptors and the Light Attack Helicoptor**, Defence Committee, HMSO, London, 1990.

28. HCP 350, **The Procurement of the Light Anti-Tank Weapon**, Defence Committee, HMSO, London, 1989.

29. MoD, 1988 *op. cit.*; and Hartley, K., **The Economics of Defence Policy**, Brasseys, London, 1991.

30. MoD, 1988, *op. cit.*

31. Hartley, 1991, *op. cit.*

32. S1085, **Defence Industry and Technology**, Committee on the Armed Services, US Senate, US Government Printing Office, Washington DC, 1989.

33. See Parliamentary Office of Science and Technology, *op. cit.* for a discussion of likely costs and benefits.

34. *Ibid.*

35. HL20, **Civil Research and Development: Volume II - Oral Evidence**, House of Lords Select Committee on Science and Technology, 1986-7, p. 491.

36. See Smith, K., **Economic Returns to R&D: Methods, Results and Challenges**, SPSG Review Paper No3, Science Policy Support Group, London, 1991, for a discussion of such general conceptual problems.

37. For example see Bresnahan, T., **Measuring the spillovers in technical advance: mainframe computers and financial services**, *American Economic Review*, Vol. 76, 1986, pp. 742-55.

38. Ministry of Defence, **Statement on the Defence Estimates**, HMSO, 1987, p.48.

39. Kaldor, M., Sharp, M. and Walker, W., **Industrial competitiveness and Britain's defence**, *Lloyds Bank Review*, October 1986, p. 31.

40. Council for Science and Society, **UK Military R&D**, Oxford University Press, Oxford, 1986, p.40.

41. Advisory Council on Science and Technology, **Defence R&D: A National Resource**, HMSO, London, 1989, p. 16.

42. *Ibid*, p.17.

43. For an interesting and novel approach to this problem with respect to aggregate defence spending see Jones-Lee, M., **Defence Expenditure and the Economics of Safety**, *Defence Economics*, Vol. 1 (1), 1990; and McClelland, W., **Comment** and subsequent **Reply** in *Defence Economics*, Vol. 2 (1) 1990.

44. The mean pay for each sector merely equals total salaries and wages bill divided by total employment, easily calculated from Table 1.11. Average remuneration for civil R&D is therefore £2609m/138000 = £18906 and for defence, £602m/38000= £15842.

45. Advisory Council on Science and Technology, *op. cit.*, p.19.

46. Fagerberg, J., **International Competitiveness**, *Economic Journal*, Vol. 98, 1988, pp. 355-374.

47. Hartley, K., and Singleton, J., **Defence R&D and crowding-out**, *Science and Public Policy*, Vol. 7 (3), 1990, pp. 152-156.

Chapter 3

Technology Dependence: The Hidden Side of Defence Research and Development

Martin Edmonds

Background

The 1990/91 Gulf War has been interpreted as the harbinger of the future conduct of war. For the first time in a major engagement between two heavily armed antagonists, the superior "intelligent" weapon systems afforded one side a decisive technological superiority and operational advantage. In the event, making allowances for issues of morale, training, and leadership, there was scarcely any serious contest. Early prognoses of casualties to both sides were proved hopelessly inaccurate. The clash between the two armies did not turn out to be "the mother of all wars" that the Iraqi Leader had promised, and the duration of the land war, a mere 100 hours, was all that was needed to bring the conflict to an end. The full extent of the casualties to the Iraqi forces remains unknown - and may never be fully accounted for - though for the Allies', bearing in mind the number of weapons employed, the losses in men and equipment were comparatively negligible.

The immediate lesson for all those participating, as well as observers of the conflict, was clear: the "emerging" or "smart" weapons technologies about which many had been writing and speculating over the previous decade had not merely arrived; with adequate logistic support, preparation time, and intelligence, they had also demonstrated that they could perform, and perform effectively, against designated targets.[1]

For future defence technology, the less obvious but nonetheless important lessons were that the United States had emerged with a commanding lead in most of these weapon systems; the technologies required to develop them were not just extremely expensive, but substantially beyond the financial and technological capacity of most nations; and the sheer logistical and organisational complexity of introducing them into the order of battle a distortion to existing military forces.

The image of future war on the Gulf model thus presented governments and service chiefs with a paradox: on the one hand defence-related "smart" technology was becoming both something that states could not do without in future conflict and therefore had to find ways of acquiring, whilst on the other hand the limited resources and technologies at their disposal constrained their ability to be able to respond adequately.

This was acknowledged by the Soviet High Command, the only military with access to the level of military spending and technology to match that of the United States, before the break-up of the USSR.[2] Now that the economies of the former Soviet Republics are in difficulty and the future of the Soviet Armed Forces remains in doubt, the prospect of "smart" weapons being developed outside the USA for many years is highly unlikely. As the former Red Army breaks up into the forces of the separate independent Republics, the economies of those Republics, with the possible exception of the Russian Federation, are not strong enough to sustain a programme of weapons research and development, even if the expertise is available.[3]

One of the principal drivers behind the Cold War, the Soviet-American arms race, has effectively lost its *raison d'etre* and former momentum: political and economic difficulties within Eastern Europe and the new Commonwealth of Independent States in the wake of the abortive coup against Mr Gorbachev in August 1991 and the end of the Soviet Union in the December, have meant that the ex-Soviet military forces are no longer regarded as a risk to Western Security. The imperative of driving defence-related technology forward has diminished even further as the Russian leader and Head of the Commonwealth of Independent States, Boris Yeltsin, makes overtures to the USA that the two countries should collaborate over "star wars" technology to their mutual advantage, seeks Western technological help to dismantle the burgeoning, but predominantly redundant, ex-Soviet nuclear arsenal, and presides over arguments between the Commonwealth Republics over future ownership of the facilities, equipment, and infrastructure of the former Soviet military machine.[4]

Future Scenarios

Nevertheless, uncertainties remain. The sense of urgency in the 1980s that characterised the search for new weapons technologies to act as "force multipliers" against a numerically superior adversary has significantly receded, but instabilities within the old Soviet Empire and elsewhere in Eastern Europe, having lain dormant for seventy years and during the cold war period, have now begun to surface. These present both East and West with new conflict scenarios and military operational requirements.

It is to these new potential threats that governments and service chiefs are turning their attention. All recognise, as the lessons of history have made clear, regional instabilities and disputes are not merely a menace to normal life. If allowed to develop unchecked they pose a threat both to the security of Europe and to that of the North Atlantic area as a whole. These are issues to which Western intelligence services must be retasked, and to which the new weapon systems technologies demonstrated to such dramatic effect in the Gulf need to be addressed, developed and applied.

The uncertainties inherent in a Europe whose past was dependent on a stable relationship between the old super-powers will have to be addressed with some urgency. Furthermore, they have to be confronted by the Europeans themselves in the first instance, since no long term expectations can be made of either the USA or the disintegrating Commonwealth of Independent States. Europe therefore has to face three critical questions, each of which bears directly on decisions all the states must make regarding their future security: first, whether the USA is likely to want to remain entangled within and be a part of any future European security architecture or will choose an isolationist role; second, whether or not the necessary resources are likely to be forthcoming to modernise military forces with smart weaponry; and last, can any consensus be found on what is needed and how it will be acquired on a European-wide, as distinct from a national, basis (see Chapter 7)?

Against these projected new scenarios must be set the expectations of a general public, both in Britain and Europe. It is generally accepted - or at least that is the popular perception - that the British population (though perhaps to a lesser degree elsewhere in Europe) has been rendered economically poorer by 40 years of military confrontation. Most would admit that they have been psychologically and emotionally bruised by anxieties and fears of nuclear armageddon. With the end to the Cold War, public expectations of "peace dividends" and the diversification or conversion of defence oriented manufacture and development to civilian products and needs, have merged with a conviction that high defence expenditure on sophisticated weapon systems has been to the detriment of overall industrial and technological competitiveness.

These impressions are supported by contrasts drawn between the economic and industrial performance of those states such as Britain, the United States, France and the Soviet Union, which have maintained a high level of military spending as a proportion of GNP for the past 40 years, and a high level of military R&D expenditure as a proportion of the total scientific and technological spending, with that of the Japanese, German, and the "Pacific Rim" States where defence expenditure as a percentage of GDP has been relatively low and industrial investment high. More recently, internal debates about "dual-use" or "dual-market" technologies have emerged, in part to explore ways of meeting both the demands of defence and the need for more resources to be allocated to commercially competitive products in the international market-place.[5]

Like Dr Doolittle's "pushme-pullyou", defence technology is being propelled in two directions. In one direction, the experience of the Gulf War emphasises the imperatives of modern, "smart" weapons. In the other, the nature of threats to national security is radically and rapidly changing. The world as a whole is becoming a more uncertain place and Europe, for long the focus of rivalry and tension, no less unstable. However, few if any national economies can afford to maintain the momentum of modern defence technology. Politically, governments would neither be allowed under present circumstances to continue to spend on military R&D at past levels of expenditure, nor would they for pragmatic reasons even entertain such a policy.[6]

Manifestly, some hard choices have had to be taken. Doubtless there will be more to come as the world adjusts to the new post-Cold War circumstances. New national security objectives will have to be defined, as will new strategic principles. More especially, new military capabilities will have to be acquired together with the more intractable problem of finding ways to afford them. Furthermore, these are the same set of choices the USA must address as its economy deteriorates, its national debt - already an annual burden on the economy - worsens, and the restless mood of its population over declining standards of living, unemployment, and industrial decline over many fronts, increases.

From Defence Independence to Defence Dependence

Over the past forty-seven years, there has been a steady, if not always acknowledged, change among the Western powers in their approach and attitudes to defence and security. The Second World War was largely fought by the armed forces of independent states in alliance through which they agreed strategies, coordinated operational plans, combined - even integrated - national military formations. For the most part they indigenously developed and produced equipment. In those instances where there was either limited production capability or poor weapons performance, the Allies looked to the United States for military aid and assistance (see Chapter 6). The "arsenal of democracy" (the US) was the only state secure from enemy bombardment with the necessary manufacturing potential to meet the equipment needs of the Allied forces. Furthermore, it was the US industrial resources that gave it a significant technological lead in specific categories of weapons, culminating in 1945 with the atomic bomb. For all the degree of cooperation during the War, perhaps the dominant characteristic was the degree of independence with which the Allied armed forces fought, albeit in combined operations, under a single Supreme Commander assisted by a combined planning staff.

After the military defeat of Germany and Japan, the allies' expectation was to demobilise and withdraw their forces as rapidly as possible back to their own states. Idealistic notions of collective security in the wake of their experience as allies were frustrated, and even attempts at regional security integration were thwarted by essentially nationalistic priorities and a state-centric view of the world. National sovereignty was not something to be lightly relinquished; and within that context, national military forces and an indigenous weapons manufacturing capability became a state's most potent symbol of sovereignty and independence, as General de Gaulle was later to epitomise.

NATO has remained a regional security arrangement between independent and sovereign states, though economic constraints and practical requirements have served to promote policies of military equipment rationalization (see Chapter 8), standardization and interoperability (RSI) among its members.[7] However, state interests have tended to prevail over the logic of combined operational planning. The extent of force structure and equipment commonality has not been as extensive as was expected, nor have either met the levels later demanded by the central NATO planners.

No simple, let alone objective, explanation can or has been comprehensively proffered for this obvious failure in allied security planning, except that most states seem to have held to the view that such an obvious initiative leading towards a process of trans-national integration was not compatible with strictly national military, political and economic interests.[8] The consequence was that the total of European security was less than the sum of the parts. At root, however, was a deep seated fear that too much military integration with other states would create a dependency. There was general belief that such a reliance on another state in such a fundamental area of national policy would impose a constraint on a state's freedom of action in the international arena.

If this has been the predominant attitude - and at least among the public there is clear evidence to suggest that this was indeed the case - then the image of military cooperation and integration within the NATO alliance has largely been a myth. Indeed, the reality has been quite the opposite. Military force, or capability, is broadly made up of three elements: human resources, (soldiers, sailors, airmen and their civil administrative support); organizations, (the armed forces units and their command infrastructure); and equipment, (weapon systems and their attendant logistic support facilities). To be sovereign in matters of national security, a state would have to be independent in all three elements.

All states largely meet the first criterion; however, states such as Britain, for historical reasons, incorporate military units from foreign states within their armed services' structures (such as Gurkhas). France is in a similar position since she employs a range of foreign nationals in military units, such as the French Foreign Legion. Smaller, Third World or emergent states look to larger, often ex-colonial, states to provide military advisers and combat units under the terms of bilateral treaties.

In the second category, that of military organizations and command and control infrastructure, there is a significant degree of loss of national sovereignty, especially in military alliances. In the NATO case there are military logistical and command infrastructures upon which all the members depend in varying degrees. An integrated command structure was judged by the NATO allies to have been one of the strengths of the old Soviet Union and its Warsaw Pact allies. In dismantling first the Warsaw Pact, and subsequently the former Soviet armed forces, those responsible are finding the problem of creating new command structures one of the most difficult to resolve.[9]

In the last, that of equipment, no state any longer, with the possible exception of the United States (and only then up to a point), can seriously claim to be wholly or even significantly independent in either defence-related technology, development or production. Progressively over the post-war period, the dependence of states upon each other in the research, development and acquisition of weapons systems has increased. In some cases this has taken the form of an interdependence, thereby establishing a synergism between the parties concerned in specific areas of technology; in others the dependence is more one way where one party is qualitatively superior to the other.

Dependence and interdependence in weapons technology and acquisition have today reached a point where even the United States acknowledges its reliance on external sources to enable it to meet the new equipment requirements of its armed services.[10] The Soviet Union may have largely been independent up to the end of 1991, but it has also had to look in recent years to foreign participation or involvement, directly or indirectly, to supply technologies necessary for meeting its new and primarily conventional military equipment requirements.[11] What then, does all this mean, as states address the uncertainties of the post-Gulf, post Cold-War scenario?

Defence Technology

Technology, defined in the OED as "the science of the industrial arts", is often confused with end products, or output. Insufficient recognition is given to the design, development, testing and manufacturing processes that lead to the end product. Thus the weapon becomes seen as the technology rather than the technological process - the know-how, skills and manufacturing processes - that brought it into being. The technocist, therefore, is one who has mastered the details and terminology of industry; the technologist is the person who understands its methodology. In sum, technology is the knowledge of how to design, develop and fabricate artifacts that meet a demand or human need. In simple terms it is know-how, and is directly concerned with the integration of manufacturing processes, product design, understanding of materials and quality control testing.

As products become more complex and complicated, so the requirements they are expected to satisfy become even more demanding. The situation becomes increasingly one of "Catch-22" and one which has been characterized as a "Baroque Arsenal".[12] Weapons systems and defence-related equipment are more complex and "state-of-the-art" than most. It is extremely unlikely that the requisite "know-how" will be found in any single person, corporation or even partnership. More probably it will reside within a wide network of associated and linked individuals and companies working together in a clearly defined and understood team.

There are few more challenging areas of technological endeavour than in the development and production of major combat systems. One result of this development is the emergence of the technologist as system or product designer and integrator, drawing together the range of technological skills necessary to complete and deliver complex products. Another is the technologist as manager and quality controller, with the skill to control a large technological programme, test complex systems, and ultimately ensure the required levels of reliability and performance.

Technology, therefore, comes in many forms and has its own taxonomy. Taken to mean a body of knowledge related to creative activity, that is to say related to industrial and manufacturing output, several types of technology can be readily identified. An "enabling" technology is one of fundamental importance and refers to the know-how without which other essential stages in a manufacturing process would be impossible. Examples of enabling technologies include the outcome of pure research into the properties of materials, or the know-how necessary to build and, moreover, programme computers.

One much overlooked but quite fundamental area of "enabling" technology is the more craft-based than strictly scientific work - such as optical coating and large section welding - which comes only as a result of long experience and natural talent. This has sometimes been referred to as "black art" technology, and one which those engaged in technological audit have identified as the potential achilles heel of costly major technology-based programmes, and a source of vulnerability in large industrial corporations.

Another category is that of "critical technology". This is generally taken to be that know-how which, when applied to existing demands, significantly and quantifiably meets certain performance and quality design criteria.[13] For example, a critical technology would be expected to enhance by a factor of three, one or more, of the following criteria: the performance of existing products; new products with new capabilities; improvements in the availability and reliability of existing products; and reductions in production costs. "Critical technologies often represent examples of cutting-edge technologies embedded in larger technology areas."[14]

Certain technologies almost always appear on critical technology lists such as micro-electronics, computer software, and materials. It is these technologies that are considered likely to make an appreciable difference to the end product or its cost; they are expected to extend the state-of-the-art, and are seen as the "star performers". However, they should not be seen independently of all science and technology strategies and developments; whilst they assume a central role and attract priority funding, they cannot and do not provide the whole answer in modern product development.

Both "enabling" and "critical" technologies apply to military and civil markets with equal importance. The highly sophisticated requirements of defence and military security, and the attendant need for secrecy, might suggest greater sensitivity where defence-related technology is concerned. However, advances in modern technologies have been such that the civilian commercial market is no less demanding in the complexity and scope of its products. Furthermore, the consequences of a failure to draw extensively on civil technological progress over a broad front, or to invest selectively in their development, is no less potentially catastrophic for the security of the state than those responsible agencies of government failing to keep abreast with the "state-of-the-art" in military equipment.

The optimum position would be to achieve technological synergism between civil and military technologies and correspondingly civil and military markets, and to break down the barriers between them erected on national security grounds.

Once referred to as "spin-off", to suggest that costly and product-specific investment in military-related technology could be justified in the light of benefits to civil product development (see Chapter 2), this synergism was found to be wanting. Secrecy, high product specificity, micro-management, overcentralization, and over-engineering have determined that in reality very little military technology research and development funding found its way into the civil sector; nor, some have argued, would it be appropriate for it to be attempted because the commercial market is simply much too dynamic.[15]

As new technologies emerged, particularly in micro-electronics, so advances in the civil sector were found to have cost-effective military applications. Their acceptability, however, was only possible after some adjustment to military prejudices and attitudes, and a sharp reduction in defence appropriations. Governments and military procurement agencies now consciously look to support "dual-use" or "dual market" technologies in order to promote synergism and cost-benefits for both sectors. Nevertheless, the perceived imperatives of both commercial and military secrecy present impediments to its progress.

The distinction between "civil" and "defence" technology is therefore largely artificial; the real distinction lies in their respective markets and how they operate. Technology as the "know-how" to design and manufacture products that satisfy a demand, and operate within a defined market, is a means. The civil/military technology distinction refers only to the market. For example, more pistols are owned and used by private citizens in the United States than are issued to members of the armed forces. Many share the same specification and use the same ammunition. What makes pistol technology `military' is the probability that it was originally researched, developed and manufactured to meet a military specification and requirement, with finance provided from the armed services directly and indirectly from the defence budget.

Some products are almost exclusively military either by dint of the law - which gives only the armed services exclusive right to have possession of them - or because of the absence of any obvious civilian demand. Submarines are not high on civil companies' list of capital expenditure, and nor would they be in the market for such products as armoured vehicles or artillery pieces. These can be identified most easily from the returns of companies with a 100% turnover derived from military contracts such as Royal Ordnance, GIAT, and DCN.[16] Nevertheless, there are likely to be hundreds, if not thousands, of components incorporated in exclusively military products such as fighter aircraft or naval ships, which are likely to be found and more or less duplicated exactly in very different civilian products. One extension of this point is the extent to which it is both misleading and largely incorrect to refer to a `defence industrial base', or correspondingly, a `defence technological base'.[17]

Technological Dependence

During 1988, the US Defense Science Board (DSB), among a number of other US Agencies, conducted an enquiry into US defence science and technology and the condition of American industry. The Board's general conclusion - and there was a high degree of consensus with the numerous reports that were tabled - was that there was a significant increase in offshore procurement of defence-related material. The DSB also noted that "globalization not only means dependence on foreign sources for raw materials, but also for manufactured products."[18] Whereas raw materials could be stockpiled for use in an emergency, "more and more defense systems require foreign manufactured components and assembly".

The one factor giving cause for concern was the absence of any reliable or comprehensive means of measuring the extent of offshore component acquisition. Without such data, questions as to how vulnerable US defence had become to outside constraint could not be satisfactorily answered. Without those answers, the necessary policies and strategies which the Department of Defense should adopt to control or remedy the problem could not be adequately formulated.[19]

The recommended approach from the Pentagon's perspective was to determine what areas of defence-related technology, irrespective of wider national industrial, economic and commercial needs, were judged not merely necessary, but absolutely fundamental, for the USA to be entirely self-sufficient. Before this could be achieved it was deemed necessary to acquire a data base on existing US industrial and technological capabilities. Whilst data were relatively easily available on prime defence contractors and the producers of major weapon systems and secondary items such as major sub-systems, it was almost impossible to discover data on sub-assemblies and components manufacture.[20]

Once this vulnerability had been established, and industrial sectors identified where there were obvious weaknesses which could jeopardise a US defence industrial production "surge" capacity in an emergency, appropriate government-led responses and action could be initiated. Options ranged from the injection of DOD funds into selected companies and industries to bring the necessary "defence-critical", "keystone" and "enabling" technologies up-to-date; to restrict DOD procurement of critical parts, components, processes etc to domestic manufacturing sources only; or maintaining or creating a new industrial capacity with public funding in areas of technology or manufacturing capability where there was a clear vulnerability and potential threat to national security.

American concern about a decline in its self-sufficiency in defence-related technology operates on two assumptions: first, it is assumed that future wars will require a production surge capability of sufficient scale, breadth and responsiveness that there should be a degree of redundancy built into American industrial and manufacturing technology; and second, that this redundancy should be indigenous. Implicit in both assumptions is a level of self sufficiency that applies to all levels of production. That is to say, there should be a critical mass of American manufacturers over a range of defence-related technologies from the prime contractor through second and third tier subcontractors to suppliers of components, parts, materials and support services, able to meet future US military equipment specifications.

Needless to say, one constraint on such a policy is that it would be extremely costly, not merely to the Federal Treasury, but also in terms of commercial opportunity cost. The ideal would be to maintain commercially competitive industries involving the technologies upon which the DOD could extensively draw, both for its weapon requirements and surge capability. Such defence demands should not prejudice the international competitiveness of those countries. It has been one of the consequences of past DOD practices that has tended to divorce civil from military research, development and production with the result that synergism is lost, competitiveness declined and technological and industrial investment diminished.[21]

The United States, however, has only recently come to address the crucial problem of foreign dependency in weapons technology. Only the Soviet Union, for reasons that have been self-evident, was in a similar position. High costs, the arms race, and the widening range of modern weapon systems with their associated technologies, have meant that neither has been able to meet their entire military needs from indigenous sources alone. The United States as demonstrated above has found its industries "buying-in" technologies from overseas both to keep costs down and to maintain quality; the Soviet Union, ironically, has sought to poach Western, especially American and Japanese, technologies where it has been unable to keep abreast through its own endeavours.[22] The only other option was to accept obsolescent equipment from its own industries.

For other advanced industrial states such as France and Britain, a decline in self-sufficiency, coupled with an acceptance of less advanced or even inferior equipment from indigenous sources, has been an accepted condition except in a small number of selected technological areas. Paradoxically, the two most commercially successful advanced industrial countries, Japan and Germany, have defence-related technologies available from industries that are primarily orientated to civil markets, but have deliberately chosen not to develop or promote them aggressively either for domestic military purposes or overseas exports.

A dependence may be defined for purposes of this discussion as the absence of self-sufficiency or the existence of a reliance in a particular area of human activity. A technological dependence refers to that situation where the industrial resources and level of research, development and manufacturing know-how of a state are insufficient to enable it to design, test and produce products without the assistance or participation of a third party. A defence technological dependence refers to the reliance of a state upon one or more third parties in the research, development and production of weapons systems and military equipment deemed necessary for national defence and security. Such a reliance can be considered short or long term; permanent or temporary; critical or benign; cheap or costly. How they are viewed depends on the degree and nature of the reliance, the technologies in question, and upon whom any particular reliance depends.[23]

The Gulf War demonstrated that the United States was able to bring many weapon systems to the battlefield that no other state could match, either in performance or in technological sophistication. This does not mean, however, that the US alone owned or controlled the technologies that went into the design, construction, or fabrication of the weapons systems that received such a high profile as the war progressed. Stealth aircraft and "smart" or "intelligent" munitions (for example, cruise missile and laser guided bombs) immediately spring to mind. Any state trying to emulate the Americans' achievements would have to wait at least a decade or longer to catch up with some of the levels of design and systems integration technology and know-how at which the Americans have already arrived.

If the Americans would agree (and it is extremely unlikely under the current international climate), the only option for other states in a time-frame that made any military sense would be to buy these new American weapon systems "off-the-shelf" from the US prime contractors. There is evidence that many have already approached the US with their defence shopping list, not least the Middle Eastern states. Alternatively, they could seek some production license agreement from the US with the intention of acquiring something by way of technology transfer. In either event, the need for costly and time-dependent research and development would be eliminated (see Chapter 6).

As far as the military operational capability of these potential customers is concerned, if either option were taken up a dependence would be created. For weapons-producing states like France and Britain, it would probably be the case that in acquiring the completed weapons systems of the United States, any residual indigenous technological capability of their own in that area would be reduced, if not wholly destroyed. The Newly Industrialized Countries, however, have a different perspective on the problem: for them, license agreements serve as an important learning opportunity in areas of technology largely beyond either their experience or their resources if operating on their own.[24]

The effect of Britain's cancellation of the AEW Nimrod in favour of the Boeing AWACS, or that of the Blue Streak in favour of first Skybolt and then Polaris, are instrumental cases in point: technologically, Britain is no longer self reliant in missile or airborne AEW/C^3 technology. More pertinently, it is entirely dependent on the goodwill of others. Assuming this to be a source of concern, yet recognizing that military equipment has to be prevented from becoming obsolete, the licensed production option offers a compromise, though confines industry more to the acquisition of production technology transfer than the more critical and enabling development technologies. Britain and France have experienced this with license agreements from the United States to produce helicopters and turbo-fan propulsion engines, respectively.[25]

A variant of acquiring complete weapons systems in which third parties have a technological stake is that of collaboration (see Chapter 8). Accepting that collaboration can assume many forms, the practice is premised on two or more parties agreeing a common specification and developing and producing the product together. Where there is an international division of labour with sub-systems contributed on the basis of comparative advantage, or any other synergistic arrangement, a mutual dependence is created. Unless there is redundant capacity, such an arrangement again reduces self reliance, especially when it is borne in mind that the rationale behind collaboration is to share the high costs of defence systems. Collaboration, however, at least has the merit of ensuring that the partners concerned share the intellectual property rights - the hall mark of technological ownership - of their combined endeavours.[26]

Acquiring others' high technology defence systems through direct purchase is, however, the tip of the iceberg. License production and collaboration comes just below the surface. Beneath that there is the dark and murky world of technological cooperation, one area of activity about which information is not just unknown, but the cause of concern in defence circles. Thus it is only when the technology of research, development and production of complex equipment is taken into account at all levels of the supply chain, from prime contractor to the smallest though not necessarily the least crucial component supplier, that the full extent and importance of dependence becomes revealed.

Starting with a prime contractor, and assuming there are no collaborative arrangements involved, the first consideration is that of ownership.[27] With a publicly owned industry, research establishment or design bureau there should be no problem because the technology involved is owned and controlled by the state. A private corporation is a different matter, particularly if it is owned by, or is a subsidiary of, a multi-national corporation. Not only is there the potential for technology transfer across state boundaries within the corporation, but there can also equally be a restriction on the transfer of technology. The situation becomes even more complex where, as is happening in Europe in particular, international holding companies are set up to coordinate the technological activities of participating companies.

No prime contractor produces a weapon system in its entirety alone. The pattern today is for prime contractors to act as system designers, integrators and assemblers. Prime defence contractors perform this function with the participation of the first tier sub-contractors, who bring to the operation their own sub-system technological skills. Though the prime contractors may well be national companies their sub-contractors might very well be foreign, thus creating a technological dependency one removed. A further trend is for companies to form a consortium - or holding company - to compete for military prime contracts drawn from a number of different countries, with each member of the consortium serving both as prime contractor and first tier sub-contractor.[28]

With increasing frequency, high technology companies with no traditional expertise in the field have tendered for military contracts on the strength of their size and high technology management skills. They do so on the grounds that these skills, and their range of contacts in the technologically advanced world, should be sufficient through competitive sub-contracting to enable them to be competitive, ensure a realistic profit margin, and be treated as a viable and serious contender.[29] The same phenomenon can be found *vice-versa* where traditional defence contractors compete for major civil high-technology contracts.

The British Ministry of Defence's weapons and military equipment procurement policy over the past seven years has been to encourage competition through its "cardinal points system", and to promote "value for money". The approach is to delegate responsibility for the conduct of weapon systems contracts to the prime contractors, and to encourage them to "shop around" for the most cost-effective solutions to technological problems in weapons development and manufacture.

One outcome of this procurement philosophy has been for the more prime contractors to enter the market. Another is for companies to look for new structural arrangements, either by partnership or forms of vertical integration with sub-contractors. Both arrangements are designed to increase the chances of being awarded the contract and to limit the extent of their individual and combined financial exposure. But the more immediate response has been to look beyond national sources for the sub-systems they require, even if to do so might be to the longer term detriment of independent national (i.e. indigenous) weapons development and production.[30]

More serious in the longer term is the potential implications of this development for the maintenance, development and ultimate international competitiveness of the UK national technological and manufacturing base. There are some, however, who feel that the effects of this policy have already left the technological and manufacturing base of the UK vulnerable, and potential prey to the direct and active involvement of foreign states and non-British industrial enterprises at all levels of the supply chain.[31] The prime contractor has as much need of knowing of these developments as the companies and suppliers have of keeping them informed. It is no longer sufficient for the prime contractor to take on much of these specialised areas of technology simply in order to limit its own technological dependency. Cost and overheads alone would make this a time consuming waste.

Recent research has revealed that UK prime contractors - those companies that figure in the government's Statement on Defence Estimates as receiving defence contracts to a total value per annum of above £10 million - generally account for no more than 25 per cent of the value-added element of a major weapons programme.[32] In other words, 75 per cent is sourced from elsewhere. It is the "elsewhere" which constitutes the "hidden" element of defence-related research and development.

It is also upon these "elsewhere" industries that those who look to "dual-use" technology for a solution to mounting costs of defence pin their hopes. However, in the case of the United Kingdom an increasing proportion of this "elsewhere" "dual-use" element comes from abroad. The issue of "defence-critical" technology highlighted in the United States is related to the question of how much, and which, technology should be retained within the country.

As European prime contractors, encouraged by their national governments, the European Commission, the NATO Conference of National Armaments Directors (CNAD) and the Independent Equipment Programme Group (IEPG) move towards closer collaboration in weapon systems design and manufacture, so they also affect the "filiere" or "cluster" of defence related industrial sectors upon which they depend. Although something is known of the defence prime contractors' various mergers and take-overs in recent years, nothing is known of the respective technological dependencies they bring with them. For example, the integration of the Thomson CSF-Ferranti Defence Systems missile activities to form Eurodynamics brings together their design and integration know-how, but does nothing to vitiate both their common dependence on externally sourced semi-conductors and integrated circuits.

Such evidence as exists points to a rationalisation of the European defence-related industries in the longer term. The pressures of new defence requirements, reduced defence expenditure, and over-capacity, coupled with the proactive policies of the European Commission and concern for future European competition with the US and the Pacific Rim states, make this almost inevitable.[33] But the focus has been almost entirely on the prime contractor, with little at all on the chain of supply. The harsh reality, however, is that the one cannot do without the other, and rationalisation of the defence-related prime contractors should be accompanied by a corresponding rationalisation of the sub-contractors and suppliers. Nothing has yet been done in this respect.

There are a number of industries that are of core importance to the research and development of major weapons systems. They lack the glamour and public attention of prime contractors, and are more likely to be less defence oriented and "dual-use" in character. Amongst the more important are investment castings, anti-friction bearings, materials, semi-conductors, precision optics (and coatings), manufacturing processes, electronics and computers

Some of the basic research related to these core technologies have been funded under European Commission programmes such as the RACE, BRITE/Euram and ESPRIT, and the European Cooperation for the Long Term in Defence (EUCLID) - a complicated arrangement between the 13 IEPG National Armaments Directors and the European Defence Industrialists Group (EDIG) of defence-related European companies. However, the level of funding is modest indeed, from the participating governments (120 million ECU) and industrial involvement is confined principally to the prime contractors. The level of participation on the eleven Common European Priority Area (CEPA) programmes is also extremely variable, depending on what the company representatives expect to gain or give away in technological know-how.

Neither EUCLID nor the EC programmes have fully addressed the crux of the problem. Even if both were to be successful and the technological know-how generated from the collaborative research proves useful, the critical issue is that of translating this knowledge into end products both to meet defence requirements, and enhance Europe's industrial competitiveness. If the research is not accompanied by support for the ability to manufacture and fabricate, the research knowledge alone is not sufficient. In this respect, the Japanese investment in the 16 megabit memory chip or the intention (rather than the experience) of the US SEMATECH programme to build a national integrated chipbuilding capability, are useful templates.

Conclusion

The point has been made elsewhere (see Chapter 7) that under the terms of the Single European Market, new pressures will bear on industry beyond those that have been driven by defence and national security considerations in the past. Government-funded research and development for defence, which in any event has not commanded a high proportion of overall spending, is likely to decrease in emphasis. A transition is therefore anticipated; the move away from defence-related technologies to those more appropriate to economic competitiveness. The problem, if this transition is likely, is to retain the dynamism of the defence sector, avoid the loss of the skills that are a feature of it, and ensure that the relevant skills are constructively transferred to meet the new challenges of the international civil market.[34]

It is the contention of this contribution to the debate that the technologies essential to defence, namely those associated with the know-how to fabricate, have largely disappeared. The defence technologies that have commanded high value-added are those of design and integration; the enabling and keystone technologies upon which defence prime contractors must ultimately depend have not only been under-funded by both industry and governments, but have also been overtaken by companies and industries located outside Europe. Collectively, the European states can point to a residual capability in many of these enabling and keystone technological areas, but for future defence and international commercial reasons they must be the target of national and government funding.

Endnotes

1. US Department of Defense, **Lessons of the Gulf War: Interim Report**, September, 1991.

2. Erickson, J., **Soviet C3**, *Defense Analysis*, Vol. 7, No. 2/3, 1991, pp. 263-4.

3. Garthoff, R., **The Military in the Soviet Union**, *Defense Analysis*, Vol. 7, No 2/3, 1991, pp. 339-340.

4. **Guardian Weekly**, 9 February 1992, p. 7.

5. Fouquet, D., Kohnstamm, M. & Nolke, M. (eds) **Dual-Use Industries in Europe Vol 1**, Brussels, Eurostrategies, 1991, pp. 134-166.

6. That said, the expectation is that France plans to increase its level of defence spending in real terms over the next five year Loi Programme, 1992-7. How much of this will be given to military R&D and procurement is not clear.

7. Metcalf, M. & Edmonds, M., **RSI and the Main Battle Tank, 1970-80**, in Edmonds, M. (ed), *International Arms Procurement*, Pergamon, New York, 1981, pp. 144-5.

8. The recent EC Lisbon Conference (28 March 1992) between the National Armaments Directors resulted in disagreement on most crucial issues (finance, specifications, etc) on precisely these grounds. See **Jane's Defence Weekly**, Vol 17, No 4, 4 April 1992, p. 553.

9. Woff, R., **Commonwealth Strategic Command**, *Defense Analysis*, Vol. 8, No 2 July 1992, pp. 179-197.

10. General Accounting Office, **The US Industrial Base, Significance of DOD's Foreign Dependence**, Report GAO/NSIAD 92-93, Washington DC UGGPO, 1991, p. 4. Also, OTA, **Holding the Edge: Maintaining the Defense Technology Base**, Washington USGPO 1989, pp. 178-182.

11. Fitzgerald, M., **Soviet Views of Future War**, *Defense Analysis*, Vol 7, No 2/3, pp. 173-4. Ms Fitzgerald alludes to a USSR claim that these technologies should be treated as universal, and not held by one country.

12. Kaldor, M., **The Baroque Arsenal**, London, Sphere, 1982, p. 18.

13. US Senate, Committee on Armed Services, **Hearings on Defense Appropriations, 1990-91 : Defense Industry and Technology**, Part 7, 17 March 1989, pp. 10-29.

14. Defense Science Board, **Critical Technologies List**, Washington DC DOD, 1990, p. 6.

15. Weidenbaum, M., **Small Wars, Big Defense: Paying for the Military after the Cold War**, NY 20th Century Fund, p. 97. (He cites **Technology and Competitiveness**, NY Japan Society, 1990, p. 17).

16. Fouquet, D. et. al., *op. cit.*, p. 6.

17. Burns, D., **What is the Defence Industrial Base?**, *Defense Analysis*, Vol. 8, No 2 July 1992.

18. The Defense Science Board, **Critical Technologies List**, Washington, DOD, 1990, p. 4.

19. Libicki, M. et. al., **US Industrial Base Dependence, Phase 2: Vulnerability**, Washington NDU Press, 1987, pp. 1-8.

20. On this point, see, Walker, W., Graham, M. and Harbor, B., **From Components to Integrated Systems**, in Gummett, P. and Reppy, J. (eds), *Relations Between Civil and Defense Technologies*, Dordrecht, Kluver, 1987, pp. 17-37.

21. National Research Council, **Manufacturing Technology**, Washington, NAP 1982, pp. 2-3.

22. For example, see the sale by Toshiba of an advanced machine tool to the Russians which the Pentagon claimed would considerably affect the capability of Western ASW abilities to detect Russian submarines by reducing their propeller noise signatures.

23. Edmonds, M., Uttley, M. and Hayhurst, G., **UK and US Dependence on Foreign Technology in Defence R&D**, *Science and Public Policy*, Vol. 17, No 3 June 1990, pp. 159-60.

24. Matthews, R., **Offset Decline for Britain's Defence Industrial Base?**, *Royal United Services Institution Journal*, Winter 1991, pp. 59-60.

25. Uttley, M., **British Helicopter Development, 1945-60 : A Case Study in Technology Transfer and Market Dominance**, *Science and Public Policy*, Vol. 18, No 4, 1991, pp. 235-243.

26. Gething, M., **With a Little Help from my Friends**, *Defence*, June 1991, pp. 25-31.

27. House of Commons Defence Committee, Report, 1987, cited in Taylor, T. and Hayward, L., **The UK Defence Industrial Base: Issues and Options**, *RUSI Journal*, Summer 1989, p. 54.

28. Tusa, F., **European Defence Giants in the Fast Lane**, *Armed Forces Journal International*, December 1991, p. 46.

29. The phenomenon can work in reverse, also: Martin Marietta, a major defence contractor in the aerospace field, was a major contender for the multi billion dollar US Government Federal telecommunications contract, FTS 2000. In the UK, IBM joined forces with Westland to compete for the RAF attack helicopter contract.

30. Edmonds, M., **UK National Security and Defence Dependence**, *Government and Opposition*, Vol. 26, No 4, Autumn 1991, pp. 439-43.

31. Mailat, D., (ed), **Technology: Key Factor for Regional Development**, Paris, Saint Saphorin, 1982.

32. Edmonds, M., *op. cit.*, (1991), pp. 445-6.

33. Reed, C., **1992, A Minefield for the European Defence Industry**, *Defence*, June 1989, pp. 409-11.

34. Gummett, P., **Restructuring the European Defence Industry: Implications of Cutbacks for European Technology**, (Mimeo) Paper prepared for the Annual PSA Conference, Belfast, April, 1992, p. 20.

Part 2

Case Studies

Chapter 4

Restructuring Civil and Military Science and Technology: The Ministry of Technology in the 1960s

Richard Coopey

Introduction

In the run-up to the general election of 1964 Harold Wilson made the plea for the modernisation of British industry, for a new Britain forged in the "white heat" of the scientific revolution. Historians have subsequently written off Wilson's call as empty rhetoric, while the Labour Party is content to leave its past undisturbed by any searching analysis. This is a pity, since, following Labour's victory in 1964, Wilson instituted initiatives through the newly created Ministry of Technology which represented a bold and radical approach to science and technology policy.[1] Mintech, as the Ministry came to be called, was an attempt to orchestrate and rationalise the government's own research an development establishments and those of industry, and to closely link British military and civil science and technology in the process.

The Mintech episode only lasted until the fall of the Wilson government in 1970. The episode may have been even shorter since the ministry's military-civil technology transfer initiative ceased to be its primary focus before this demise. Nevertheless the relatively short life of this set of policy initiatives provides us with an interesting test case for a number of issues. These include the general question of whether government, or government establishments can interact with or define commercial markets, but also more specific questions of the relationship between civil and military science and technology. To what degree does spin-off occur and how, if at all, can this be enhanced? In what ways are technologies, or the institutional structures within which they develop, specifically military? Does the military procurement process carry its own market logic, radically different from civil markets, and can defence establishment staff (administrators, scientists or technicians) instigate and maintain effective commercial criteria?

Mintech was set up with overall responsibility for the Department of Scientific and Industrial Research (DSIR) research stations, the National Research Development Corporation (NRDC - later to become the British Technology Group), and the Atomic Energy Authority (UKAEA). The latter comprised the very large resources at establishments like Harwell and the Atomic Weapons Research Establishment (AWRE) at Aldermaston. Later, in 1967 Mintech absorbed the Ministry of Aviation, bringing under its control the considerable resources of centres including the Royal Radar Establishment (RRE) and the Royal Aircraft

Establishment (RAE). (In the mid 1960s the RRE was the largest centre of electronics research in the country.) Importantly, in taking over the Ministry of Aviation, Mintech gained control of a major portion of the defence procurement budget and it was envisaged that this would enable the rationalisation of industry through contract discrimination.

In setting up the ministry with this configuration, Wilson was responding to what he perceived as the long term imbalance in British science and technology which had previously favoured the military sector and interlocking "prestige" projects in the aerospace and nuclear sectors. To be sure, Wilson had other motives: the immediate popular appeal, for example, of a seemingly meritocratic, technologically literate government. In some ways Wilson was also making a virtue out of necessity since both the aerospace and nuclear sectors were facing a period of run-down in the early 1960s, due to defence restructuring and the completion of much of the research phase of nuclear energy. In attempting to redirect or commercially exploit expertise in establishments such as the RRE and AWRE an alternative to closure and permanent loss of capacity presented itself. It would be wrong, however, to characterise Mintech as entirely a pragmatic response to pressing problems. It was as much the result of considerable discussion among Labour politicians and industrial and scientific advisors, a process which intensified from the late 1950s onwards.

This chapter will focus on key aspects of the Mintech initiatives, primarily through two case studies. The RRE at Malvern and the AWRE at Aldermaston were both central to the Mintech strategy and undertook important programmes aimed at enhancing "spin-off" from defence work in both products and methods, and switching key staff to commercially viable projects within the establishments. In concentrating on the experience of these establishments the success of various initiatives are highlighted, and also the impediments and constraints inherent in a programme such as Mintech.

The Atomic Weapons Research Establishment, Aldermaston

The Atomic Weapons Research Establishment at Aldermaston was one of the earlier centres to be subjected to the Mintech initiatives. Optimism about the capability of the scientists and engineers at the AWRE was high. A preliminary report by the establishment's chemistry division for example, stressed the range of expertise which could be mustered in physical, inorganic, analytical (including radiochemical) and organic fields. Equipment at the AWRE was also held to be the best available. In addition the report noted that, unlike most industrial chemical organisations, the Aldermaston chemists would be able to draw upon the resources of divisions "of similar standing" in physics, mathematics, and engineering.[2] There was confidence too in the ability of AWRE scientists and engineers to bring a fresh perspective to industrial problems:

"Experience to date has shown...there are frequently historical or organisational reasons why a particular problem appears to be dominant, but an objective analysis by a body not wedded to these may bring a different slant to the problem."[3]

Diversification initiatives at Aldermaston featured three major areas of activity - computerised engineering, rationalised production methods and biomedical applications. The first of these came under the aegis of the newly commissioned Aldermaston Project for the Application of Computers to Engineering (APACE). Based "outside the wire" at Blacknest, a country house two miles from the AWRE, the centre came into operation in October 1966. APACE had a fairly broad remit, conducting courses and providing services based on the computing facilities and expertise at Aldermaston. Principle activities centred around the numerical control of machine tools, computer aided design and workshop production scheduling.[4] Courses ranged from basic "Computer Appreciation" to more advanced instruction.[5] Computer services were based on the utilisation of the AWRE's powerful hardware including an IBM 7030 (Stretch) and an ICT Atlas 2 - resources clearly beyond the budget of most firms in Britain. Visiting engineers were given practical demonstrations, and could be provided with resources to work independently on their own problems using the Blacknest facilities.[6]

The AWRE was in advance of British industry in both hardware and software development. For example, Aldermaston had the first computer aided design (CAD) visual systems in the country.[7] The establishment imported the latest advances from the USA where necessary. This included the Automatically Programmed Tools (APT) system for NC work, which had been developed by the Illinois Institute of Technology. In this, as in other fields, the AWRE was ahead of British industry in bridging trans-Atlantic "technology gaps", being "assisted by close contacts with sections of US industry where APT is in wide use."[8] (Unfortunately these links could also generate significant conflict, as we shall see, with the Mintech ideal of support for British computer technology.) In-house developments were also disseminated, for example AWRE's own production control analysis systems. One of the crucial advantages of an establishment such as the AWRE was its interest in all stages of manufacture, from R&D through to production. AWRE had developed its own system, Problem Analysis By Logical Approach (PABLA) for systems analysis, which was developed in consultation with employers associations and promoted through courses available. Attempts were also made to integrate this system with work design systems of other establishments and institutions.[9]

The APACE centre was thus one of the central Mintech initiatives, marshalling information and expertise which drew on the AWRE's home-grown or bought-in resources and also acted to channel developments from other institutions in the Mintech network, such as the CAD developments at other AEA establishments, the Mintech Atlas Centre at Cambridge, or the National Engineering Laboratory.[10] It was to be a "school" for industry to foster the use of the computer in all aspects of engineering. In addition it was to act as a bureau, providing services to government and industry. It went beyond simply unlocking existing AWRE knowledge of computer applications, as up to 60 per cent of staff time went into improving software specifically for industry.[11]

The APACE centre did fairly brisk business from its inception and was expanded in November 1967. Services were publicised through the national press, technical publications, training boards and engineering institutions. Charges were kept to a minimum where possible. Until March 1968 for example the first day of consultation was given free of charge. Course attendance reached 526 by 1968 and general enquiries numbered 155,000 in 1967. These figures disguise a significant failure however. Of those attending courses between 1967 and 1970 less than 30 per cent came from industry. Around the same number came from government departments, while the largest group, nearly 32 per cent, came from within the AWRE itself.[12] This failure to reach outside industry directly had a major impact on the viability the centre. APACE was not initially intended to make money, rather it was to provide a service. On expansion in 1967, however, the Treasury intimated that it should at least be self-supporting.[13] This was to be a constant problem for senior staff. Operating costs were continually well in advance of income generated. Money recouped from industry rose steadily between 1967 and 1970, but never exceeded 12 per cent of operating costs. The centre's largest single source of income was the Ministry of Technology itself, but even with this APACE could only cover a fraction of total costs. There was also a hidden cost in Mintech's patronage. The type of work which they contracted at APACE involved using senior staff to appraise projects and act as project officers. This meant less time to train junior staff at the centre in the crucial early stages.[14]

It is interesting to note that pressure on the APACE centre to generate profits existed while the Mintech initiatives were at their height. The original proposal had been more pragmatic, envisaging only 50 per cent of costs as recoverable.[15] As pressure mounted, senior staff at APACE reacted strongly, seeing their work in pioneering terms. As APACE Project Manager Fred West stressed in 1969, "I have always argued that this is missionary work and the real results will only be seen through the national economy, possibly years after the event."[16] Had they wanted to make a profit APACE could arguably have narrowed its focus to concentrate on NC machine tool software or CAD technology. West insisted that, although less profitable, a wide range of activity was essential. Production control, for example, was an area of extreme need: "a multi-disciplined structure as we have with APACE is right for the future of the economy if system trends are to be encouraged."[17] As late as 1970 West put a "realistic ceiling" on income at a maximum of 40 per cent, insisting that "one should judge the success of APACE by the spread of its evangelism."[18] West was emphatic that the Mintech ideal should put priority on promoting computer literacy and systems thinking among the engineering community and not covering the cost of AWRE staff activity. Industry for its part had to be persuaded of the value of the kind of systems approach which

APACE was propagating. Even where persuaded, many firms expected something for nothing from a Government organisation, as evidenced by ICL's reluctance to pay for transcribing AWRE programmes.[19]

Although it was clearly unrealistic to expect APACE to be profit making, at least in its early stages, there were significant weaknesses in the centre. The team assembled had considerable expertise, comprising mostly engineering and technical officers from the higher grades.[20] The staff may, however, have lacked commercial experience and an appraisal list compiled in 1970 contains revealing comments:

"Good applications software man but avoids industrial liaison...Academic, management sciences man. Good computer knowledge, totally unsuited to industrial liaison."

This comment on the reluctance or inability to liaise with industry reoccurs throughout the appraisal list.[21] There were still perceived to be barriers within the APACE team, with people adhering to narrow specialisms. Programmers, systems implementation staff, and most significantly, marketing staff were deemed to have insufficient contact with each other.[22] In spite of this problem the team did contain considerable expertise, particularly in applied engineering. This was reflected in the decision to replace mathematicians on the staff with engineers.[23]

The expertise of key members of the APACE staff created a further problem, endemic among such initiatives. As personel developed expertise and gained closer contacts with industry, so industry began attempts to recruit them. Firms such as Plessey were calculated to be between one and two years behind APACE in computer applications. The "key man on Post Processor writing - the leader" at APACE resigned to go to Plessey in 1970, taking other supporting staff with him. Another team leader went to Systems International around the same time. The APACE management viewed these developments with equanimity and "noted (and applauded) the fact that trained APACE staff are attractive to industry."[24] Nevertheless the centre was left with disproportionate running costs owing to the high level of training costs necessary in replacing lost staff.

APACE also faced constraints imposed by Mintech competition policy which obstructed attempts to import technologies. When the APACE team organised a syndicate of manufacturers to purchase American software for electronic circuit design, Mintech withdrew funding for electronics CAD altogether. This was because Racal were working in the same area in Britain and "it could not be countenanced that Mintech should separately fund a potential competitor to Racal."[25]

In addition APACE encountered difficulty in its relationship with other establishments in the Mintech group. This was highlighted in a conflict which developed in 1970 with AEA Harwell when the latter complained that APACE was not promoting their production control software. APACE engineers, in tune with the needs of industry, thought the Harwell software too complex. Fred West's comments reveal the pragmatic shop-floor orientation of some of the centre's thinking:

"Most of my customers are not interested in sophisticated systems, they have their eye on computer costs and simplicity in understanding by the average workshop staff...the acid test is what will work in the practical environment and do the job required most cheaply, no more, no less."[26]

Correspondence with Harwell also reveals difficulties experienced by Aldermaston-based staff in controlling APACE work undertaken at Harwell.[27]

APACE was effectively wound up with the demise of Mintech in 1970. The familiar arguments about profitability were used again to justify dismemberment, as separate divisions within the AWRE took over the remains of production control and NC machine-tool software projects. Support for training activity was discontinued in favour of a purely consultative role and in-house software development was curtailed. Managers at APACE had seen the balance sheet principle triumphant: "Clearly the DTI have an eye more on a convincing revenue proposal to the Treasury than on the realism of industrial support operations."[28] The DTI had earlier intimated that AWRE might support APACE if it wanted, but this was unlikely to be seriously considered.[29] Ieuan Maddock made one last attempt to save the centre, offering for funding the strongest proposal he could find. It was summarily dismissed and he reported that "axes were swinging" and strongly advised against raising any new proposals.[30] Late in 1971 APACE was renamed the Production Control Group and continued to operate as a demonstration centre throughout the 1970s, on a greatly reduced basis and with little publicity.[31]

The second major Aldermaston Mintech project was in the related field of group technology. This was aimed at speeding work-flow using computer techniques. The system operated on the basis of classifying parts to be manufactured into a system of digital codes. Features such as size, geometric definitions, material type and so on were coded in order to group components into families. These codes were then matched to information on machine loading to give optimum scheduling through workshops. Machine tool grouping could also be reconfigured following analysis using coded information. The system offered additional saving in throughput time by reducing adjustment of tools in the setting up process. The resulting database of components meant that similarities could be identified in parts, avoiding duplication at the drawing stage. The group technology initiative reflected Aldermaston's interest in manufacturing systems as a whole process. It was an attempt to use computer aided information systems to bridge the gap between flow-line production of mass produced parts and batch production of specialised parts. Rational organisation of parts and tools could significantly reduce both labour costs and time. Group technology could also eliminate the practice of manufacturing large batches of components and stockpiling those not immediately needed, thus reducing inventory levels.[32]

Work on the principles of group technology was at its most advanced in the Soviet Union. This had begun in 1939, although little progress had been made until the late 1950s. Between 1957 and 1965 there had been a major advance in the application of systems, particularly that developed by Mitrafanov. In 1963 for example, there were estimated to be over 100 factories in Leningrad alone working under group technology, processing over 500,000 different parts. A report compiled by the AWRE Weapons Design Division estimated savings to be considerable.[33] It must be remembered that in the early 1960s, unlike more recently, there was a strong belief in the efficiency of some sectors of Soviet manufacturing. Soviet developments in the application of mathematics could be seen to compensate for more limited advances in computer technology.

Unlike the APACE initiative the Group Technology Centre was never expected to pay its own way: 75 per cent of operating costs were expected to be written off until well into the 1970s.[34] It operated on similar lines to APACE, conducting training sessions and undertaking consultancy. Impressive claims were made on behalf of the system as total component times were held to be reduced by a factor of 4 or 5. One reported example of a company applying group technology techniques was that of Serck-Audio, where average manufacturing time was estimated to be reduced from 12 to 4 weeks.[35] Potential savings were more significant in the light of estimations that 80 per cent of engineering components were manufactured in batches.

The group technology initiative at Aldermaston is interesting in that it represents an example, not of diffusion of technology or technique, but rather a case of an attempt by staff to become consultants in an area which was in fact an innovation for the AWRE. Group technology principles were never in fact used at Aldermaston.[36] After the Mintech takeover the Director instructed key members of staff to prepare feasibility studies on projects to assist civil industry. Following a series of conferences, papers etc. and an unclassified exhibition for industrialists, initiatives including group technology were chosen for funding. The mathematical element of the system clearly had an appeal to staff at AWRE. The system was actually developed, as noted, from Soviet work, and also in collaboration with Birmingham University[37].

The third major area of diversification at Aldermaston was that of biomedical technology. The establishment began a programme of extensive work including research into the materials and design for surgical implants, components for kidney dialysis machinery, patient monitoring systems, heart pacemaker development, surgical lasers and toxicity in plastics.[38] Many of these were new applications for AWRE expertise, although some areas represented a diffusion of work already undertaken. In some cases, such as toxicology, the establishment hoped to achieve a form of reverse spin-off, gaining extra knowledge of the effects on workers of hazardous radiochemical materials and improving safety and accident procedures. No special centre was set up as in the case of APACE; instead, staff on medical projects worked separately in their original locations. This method of working was criticised by some researchers who felt they would have benefitted from more closely-knit group activity.[39]

The programme was initiated in 1965, and by 1969 the AWRE was working in liaison with 27 hospitals. Between 1967 and 1969 seventeen patents were filed on behalf of the establishment including a laser beam manipulator, thermograph scanner modifications and artery clearance equipment.[40] The biomedical programme generated the most publicity of all the AWRE activities. In addition to exhibitions, symposia, and articles, the project achieved national press and television coverage. This was a particularly visible "swords to ploughshares" programme and both the government and the AWRE were keen to promote the idea of weapons engineers working to the benefit of medical science. Perhaps the most highly visible example of this was publicity given to the work on artificial limbs. The AWRE engineers produced a working prototype of an artificial hand utilising servo motors and control mechanisms originally developed in missile guidance. This achieved widespread publicity in the wake of the Thalidomide tragedy. Interestingly, as with group technology, engineers at Aldermaston liaised closely with Soviet engineers and medical personnel, examining prototypes and inviting speakers to lecture at the establishment.[41]

Despite the many advances aided by AWRE work in medical engineering there were significant barriers facing the overall success of the initiative. Cost effectiveness was always a stumbling block, and the Ministry of Health could not afford to pay for many of the products which were proposed. The artificial hand for example cost in excess of £5000 - far beyond the budget of the health system. Similarly, the life support monitoring system proved to be too expensive. Part of the problem lay in the fact that the AWRE tradition involved identifying a problem and then engineering the optimum solution. Budgetary constraints were not necessarily given primacy. Thus the Head of Weapons Development at the AWRE was surprised to find that by comparison to the AWRE, the Ministry of Health budget for technical developments amounted to "peanuts".[42] The National Health Service's own R&D facilities for artificial limbs were judged by AWRE staff to be "pitifully small".[43] This problem was exacerbated by the small production runs and customised nature of many medical products.[44]

As with the APACE initiative, medical engineering was given low priority after 1970, being almost entirely discontinued by the mid 1970s. A statement in Parliament by Minister of Defence, William Rogers in 1976 that defence work might somehow be used for the benefit of disabled people provoked enquiries from AWRE hoping the programme might be revitalised. This drew a rather weary response from officials at the Department of Health and Social Security:

"I note your reference to the assurance which your Minister gave regarding possible "spin-off" from defence research which might benefit disabled people. I fear that I have a long-playing record about solutions in search of a problem and I will never cease to stress the importance of identification of problems which need a solution and then looking for a technology which will provide the best solution".

A later memo from the same source concluded that "We seem to have done our stuff and can rest upon it."[45]

Further projects were mooted during the Mintech years in addition to those previously outlined. A series of initiatives was proposed by Ieuan Maddock who moved from the AWRE Director's post into the Ministry itself as a controller. Maddock frequently turned to what he termed his "old establishment" for advice on the feasibility of new programmes. In 1969 for example, Maddock approached the AWRE to set up "a small team of enthusiastic chaps to act as a "mini-directorate"" overseeing an intermediate technology initiative. This comprised a holistic approach to manufacturing: "Our line of arguing here is that the average manufacturing plant of the future will be as complex as the Radar site of today".[46]

If vertical links between Mintech and Aldermaston were fairly direct, horizontal communications with other parts of the Mintech technology empire may have been less effective. There was certainly a degree of rivalry between Aldermaston and other research institutions. As noted above, the APACE team had difficulty in controlling work undertaken at Harwell. There were also difficulties in gaining full cooperation with existing civil research organisations such as the NRDC and MRC. The NRDC at one point insisted on the right to monitor all papers on medical work prior to publication, while the MRC sought to limit AWRE activity to what was perceived as "natural" spin-off, and were concerned that activities did not bring the establishment into competition with industry.[47] Liaison between AWRE and the DHSS Biomedical Research and Development Unit "proved a stumbling block", there being a "certain amount of mutual disenchantment." There were also general complaints that staff at the AWRE did not communicate with staff at the DHSS.[48] Furthermore, the internal communications networks which Mintech set up to diffuse information did not always function effectively. There were, for example, a number of "sooty blushes" when it was discovered out that two institutions within the Mintech group were working on pressure die casting research, totally unaware of each other.[49]

The confidence of the AWRE scientists and engineers in their own abilities may have been taken for arrogance by other organisations. There was certainly no doubting the ebullience of the Aldermaston staff involved in the Mintech strategy. Some evidence of this can be seen in the reports of investigations by a team from Aldermaston into possible improvement in the performance of the textile industry. In conjunction with the Hosiery and Allied Trades Research Association, the AWRE sent a team to the factory of E.L. Bastow Ltd. who, among other lines, produced undergarments for Marks and Spencer. The team included staff from APACE, adhesives experts from the Chemical Division and the head of Weapons Design. Undaunted by the fact that Marks and Spencer were at that time being trumpeted by Mintech as the ideal consumer for its policy of forcing suppliers to modernise and rationalise production, or by the fact that M&S underwear was one of the most unassailable consumer goods on the market, the AWRE team felt able to recommend a list of improvements. This included greater automation and rationalisation of production flow. Perhaps the most startling recommendation was a proposal to dispense with the process of sewing altogether in favour of gluing the underwear together, thus obviating troublesome and expensive foreign-manufactured sewing machines. The AWRE proposal meant a return to first principles, a hallmark of the AWRE approach to problem solving. As Peter Jones, Head of Weapons Engineering, suggested, "ideally one should think afresh on garment design including material utilisation if alternative bonding techniques are to be attempted."[50]

There was undoubted enthusiasm among staff assigned to various diversification and diffusion programmes during the period. Most of the personnel interviewed in the course of this research recalled this as a time of great optimism and interest. It would be going too far to suggest that this was primarily attributable to a relief engendered by working away from weapons, since most were, and remain, unequivocal about the need for work in this field. Enthusiasm centred instead on the recognition of staff expertise and the satisfaction of working towards the `improvement' of British industry. In some ways it removed the veil of secrecy surrounding weapons manufacture which previously meant that workers at establishments like Aldermaston got little public recognition, or cognisance among peers in civil industry. Secrecy did remain as an obvious barrier to the success of many of the programmes. Staff on industrial projects were warned that certain materials and names were classified and should not be discussed outside the establishment, or indeed, within the establishment unless there was a "need to know".[51] Mechanical CAD developments were to be openly available, but there were continuing difficulties disclosing advances in electronics. This was only partially overcome by offering bureau services in this area.[52] For many other industrial applications this was not a significant problem, staff being pleasantly surprised at the degree of openness allowed in promulgating their work. Indeed, as with the Royal Radar Establishment, secrecy was a greater problem in respect of commercial confidence and the restrictions placed on diffusion by firms which contracted their research to Government establishments.[53]

Evidence suggests that staff assigned to permanent project teams were more highly motivated, or found their task easier. The contrast has been noted above between the APACE staff and the fragmented work done in medical engineering. The idea of establishing group activity represents one of the Mintech general initiatives in microcosm: that is, avoiding the break-up and dispersal of centres of excellence in the defence field. Where specific teams were not set up there were problems of communication and interchange of ideas. Also, it became difficult to completely segregate civil and defence work. In busy periods individual staff on the diversification budget were found to have been seconded to weapons work, and some diversion projects proposed by industry were refused.[54]

The Royal Radar Establishment

Study of another major research establishment, the ex-Ministry of Aviation Royal Radar Establishment (RRE) at Malvern reinforces many of the points made about

AWRE. The RRE in the mid-1960s was the largest centre for electronics research in the UK. Its activities were divided into groups comprising solid state physics and an electronics group whose function was to link basic research to, finally, a Military and Civil Systems Division.[55]

There were a number of aspects of the establishment's work which were applicable to civil industry. Basic research was carried out into solid state materials, semiconductors, low temperature and high magnetic fields, infra-red and lasers. Applied techniques included computer circuits systems and programmes, machine tool controls, microwave oscillators and display techniques. Applications developed included radar and radio astronomy, and air traffic control systems. An Industrial Applications Unit was set up in February 1967 as a channel through which RRE technologies could be diffused to industry. The establishment also set up an Electronic Materials Unit to concentrate on the commercial exploitation of work such as that carried out on high-quality single crystal materials.[56]

Unlike the AWRE, work at the RRE stopped short of full engineering development, industry being expected to take up and fully develop promising products. A series of open days and circulated bulletins were used to publicise work on a range of technologies including a compact short-range radar based on the Gunn oscillator, for use in burglar alarms or ship navigation. Infra red detectors, pioneered at the RRE for night-time fighting and reconnaissance, were also seen to have applications ranging from medical scanning to aeriel photography of power station outfalls. Further civil development of air-traffic control systems was envisaged. This encompassed work on complex data handling systems in addition to work on interactive operator-computer communication, both of which had potentially wide-ranging civil applications.[57]

The market potential of some of these developments was held to be very large indeed. The civil market for infra-red applications for example, was expected to exceed the military market by the early 1970s.[58] There were voices within the establishment, however, urging caution with press statements, in case claims exceeded the investigated possibilities of some technologies. Whatever the outcome the RRE certainly attracted the attention of many of Britain's major manufacturers.[59] A typical visit was that arranged for a team from ICI in early 1968. Eleven possible applications for infra-red were noted, the most promising being hot bearing detection, effluent and water pollution detection, thermocouple substitutes and enclosed space measurements. These applications were subsequently allocated to RRE staff for further investigation.[60]

Since much of the development work connected with RRE technologies was contracted out, the post-1967 publicity campaign had the effect of turning the RRE into a promotional mechanism for some sectors of British industry - putting users in touch with producers. In fact this brought out into the open a process which, to a limited extent, was already taking place. As one of the RRE staff involved at the time recalled:

"In effect we were acting as honourary salesmen for some of these firms. In the Mintech period it was made a more respectable activity whereas before it went on more or less on the side."[61]

Similarly the diffusion of information about RRE advances in electronics materials had also been under way, requests being met "legitimately" or by "old-boy trading". Many requests had to be refused however, and it was hoped that the Mintech initiatives would bring a new level of openness.[62]

An examination of one technology in particular reveals something of the dynamics and relative success of the diffusion process during the Mintech period. Infra-red techniques were seen to have a great potential for civil applications, and an exploratory working party was set up immediately the new initiative began. Two basic processes were distinguished - simple detection of hot objects and thermal imaging. A wide range of applications seemed possible to RRE staff including monitoring processes and quality in smelting metals, particularly steel and aluminium; plastics and ceramics; electricity power station inspection and monitoring; hot axle-box detection for the rail system; detection of overheating in coal mines and tips; medical thermography; prison security; and-on line analysis in chemical plants. It was also hoped that the British instrument industry would subsequently pick up an increasing volume of orders for instruments and components relating to pyrometry and thermal scanning.[63]

Early reports stressed the need for a process of education to "make industry conscious of what infra-red can do".[64] Visits by RRE teams to plants in the rubber and plastics industry had revealed a general "lack of appreciation of what infra-red techniques could do". One major obstacle seemed to be industry's reluctance to invest in development, evidenced in the case of steel:

"This, the working party was told, is because the management of the steel industry does not regard itself as responsible for the development of instruments but simply as the user of what instruments manufacturers are willing to supply."[65]

By 1968 approaches by industry to the RRE had picked up considerably, but RRE staff were still advocating further visits to industry to spread the gospel of infra-red.

The awareness of possible applications which was generated in infra-red technology produced an interesting reaction among firms supplying the RRE. While staff at the RRE were keen simply to boost the flow of information about infra-red and involve as wide a circle of manufacturers and consumers as possible, the group of key firms involved in supplying infra-red technology had other ideas. They sought to protect their exclusive position and, in order to achieve this, set up the British Infra-Red Manufacturers Organisation (BIRMO). This group, consisting of Barr and Stroud, EMI, Hawker Siddeley Dynamics, Hymatic Engineering, Mullard and STC, then demanded that all enquiries received at the RRE be passed on exclusively to them by reason of their "special, perhaps even privileged position."[66] Although BIRMO gave assurances that it was not their intention to be in any way restrictive, the RRE continued to limit information passed on.[67] Matters came to a head in June 1968 when representatives of RRE and BIRMO were called to Mintech headquarters following complaints by BIRMO to one of the Mintech Ministers.

At this meeting the RRE put the case that some user firms, while prepared to discuss applications and processes with the RRE in confidence, were often reluctant to discuss them with industry.[68] This was accepted and the meeting ended amicably, but there were deeper reasons for the RRE's stance. Senior staff at the establishment saw their role in relation to infra-red suppliers in the broadest terms and were seeking to use their position to force through rationalisation of the industry as a whole. They were unhappy that BIRMO seemed to represent a predominance of electrical firms to the exclusion of instrument manufacturers, and also that by its nature, the organisation would fragment development in an inefficient way.[69] Earlier, in 1967, the Director of the RRE had raised the possibility of rationalising the industry by favouring one or two firms, in line with policies pursued by Mintech and the IRC designed to force concentration. This was rejected by staff at the RRE as impractical at that time since each of the six BIRMO firms had their own specialised field: Smiths in medical applications, for example, and Barr and Stroud in imaging systems. Nevertheless it was agreed that RRE's "final aim should be to concentrate activity in one or two firms"[70]. In the interim the RRE retained its role as general overseer and regulator of the infra-red industry in its fragmented form.

In general the RRE diffusion experiment illuminated two general sets of problems, one internal and one external to the establishment. External problems involved the inability or reluctance of British industry to take up the innovations on offer. Reasons for this range from attempts to erect barriers to general diffusion as in the case of BIRMO, to a more general aversion by firms to form links with external organisations such as the RRE. It may on the face of things seem ironic, but many firms approached by the RRE and the AWRE expressed concern about the security of work undertaken at government establishments. It was noted at the time that "Scientists at Malvern have found to their great surprise that the commercial `security curtain' is often far harder to lift than the defence one."[71] Where work was undertaken, firms often insisted on sole access to information resulting in an elaborate system of "Commercial in Confidence" reporting within the RRE, limiting the diffusion process. This phenomenon was perhaps to be expected given the nature of competition in a capitalist economy, the inhibitive secrecy of which had been noted many years before by Bernal.[72]

Although the Mintech initiatives were aimed at integrating technology centres within government establishments and industry, rigid divisions remained an impermeable barrier in many cases. RRE staff frequently complained that British firms were too compartmentalised - that research was cut off from development and production[73] - yet the establishment itself presented one of the biggest problems in this respect. Staff at the RRE had never given priority to production in a strictly commercial sense; still less did they have any real notion of markets for commercial products. These constraints for example were revealed in work on induction heating developments for furnaces, and also noted by the infra-red group.[74] This was, and remains, a perennial problem of government research establishments, and had been identified in a report on the eve of the Mintech takeover of the RRE which stressed the necessity of "the right sort of applied scientists", which were lacking in the RRE labs.[75]

There were further problems which affected the RRE and AWRE, in common with other defence research establishments. Central was the degree to which effective spin-off from defence technology was possible at all, in any commercial sense. It was observed early on for example, that extensive markets for infra-red technology on a cost-effective basis might be limited.[76] Ernest Putley, one of the central figures in the development of this technology commented recently that "national security criteria meant people looking at problems from a sort of academic point of view rather than a commercial point of view."[77] This defence specific function, and resultant "baroque" technology development can be applied to the rationale for the whole of an establishment like the RRE; its location, the skill profile of the staff, the avenues of research and development pursued and so on. As Sir George MacFarlane, RRE Director and Mintech Controller during the period notes, "the reason for these establishments to meet a Government need...not industry, not markets or anything else. The defence "marketplace" operates on the basis technical superiority, not price."[78] These sentiments echo those expressed by Sir John Hill, Atomic Energy Authority (UKAEA) chairman during the Mintech years.[79]

Conclusions

These latter criticisms, pointing to the structural problems facing any defence-civil diffusion strategy, represent the strongest challenge to the Mintech initiatives. Yet it is difficult to see what the alternatives might have been. Given that the Labour Government had identified the imbalance in the British technology resource base with its preponderance of effort in the government defence related research establishments, only two alternatives presented themselves: an attempt to redirect resources, recognising the value of keeping teams together within establishments; or alternatively close down sections within the establishments and hope that British industry would absorb the resultant increased supply of scientists and engineers on the labour market. The second, non-Mintech, strategy would arguably have presented an even greater range of problems of its own. First, research teams' collective expertise would have been diluted if teams were broken up. This collective expertise may not have been equivalent to a well-rounded commercial competence, but in technological terms it meant the ability to stay abreast of critical defence related technologies. Re-entry barriers in advanced technology fields were perceived to be too high to risk dropping out, even if costs were prohibitively high. In addition, there was no guarantee that scientists and engineers released onto the labour market would be taken up by British industry. Capacity to absorb the new influx was doubted and it was widely held at the time that the "brain drain", particularly to the USA, would be a more likely destination.

The Mintech experiment points to the difficulties which face any political initiative aimed at restructuring national science and technology, and effectively linking this to industry policy. Varying degrees of compliance, inertia or resistance will be encountered throughout a hierarchy which extends from Ministry staff down to the level of scientists and engineers working in individual research establishments. Linking technologies to markets presents another set of structural impediments to change. Yet Mintech was at least a coherent attempt to come to grips with the military-civil legacy which arguably distorted post-war British science, technology and industry.

Mintech's primary focus moved away from military-civil transfer during the later years of the Wilson government as the ministry expanded to absorb the functions of the defunct DEA, and the Ministry of Fuel and Power. Mintech in effect became a Ministry of Industry, responsible for virtually the whole of Government industial policy. It might be said that this was a welcome development, linking science and technology policy directly to general industry strategy such as regional development or the nationalised industries. In effect however, it meant that the Ministry's remit became too large and unwieldy. Patrick Blackett, in helping to formulate the Mintech strategy prior to 1964, had warned against overextending the scope of such a ministry. Blackett had also maintained that such an initiative was essentially long-term. The demise of Mintech can perhaps be interpreted as much in the inability of governments to wait for long-term pay-offs. Just as Mintech in its original form was an attempt to restructure what was immediately available - a preponderance of science and technology in military and "prestige" sectors - so too, decisions to broaden the focus of Mintech and give a lower priority to the kind of projects under way at the AWRE and RRE reflect immediate pressures on the Labour government in power after 1964.[80]

Quantifiable indicators of the success of the projects at establishments like the RRE and AWRE were, and remain, problematic. The foregoing analysis suggests that there is some truth in the assertion that technologies like infra-red, in the form which they are developed, carry predominantly military characteristics. Evidence also seems to support the notion that commercial expertise in terms of production criteria or marketing may have been underdeveloped in establishments. Yet there is evidence too that staff at these establishments were well aware of, and were in the process of correcting these shortcomings. Certainly the scientists and engineers were not lacking in enthusiasm for the Mintech programme.

The problems of conversion remain unresolved in the 1990s and restructuring of national defence priorities has forced questions of civil-military transfers back to the top of the political agenda. Precise circumstances are of course substantially different from those of the early 1960s. Yet in broad terms the Mintech initiatives can provide a useful guide to some of the constraints facing government policy aimed at restructuring defence and civil science, technology and industry.

Endnotes

1. I would like to thank David Edgerton who originally identified Mintech as an important initiative and whose advice has been invaluable. Also invaluable has been the help of Janet Dudley, archivist at the RSRE and Adrian Willson, archivist at the AWRE.

2. AWRE SSCD/65/212/008/01, **Potential of Chemistry Division in a Diversification Programme**, 1965.

3. *Ibid.*

4. **New Technology**, 5 May 1967, p.6.

5. Apace Project, **Atom**, 126, April 1967, p.67; Apace Centre Courses, **Atom**, 134, December 1967 p. 323; 159, January 1970, p.11.

6. **APACE**, *AWRE News*, April 1967, pp. 14-16.

7. Latham, R.L., ex-Head of Weapons Engineering Division, AWRE Interviewed 27 March 1991.

8. AWRE W0199, **Alden Project A.C.E.**, (undated)

9. See for example the report prepared by Terry, G.J. of APACE, **The Institute of Operational Research Design Management System (Analysis of Interconnected Decision Areas)**, AWRE W0199, July 1967.

10. **Computer Aided Design**, *Mintech Review*, May 1969, pp. 10-11.

11. AWRE WO119, **Report to Directors Advisory Committee**, Hopkin, G.L., 27 February 1970, pp. 3-4.

12. AWRE WO199, **Hopkin, G.L., "Report to the Directors Advisory Committee"**, 27 February 1970.

13. *Ibid.*

14. AWRE D/99/04, **West, F.L. to Rock-Carling, F. letter, 1969**; K2984/001

15. AWRE WO199, **A Proposal for an Aldermaston Project for the Application of Computers to Engineering**, 1966.

16. West, F.L. to Rock-Carling, p.2.

17. *Ibid.*

18. AWRE WO199, **West, F. to Maddock, I.**, 6 April 1970, pp. 4-5; AWRE WO199, **Note of the APACE Review Meeting on 15 July 1970**, p.1.

19. West to Rock-Carling, (e)iii, (h)iii.

20. AWRE K2984/001, **Newley, E. to West, F. "Deployment of APACE Staff"**, 8 October 1969.

21. AWRE WO199, **DTI Support to APACE**, report, 3 December 1970.

22. AWRE WO199, **Note From APACE Review Meeting on 15 July 1970**.

23. AWRE WO199, **Hoskin, N.E. "The Mathematician's Role in APACE"**, 3 April 1970.

24. AWRE WO199, **Apace Staff Training and the Impact on Revenue -Viability Measurement**, 20 July 1970; AWRE WO199, **DTI support to APACE**, 3 December 1970.

25. AWRE WO199, **Llewelyn, A.I. to West,F.**, 24 August 1970.

26. AWRE WO199, **West, F. to Trusler, J.D.C.**, 23 June 1970.

27. AWRE WO199, **West, F. to Cheshire, I.M.**, 11 November 1970.

28. **"Notes on a Discussion with DTI, SA Division"**, 23 November 1970; AWRE WO199, **DTI Support to APACE Year 1971/72**, 3 December 1970.

29. AWRE WO199, **Nichols, T.W. to Newley, E.F.**, 6 November 1970.

30. WO199, **West, F.L. to Hopkin, G.L.**, 11 December 1970.

31. AWRE K5967/002, **Lingard, R.A. to Cardwell, D.**, April 1979; Blacknest Centre Production Control Group, **11th Quarterly Report**, 17 February 1975.

32. Mintech, **The Group Technology Centre**, September 1970; DTI Group Technology Centre, **The Principles and Practice of Group Technology**, 3, September 1972.

33. AWRE K2984/001, AWRE Weapons Design Division, **Report to the Ministry of Technology Relating to Contract ME/47/03. Group Technology**, September 1967.

34. AWRE WO199, **Coleman, R.F. to Burkitt, R.W.**, 15 October 1970.

35. Bennett, D. **Group Technology**, *Atom*, 158, December 1969, pp. 310-316.

36. Latham, R.L., interview.

37. Grayson, T.J., **Group Technology: A Comprehensive Bibliography**, (UKAEA, 1972).

38. AWRE WO231, **Whiteway, F.E. to G.E. Gale**, 12 March 1969; **Biomedical Technology**, *Atom*, 144, October 1968, pp.260-267; **AEA Work in Medical Engineering**, *Atom*, 150, April 1969, pp.100-107; **Laser Surgery**, *Atom*, 166, August 1970, pp.168-171.

39. Bultitude, F., interview.

40. AWRE WO231, **Whiteway, F.E. "Collaboration, Commercial Exploitation and Publicity Connected with the Biomedical Technology Programme"**, 18 September 1969.

41. **Vincent, C.H. to McKenzie, D.C.**, 22 July 1965; **Notes on Seminar "New Horizons in Rehabilitation" 12/7/65**, pp. 2-3.

42. Jones, P., ex-Head of Weapons Development, AWRE, Interview, 11 October 1989.

43. AWRE JO850/006, **Dawson, J.A.T. to Maddock, I.**, 16 August 1965.

44. **Walker, R.D.J. to Maddock, I.**, 1 July 1965; AWRE JO850/006, 8 July 1965.

45. **Harms, P. to Whiteway, F.E.**, 4 January 1977; AWRE K4909/001, **Eastwick-Field, G.G. to Challens, W.J.**, 12 January 1977.

46. **Maddock, I. to Newley, E.**, 7 August 1969; **Newley, E. to Hopkin, G.L.**, 12 August 1969; AWRE K2984/001.

47. AWRE J0850/006, **Minutes of a Meeting with MRC representatives at AWRE**, 2 May 1965; AWRE K0113/008, **Minutes, Branch Management Meeting, STC**, 3 December 1968.

48. AWRE K4909/001, **Whiteway, F.E. to Harms, P.M.**, 20 December 1976; K0113/008, **STC Branch Management Meeting, Minutes**, 17 December 1969.

49. **Hood, St. Clair C. to Jackson, R.F.**, 11 May 1970; AWRE W0199, **Hopkin, G.L. to Hood, St. Clair C.**, 18 May 1970.

50. AWRE W0199, **Jones, P.M.S., "Visit by AWRE Team to Hosiery and Allied Trades Research Association"**, 2 March 1967.

51. AWRE K0113/008, **STC Minutes**, 4 November 1970.

52. AWRE D/99/04, **West, F. to Rock-Carling, F.**, 17 September 1969.

53. AWRE K0113/008, **STC Minutes**, 3 December 1968.

54. AWRE K0133/008, **STC Minutes**, 14 December 1970; 23 January 1968; 30 July 1971.

55. Dummer, G.W.A., **A History of Microelectronics Development at the Royal Radar Establishment**, *Microelectronics and Reliability*, 4, 1965, pp. 193-4.

56. **Mintech Review**, September 1967, p.11

57. *New Technology*, 3, March 1967, p.1; **Diversification in a Government Laboratory**, *Nature*, 216, November 11 1967, p. 542; **R&D Pay-off at the RRE**, *Electronics Weekly*, November 8 1967, p. 5; **Spin-off to Industry from Malvern**, *Engineering*, 10 November 1967, pp. 739-40.

58. Benn, T. **Speech at Woolwich Polytechnic**, 15 February 1968, transcript Benn Archive.

59. RRE, Parkinson, D.H., **"Press Day RRE", memo**, 9 August 1967; **"Visit of Senior Industrial Staff"**, 18 October 1966.

60. RRE, **ICI Billingham Visit**, 29 January 1968.

61. Putley, E., interview, 12 April 1991.

62. **RRE Newsletter and Research Review**, 7, 1968, p. iv.

63. RRE, **Report of the Working Party on the Civil Application of I.R. Techniques**, annex, 4 April 1967.

64. *Ibid.*

65. RRE, **Report of Working Party on Civil Applications of Infra-Red Techniques**, 31 March 1967, p. 3; RRE, **Putley E.H. and McLean T.P., "Industrial Application of Infra-Red Techniques. App. A., Visit to Spencer Steel Works (Richard Thomas and Baldwin)"**, 13 December 1966, Physics Group.

66. **Morris, G.E. to Oakley, B.**, 12 January 1968.

67. RRE, **Morris, G.E. to Lawson, W.**, 1 January 1968; RRE, **Oakley, B.W. to Scrimshaw, F.H.**, 19 June 1968.

68. RRE, **Meeting Between BIRMO and Mintech Representatives**, 21 June 1968.

69. RRE, **Note of meetings at Castlewood House**, 6 February 1968.

70. RSRE, **"Industrial Infra-Red Symposium and Exhibition", memo, Glazier, E.V.D. to Larson, W.D.**, 6 June 1987; **Putley, E.H. to McLean, T.P.**, 13 June 1967; **Maclean, T.P. to Glazier, E.V.D.**, 16 June 1967.

71. **Spin-Off to Industry from Malvern**, *Engineering*, 10 November 1967, p. 739.

72. Bernal, J.D., **The Social Function of Science**, (MIT, 1967).

73. Putley, *op. cit.*

74. RRE, **Work on Civil Electronics**, January 1967, p. 82; RRE, **Notes From a Meeting at Castlewood House**, 6 February 1968.

75. RRE, **"Industrial Aspects of Electronics Research", Report by Mallett, E.S. Ministry of Aviation**, 24 February 1966.

76. RRE, **Roberts, V. to Glazier, E.V.**, 1 March 1967.

77. Putley *op. cit.*

78. Sir George MacFarlane, interview, 5 March 1991.

79. Sir John Hill, interview, 18 Feb 1991.

80. Coopey, R. **Industrial Modernisation** in Coopey, Fielding, Tiratsoo, *The Wilson Governments*, (Pinter, 1993).

Chapter 5

The Technological Impact of a Defence Research Establishment

Donald MacKenzie and Graham Spinardi

Introduction

Defence research establishments, such as the Los Alamos and Lawrence Livermore National Laboratories in the US, or the Ministry of Defence Research Establishments in the UK, are of interest for a number of reasons. They represent substantial concentrations of research and development expertise and expenditure. Does this, in combination with their defence remit, shape the wider development of science and technology in the fields in which they operate? Are their research agendas dictated by military needs, or by scientific and technological opportunity? What role do they play in the `politics of weaponry'? And are they, for example, neutral advisors on technical feasibility, or are they active advocates of new weapon systems?

Recent radical changes in world politics place new emphases on these questions. Will the end of the Cold War mean `business as usual' for these establishments, a shift of emphasis (perhaps to civil work), or decline and even closure? In the UK, at least, institutional arrangements are also changing as fast as the international environment. The four major non-nuclear defence research establishments have been brought together into one corporate organisation, the Defence Research Agency (DRA), and management of the Aldermaston Atomic Weapons Establishment is being contracted out to a private consortium.

This chapter reports the results of one part of a wider study of defence research establishments.[1] Our concern here is with the effect of these establishments on the general development of technology. This is still an extremely broad topic, one where there is little previous academic work to guide us,[2] and where publicly available data is sparse in the extreme.[3] So in approaching the issue we have had to adopt a case-study approach, focusing on one particular establishment,[4] and gathering information by interviewing those involved.

Our chosen establishment is the UK Royal Signals and Radar Establishment [RSRE], now the Electronics Division of the Defence Research Agency. Located in Great Malvern, RSRE was formed in two successive mergers, in 1953 and 1976, of four separate establishments with roots in the Second World War and earlier.[5] RSRE had and has a good claim to be Britain's premier concentration of research and development expertise in electronics and various related aspects of information technology. Its significance is such that, for example, one of the few television programmes to investigate the connections of military and civil technologies was titled `The Malvern Link'.[6]

RSRE's remit of course extends beyond `information technology' as conventionally conceived. The place of its predecessor establishments in the overall history of the twentieth century will rest on their radar research in the late 1930s and early 1940s, and that radar work continues, as, for example, does work on guided weapons. We chose, however, to focus on aspects of RSRE's research that are more `upstream' in application: fundamental work on aspects of information technology such as semiconductors, computer architectures and programming languages. Importantly, this is work not intrinsically tied to military applications (in contrast, for example, to guided weapons activities).

It is, therefore, work where the questions of interest to us are open. Do military needs shape what RSRE does? If so, in what sense? Are developments at RSRE exploited commercially - especially in the civil market? And what seem to be the determinants of success and failure in this respect?

These questions are not as simple as they may appear. In particular, the influence of military needs on the history of particular forms of technological development is not ascertainable by straightforward empirical means. It is not enough simply to note the involvement of a defence organisation or applications to defence purposes. Rather, the crucial issue is whether the history of the technology in question would have been different in some fundamental technical respect had the defence organisation or application not existed. Because that necessitates hypothesising a counterfactual alternative history, it involves delicate questions of judgement rather than empirical investigation alone.

This research draws on more general work on the development of information technology conducted under the aegis of the Programme on Information and Communication Technologies (PICT) at Edinburgh University. The wider research enables us to place assessments of RSRE's influence in context and helps us to judge the significance of the relative importance of RSRE's work compared to other organisations.

Somewhat artificially (because there are strong links between the different areas discussed), we divide our data into ten case-studies. Three are in the area of semiconductor development: infrared sensor technology, gallium arsenide and silicon integrated circuits. A further three lie broadly within the field of computational architectures: systolic arrays, and two forms of parallel computing. Three more concern computer security, `static analysis' of software, and hardware verification. The final study is the technology of liquid crystal displays.

The ten areas are reported in the same way. After a brief description of the technical area in question we give a short account of relevant RSRE work. We assess whether and how military needs have shaped this work, and then describe efforts to commercialise the technology. After the case-studies follows an extended discussion of the technological impact of RSRE, including some reflections on the current situation in the establishment.

To keep the length of this chapter reasonable we are forced to summarise our ten cases. Each technology, it is worth remembering, can represent a significant part of the lifetimes' work of several (sometimes many) people; people we have often avoided even naming for fear of failing to give due credit to all those involved. So any summary is bound to be unsatisfactory as history, given that it must omit both important developments and important people. We hope, however, that our accounts give accurate answers to the questions that interest us.

Case 1: Infrared Sensors

The Technology

Thermal imaging is based on the detection of the infrared radiation which is naturally emitted by all objects warmer than absolute zero. Because they suffer least from atmospheric absorption, two wavelength bands are of particular practical interest: mid infrared radiation (wavelengths 3 to 5 microns), and far infrared radiation (8 to 14 microns). Objects at room temperature (20°C) have a peak emission at 10 microns, and thus detectors operating in the far infrared waveband are more commonly used for imaging people and natural scenes. Hotter objects, such as an electric fire or the exhaust from a jet engine, emit much more radiation and have a peak of emission at shorter wavelengths. Detectors of such objects do not need to be so sensitive, and generally operate at around 3 microns.

Two types of technology have found major use in thermal imaging. One is based on the optoelectronic properties of certain semiconductors — notably cadmium mercury telluride (CMT) — which generate an electrical potential or current when irradiated at the appropriate wavelength. The other depends on the pyroelectric properties of certain materials which generate a potential when warmed.

Cadmium Mercury Telluride and the TICM Programme: RSRE's Work

Although the fundamental concept of infrared detection emerged at the start of the century, the first practical military device was developed by the Germans during the Second World War. Based on a lead sulphide cell, this device did not respond to radiation beyond 3 microns so its use was limited to detecting relatively hot objects such as aircraft engines.[7] Postwar research at one of RSRE's predecessor organisations, the Telecommunications Research Establishment (TRE), focused on finding detectors which responded to the far infrared radiation of objects at normal ambient temperatures. As an article in the *Times* of 9 January 1948 noted:

'The trend of research at T.R.E. has been to make photoconductors, as these detectors are called, work on longer wave-lengths, with the ultimate aim of reaching 10 microns, so that it may be possible to see relatively cool things, such as the human body and trees, in the dark'.[8]

Lead sulphide detectors proved difficult to manufacture, and initial work at TRE concentrated on the study and replication of the German manufacturing process. Research then began on other materials including lead selenide and lead telluride. At a time when most other semiconductor research was still working with polycrystalline material, Bill Lawson of RSRE had grown single crystals of these compounds by about 1950.[9] Other compounds investigated included indium antimonide, lead telluride and gallium arsenide, before the discovery of cadmium mercury telluride's (CMT) photoconductive sensitivity to infrared at the crucial 10 micron wavelength.

By the time this was synthesised in 1957, however, the official decision had been taken to abandon further research into thermal imaging as — strange though it seems in retrospect — there was no practical usage envisaged by the Ministry of Defence. According to the Royal Radar Establishment's ***Review*** of April 1958:

'Some success has been achieved in the development of detectors sensitive to a wavelength of the order of 10 microns . . . This work has now ceased as there is no operational requirement for a detector sensitive to such wavelengths'.[10]

In actual fact work had not ceased. Those interested in thermal imaging — particularly Lawson — simply fitted in 'Friday afternoon experiments' to carry on the research. With the establishment's funding provided en bloc by annual parliamentary vote, there was little the Ministry of Defence could do to stop research that had strong advocacy by individuals within the establishment. In the event this proved fortunate, as expertise was maintained in a technology that was about to gain practical recognition during the American war in Vietnam.

The US pursuit of thermal imaging reawakened interest in the UK. It also probably led the UK to concentrate on CMT (like the US) rather than a potential alternative material, lead tin telluride. On technical grounds alone the choice was 'six of one, half a dozen of the other', but the demonstration of practical CMT detectors in the US made that the safer approach.

The Influence of Military Needs

It was only in the mid-1970s that the military usefulness of the technology at last received sufficient recognition to generate concrete service requirements in the UK. These requirements were diverse, however, with 18 different thermal imaging designs produced by the Ministry of Defence by 1974. Analysis at the Radar Research Establishment (RRE) indicated that there was considerable commonality in the basic thermal imaging requirement, and favoured an approach based on common modules, as had already been adopted in the US. A number of factors militated against actually buying the US technology. First, it was considered by UK scientists to have significant technical weaknesses, and to be unsuited to UK requirements. Second, the UK could become dependent on the US for supply, and perhaps suffer delays or cost increases. Third, sales to third parties of weapons systems incorporating the thermal imager would be subject to US embargoes. Fourth, though probably not a major factor in the decision, the benefits of a UK development programme for spin-off into civil products would be lost if systems were simply bought from the US. Possible collaborative programmes with France and Germany did not come to anything, and the UK Thermal Imaging Common Modules (TICM) programme was set in motion in 1977.

The common modules approach offered several advantages — notably in unit cost and servicing — but created one serious difficulty: who would fund it? According to a history of the programme written for the Cabinet Office:

'The common modules in themselves did not constitute a weapon, its platform or even a sight system. They were more in the form of an enabling technology which would find application across the three services. Therefore they did not qualify for the status of a Staff Target or Staff Requirement and consequently funding for the programme could only be provided by those individual projects which had an endorsed need for thermal imaging equipment. So here was a new technology offering widespread application across many diverse projects yet that very diversity meant that no single source of funding could be identified. Furthermore, Project Managers were naturally cautious about relinquishing control of any aspect of their project and were certainly reluctant to risk subordinating their needs to the demands of commonality'.[11]

In the end the Directorate for Surveillance and Instrument Projects (DSIP) was selected as the project office for TICM. Funding was provided by two projects: the Short Range Surveillance and Target Acquisition System, which was the responsibility of DSIP; and the Main Battle Tank, MBT 80. Both these projects were subsequently cancelled, but the funding arrangements were reorganised. Rather than pooling funding from particular projects, it was decided to divide up the costs to each service in proportion to its expected uptake of TICM. This proved unacceptable to the RAF, however, and the eventual funding breakdown assigned 90 per cent of the bill to the Army and the rest to the Navy. In the end the RAF would turn out to be a major user of TICMs.

Full development began in January 1980, and production in 1983. Two categories of TICM were developed, one man-portable, the other vehicle-mounted. TICMs are now in use with all three services, and have also been sold to seventeen other countries. RSRE's work on CMT technology also resulted in a Queen's Award in 1983 (jointly with the ElectroOptic Division of Mullard Ltd).

Commercialisation

In 1967, the same year as the first demonstration of a real time thermal imager, RRE became part of the Ministry of Technology. A Working Party was set up to examine the commercial potential of thermal imaging, and the technology was demonstrated to about twenty companies. However, the expense of the technology and its small civil market meant that none was prepared to make substantial investment.[12] Industrial interest depended on extramural funding from RRE which supported work at Mullard (detectors), Hymatic (coolers), Rank and Barr and Stroud (optics), and a range of electronics companies.

As the TICM programme came together in the late 1970s, the possible commercial benefit of an indigenous UK thermal imaging sector was seen as an explicit, if subsidiary, justification. According to the Cabinet Office history of TICM:

'An important factor in the selection of the TICM contractors was the determination and organisation of the companies to compete in overseas thermal imaging markets'.[13]

However, although the military utilisation of CMT technology in TICMs seems to have been very successful, the civil exploitation or `spin-off' has been limited by the high price. Some civil users can afford to pay for the capability: the Central Electricity Generating Board for example, bought three TICMs which it uses to check the integrity of inaccessible power cables by helicopter. But in general a large civil market for the technology depends on lower cost, which in turn requires technology which does not need cryogenic cooling. RSRE is working on uncooled CMT technology in a programme called the New Detector Initiative (NDI), but as the Cabinet Office history notes, `progress in this area is limited not by ideas but by resources'.[14]

Low-Cost Infra-red Sensing: The Pyroelectric Effect: RSRE's Work

At about the same time that CMT research was officially revived in the mid-1960s, work also began on infrared detectors based on pyroelectric materials. There were still doubts about quantity manufacture of CMT devices and so this alternative approach was pursued.

Pyroelectric devices offer a cheaper, less powerful approach to infrared detection. Although CMT offers superior quality it typically requires an expensive and heavy cooling system to reduce the detector to very low temperatures (about 80°K). It became clear that pyroelectric devices, though initially examined for military applications, were being superseded in most such uses by CMT, and would be more suitable for civil applications where cost took precedence over quality.

The Influence of Military Needs

Pyroelectric technology does not seem to have been greatly shaped by development at a military establishment or by defence requirements. Indeed, in the light of the cancellation of funding for other technologies (such as that of light emitting diodes which ceased in the mid-1970s), the pyroelectric work may have survived in spite of, rather than because of, the military's perceived interests.

Actual military applications of the technology seem to have followed its success in civil uses.

Commercialisation

Pyroelectric devices have been developed for two main types of usage. One is simply as infrared sensors which respond to a change in an infrared beam directed at them. Some of the most successful products of the work that RRE sponsored in industry — particularly at Mullard and Plessey — have been intruder alarms, automatic doors and other infrared operated systems.

The other main category of applications is in thermal imaging. In 1967/1968 a joint programme between RRE and the English Electric Valve Company (EEV) at Chelmsford was initiated to do research on a pyroelectric vidicon. The pyroelectric cameras thus developed were tested in civil applications in the late 1970s. These included fire fighting, medical thermography and site surveying.[15] This led EEV, with sponsorship from the Department of Trade and Industry, to develop a specially engineered vidicon for the fire services, which has been used to locate injured people in collapsed buildings following gas explosions and other disasters. This civil application of the technology then in turn prompted its uptake by the military in response to the onboard fire-fighting experiences of the Navy in the Falklands. For its pyroelectric infrared detector work RSRE has been the recipient (jointly with the relevant companies) of two Queen's Awards for Technological Achievement. In 1982 it was awarded for the pyroelectric detector, and in 1987 for the pyroelectric vidicon, particularly its exploitation in the Fire Service Camera developed by EEV.

The latest developments in thermal imaging technology, both for CMT and pyroelectric detectors, are concentrated on staring arrays. These are analogous to the modern solid-state TV cameras which can now be bought cheaply on the high street. Staring thermal array cameras avoid the complexity and expense of opto-mechanical scanning systems and are therefore much smaller and lighter. Also, because each detector spends more time `staring' at a particular part of the scene it absorbs more radiation, and consequently it is more sensitive. In pyroelectric cameras, this increased sensitivity leads to a performance more comparable with cooled CMT imagers, hence the growing interest in this technology. In high performance cameras using CMT this senstivity gain can be traded for higher temperature operations or smaller optics - items of key interest in smaller lightweight systems for hand-held thermal imagers or smart weapon applications.

Case 2: Gallium Arsenide

The Technology

Gallium arsenide has long been recognised to have properties which offer advantages over silicon in semiconductor use, but it is not yet in wide usage because of other disadvantages. `Gallium arsenide', according to a well-known aphorism, `is the technology of the future, always has been, always will be'.[16] It differs from silicon in four main ways that offer potential advantages. First, Gallium Arsenide's crystalline structure attracts moving electrons less strongly than those of silicon, making it inherently faster and also able to operate at higher frequencies (which allows for lower noise operation that is especially useful in signal detection applications).[17] Second, it is much more amenable to band-width engineering than silicon. Third, the difference in band gap properties also means that gallium arsenide has the capacity to radiate and detect near-infrared radiation. The potential energy of an electron moving from the conduction to the valence band can be given up as a photon. Light emitting diodes (LEDs) make use of this property. In the reverse process gallium arsenide is a very efficient fast photodetector, whose wavelength sensitivity can be tuned by band-width engineering. Fourth, devices fabricated from gallium arsenide tend to be less susceptible to damage from radiation (for example from a nuclear explosion) than devices made from silicon: gallium arsenide is `radiation hard'.

Set against these benefits are manufacturing disadvantages which have prevented the widespread uptake of gallium arsenide. First, gallium arsenide has no usable counterpart of the insulating oxide that silicon forms when heated in air. This easily produced layer makes silicon much easier to work with, providing both insulation and a masking agent for etching and doping particular regions. Other, less convenient means must be used when working with gallium arsenide. Second, because gallium arsenide is a compound, it is more difficult to remove crystalline imperfections from it than from elemental silicon. Silicon can be annealed at high temperatures (nearly 1000°C), whereas gallium arsenide is susceptible to the selective vaporisation of arsenic before effective annealing can take place. Also, heating gallium arsenide can result in the loss of dopants which are retained in silicon by the silicon oxide layer. Thus, device characteristics tend to vary across a gallium arsenide chip. Along with other factors, this means that the level of integration available with gallium arsenide is currently several orders of magnitude lower than that available with silicon. A square centimetre silicon chip can hold more than a million transistors, whereas one of gallium arsenide can manage only tens of thousands.[18]

RSRE's Work

Although semiconductor research seems to have begun earlier at the Telecommunications Research Establishment in connection with infrared detection, the bulk of early gallium arsenide work was done at the Services Electronic Research Laboratory (SERL) at Baldock. In 1952, a Semiconductor Devices Division was set up there, looking first at germanium and silicon, but within a year also at intermetallic semiconductor materials such as indium antimonide, gallium phosphide and gallium arsenide.

Of these, gallium arsenide was to become the dominant material at SERL. Initially chosen primarily as a transistor material for its high temperature and frequency properties, it was in the end never used in junction transistors.[19] Instead, it found application in a number of more specialised uses in connection with light emission and detection, and microwave generation and amplification. Early examples of light emitting diodes (mainly using gallium phosphide or gallium arsenide phosphide) were developed at Baldock, but this line of work was eventually terminated in the mid-1970s because the services had no system requirement for such technology, nor was there any commercial interest.

In late 1959 an Electronic Materials Division was also set up at the Royal Radar Establishment (with which SERL would merge in 1976) at Malvern. RRE and SERL contracted out work on gallium arsenide to companies interested in the material, and this was funded through the Ministry of Defence's Components, Valves and Devices (CVD) programme. In 1966 it was institutionalised through the formation of a Gallium Arsenide Consortium, whose first chairman was Dr Cyril Hilsum of SERL.[20] As well as SERL and RRE, the consortium included Plessey, STL, BDH, Mullard and GEC.[21]

Almost all of the funding for early UK research into gallium arsenide was provided through the CVD under the aegis of the consortium. Precompetitive collaboration between companies was unhindered by commercial confidentiality because the basic technical problems ruled out any immediate industrial exploitation. Much of this work involved developing techniques for producing suitable materials and for characterising their properties.

One particular device that came out of the gallium arsenide work was an image intensifying photocathode. Begun in the late 1960s at SERL, this led to the development of night goggles that went into service in the mid-1980s and were used in the Gulf War. For this, RSRE and English Electric Valve Company were jointly awarded a Queen's Award for Technological Achievement in 1987.

The Influence of Military Needs

Although gallium arsenide's potential military advantages as a semiconductor material underpinned the interest of RSRE in it, the funding of UK industry through the consortium seems to have been at too basic a level to reflect any particular military bias (such as an emphasis on radiation hardness). Without the military rationale of RSRE (and its predecessor establishments) the work would probably not have taken place, at least on such a scale, but had funding been available from a civil source it would not have taken developments in a significantly different direction.

Commercialisation

This lack of specific military orientation is reflected in the most concrete success story that can be attributed to the consortium and CVD funding. Metals Research Ltd (now Cambridge Instruments Ltd) were funded in the growth of semi-insulating gallium arsenide substrates using the liquid encapsulation Czochralski (LEC) technique pioneered at RRE in the late 1960s. Collaborative study of the properties of the gallium arsenide produced by this method, which required heavy doping with chromium to achieve the semi-insulating behaviour, revealed some thermal instability. This could be eliminated by another method of producing semi-insulating material which required no doping. Instead of pulling presynthesised chromium-doped gallium arsenide crystals, it was found that pulling the gallium arsenide as it was synthesised from elemental arsenic and molten gallium produced semi-insulating material. However, whereas the former operation could be carried out at low pressure, the latter required the puller to be kept at high pressure. For this Cambridge Instruments used high pressure pullers they had developed for gallium phosphide based on designs that originated at RRE: the Malvern MsR6 and the Melbourn.[22] According to the consortium chairman at the time, Dr. Don Hurle:

'These pullers quickly came to dominate the world market for pressure pullers and the materials base for a gallium arsenide IC technology was founded. ... This would not have happened (at least in the UK) without two ingredients; CVD funding and the provision of device-relevant characterisation by the consortium'.[23]

Attempts to extend collaboration to device fabrication technologies were not so successful, being hindered by a lack of access to fabrication facilities. An attempt to overcome this difficulty was made in 1982 with the formation of the 'III-V IC Technologies Consortium' under the chairmanship of David Colliver of RSRE. Membership comprised device development managers from GEC, Plessey, STL and BTRL, with Don Hurle representing the Gallium Arsenide Consortium, and also representatives from CVD and the Department of Trade and Industry.[24]

One successful device, in the specialised optoelectronic field, was the photocathode built by English Electric Valve Company after many years of work at RSRE and its forerunners. However, although the photocathode night goggles built by EEV comprise an annual turnover in excess of £1 million, most of this comes from military customers.

Case 3: Silicon Integrated Circuits

The Technology

The silicon integrated circuit is at the heart of modern information technology. Many aspects of that technology would not be possible, or not economic, without the capacity to replace collections of separate electronic components such as transistors with entire circuits (now of very great complexity) fabricated on a single piece of semiconductor.

RSRE's Work

The idea of the integrated circuit seems to have been first put forward in 1952 by an Royal Radar Establishment employee, G.W.A. Dummer, following discussion with staff at the Caswell Research Laboratory of Plessey Company Ltd. Although during the 1950s there were sporadic development efforts at the Establishment and (funded by it) at Plessey, the decisive steps towards making an integrated circuit possible were first taken in the US, following the pioneering work at the end of the 1950s by J.S. Kilby of Texas Instruments and R. Noyce of the Fairchild Corporation. Despite important research and development work at RSRE and elsewhere in the UK, the US industry - and, by the 1970s, Japanese industry - soon far outstripped British industry's efforts in the area.[25]

RSRE, however, continued both its own work and also its sponsorship and co-ordination of wider research and development efforts. The latter have been of particular importance in the 1980s. Early in that decade, RSRE began coordinating for the Ministry of Defence a programme of largely industrial research and development on Very High Performance Integrated Circuits (VHPIC), a programme that began when it became clear that the UK was not to be allowed access to the US Department of Defense's Very High Speed Integrated Circuits (VHSIC) programme. VHSIC technology `was going to wipe us out in the UK unless we did something', says one RSRE staff member.

Basic work under the UK VHPIC programme, however, was largely subsumed into the wider Alvey Programme (a separate Ministry of Defence VHPIC Applications Demonstrator programme was established to develop uses of VHPIC/Alvey technology in military systems). Alvey, which ran from 1983/84 to 1988/89 (with a small amount of expenditure continuing for a couple of years afterwards), was a major UK government effort, prompted by the Japanese Fifth Generation Programme, to maintain and increase the British stake in advanced information technology. Silicon VLSI (Very Large Scale Integration) was one of the four main Alvey technologies. Alvey's overall Director, Brian Oakley, was a former member of staff of RSRE, although one who had had several other posts in the interim, and who came to be critical (unfairly, in the view of RSRE staff) of RSRE's role in Alvey.[26] Alvey VLSI Director, Bill Fawcett, moved to the post from being head of the physics group at RSRE, and RSRE staff played a major role in the coordination, monitoring and evaluation of the Alvey VLSI programme.

The Alvey VLSI programme supported development of six integrated circuit production processes. Three - at GEC, Plessey and STC - were devoted to the most popular silicon integrated circuit technology, CMOS (Complementary Metal Oxide Semiconductor). Two - at Ferranti and Plessey (Caswell) - were devoted to the faster, but more complex and less highly-integrated, bipolar chips. The sixth Alvey integrated circuit technology, developed at Marconi Electronic Devices Limited, was devoted to CMOS/SOS (silicon-on-sapphire) used primarily for radiation hard military applications. RSRE's role in the Alvey VLSI programme was to provide the scientific research into the basic substrate materials and into the layer processing steps, such as dry etching.

The Influence of Military Needs

The pervasiveness of the applications of the silicon integrated circuit, and the numerous benefits from having faster, more highly-integrated circuits, mean that in most of its aspects neither the Alvey VLSI work, nor RSRE's own research, can be seen as being underpinned by specifically military needs. It is true that the goal of this work was not truly general-purpose products: memories and standard microprocessors. Instead, VHPIC and Alvey VLSI work concentrated on supporting technologies to boost the UK position in the more specialised Application Specific Integrated Circuits (ASICs). These are of great importance in modern defence electronics, but they have civil applications as well, and furthermore a strategy to boost direct competition in volume products would have been beyond the scope and resources of a programme like Alvey.[27]

The most plausible example of the influence of defence needs is thus the presence within Alvey of the radiation-hard silicon-on-sapphire technology, which some observers have criticised.[28] RSRE staff point out, however, that silicon-on-sapphire was merely one integrated circuit process amongst six supported by Alvey, and that in the early 1980s there was a glimmer of hope that silicon-on-sapphire technology and its derivatives would be useful for high performance commercial applications (the latter has proved not to be the case).

Commercialisation

Most of the VHPIC/Alvey work with which RSRE was involved took place in firms, and it fed directly into state-of-the-art production facilities in bipolar and silicon-on-sapphire technologies. The takeovers by GEC of Plessey and Ferranti mean that these facilities are now largely concentrated in one firm, GEC Plessey Semiconductors, which has a portfolio of production technologies including one micron CMOS, one micron silicon-on-sapphire, and two bipolar technologies. GEC

Plessey Semiconductors claims to be Europe's largest ASIC producer, and the Alvey programme provided valuable input to all these production processes. So the VHPIC/Alvey work helped UK industry retain a relatively strong position in ASICs.

The UK remains largely excluded from the mainstream semiconductor integrated circuit market. As noted above, however, ending that exclusion was not (and realistically could not have been) a goal of the Alvey programme. For any European firm to compete in that market, especially with the Japanese suppliers of large density memories, is difficult enough, and during the period of the Alvey programme it remained the case that `the scale of [UK firms'] financial investments in SCs [semiconductors] falls far short of other major European companies'.[29]

Case 4: Systolic Arrays

The Technology

Systolic arrays form a kind of bridge between RSRE's silicon integrated circuits work (case 3) and its computer architecture work (cases 4 and 5). In a systolic array, the structure of a very regular computation is mapped directly onto the silicon of an integrated circuit. Chunks of data can then be `pumped' around processing elements on the chip, with the array of results of one set of operations being fed directly as input to the next, without any need to store intermediate results in global memory. The adjective `systolic', descriptive of this pumping, derives from the biological term `systole', the rhythmical contraction of the heart.

RSRE's Work

RSRE became involved shortly after the concept was first formulated in 1978 by H.T. Kung and C.E. Leiserson of Carnegie-Mellon University.[30] John McWhirter of RSRE, together with staff at the established electronics firm STC Technology Ltd., realised the potential of systolic arrays for the fast, repetitive calculations needed for signal processing (much of which, in the 1970s, was still being done on analogue hardware). Two main areas of work have been pursued at RSRE.[31] One is the development of an `adaptive beam-former', based around an RSRE-designed systolic array, that can by calculation suppress unwanted signals arriving at a radar receiver. The other concerns `bit-level' systolic arrays. Even with 1980s chip integration levels, developing a single systolic array chip to perform a major signal processing operation is difficult, unless the complexity of the problem is reduced by processing information in units of individual binary digits (`bits'), rather than in `words' of many bits. The concept of the bit-level systolic array originates from RSRE. The Establishment has done significant work on transforming signal processing algorithms into the appropriate forms, and has been responsible for the production of silicon implementations of several bit-level systolic arrays.

The Influence of Military Needs

Systolic arrays could be applied to a wide range of real-time computing problems, military and civil (some enthusiasts see them as a potential replacement for orthodox computers even in non real-time uses). Adaptive beam-forming is a largely military application, since the most obvious unwanted signal is enemy jamming. But `application' is the appropriate word. The defence connection has helped make real what otherwise might have remained merely paper designs, and it has affected the choice of applications and materials in which to implement arrays (see below). But if RSRE had been a wholly civil institution, there is little reason to think it would not have done systolic array work, nor that this work would have been fundamentally different in direction.

Commercialisation

The RSRE-STC adaptive beam-former was a `proof-of-concept' prototype, using existing chips. As part of an RSRE-run VHPIC Applications Demonstrator project (see case 3), STC has gone on to develop a fully custom `node processor chip' for that and similar applications. Once the project is complete (further funding is being sought to complete it), this is intended as a `lego block' for high-performance signal processing. STC will, however, probably not sell it as such - the firm does not see its business as selling chips and instead it may sell systems incorporating it, and possibly license the design. In the defence market at least, the prospects of success seem reasonable. An Intel programmable systolic array chip, iWARP, is, however, about to enter the market. iWARP may be unduly complex for many signal-processing applications: in some respect it resembles the Inmos transputer (case 6). But the economies of scale possible in a more general-purpose chip, actively marketed as a product in its own right, not just as a component of systems, will be a major factor.

In bit-level systolic arrays RSRE collaborated with Marconi Electronic Devices Ltd., part of GEC, with RSRE funding the development of two signal processing chips. These have a specifically military market, being implemented in radiation-hard silicon-on-sapphire (case 3). One is now in use in a range of military equipment. GEC has not, however, developed civil versions. In Germany, bit-level systolic array chips, implemented in conventional CMOS (see case 3), are already being marketed, primarily for civil uses. RSRE manages a Department of Trade and Industry funded IED [Information Engineering Directorate] collaborative project in CMOS bit-level systolic arrays (with Plessey Semiconductors, Racal, STC and the Queen's University, Belfast). Products with a commercial potential are the goal, but despite the continuing strength of UK theoretical work in the area, the UK technological lead has been lost and the companies involved are trying to catch up.

Case 5: SIMD Parallel Computing[32]

The Technology

The `architecture' of a computer refers to the way its different components are organised and interconnected. It is at least as important to the computer's performance as those basic components. In recent years, an important theme in the development of computer architecture has been parallelism. Instead of a single processor operating sequentially, a parallel computer has several (in `massive parallelism', many) processors working simultaneously.

There are plethora of different parallel architectures, and here we follow the terminology proposed by Michael Flynn.[33] First we consider single instruction stream, multiple data stream (SIMD) architectures. In these, all the different processors are in `lock-step', simultaneously executing the same instruction on different items of data.

RSRE's Work

RSRE's involvement in SIMD parallel computing has been with by far the most important British SIMD project, the Distributed Array Processor (DAP). The DAP, developed at International Computers Limited (ICL), following work there in the early 1970s by S.F. Reddaway, is a `classic' SIMD computer, in many ways reminiscent of the earlier ideas of American SIMD pioneer Daniel Slotnick. A large number of very simple processors (4,096 in the 1980 ICL production version of the DAP) operate in lock-step on tiny fragments of data.

This early ICL DAP did not work on its own, but only in conjunction with an ICL 2900 series mainframe computer. Indeed, it was designed to emulate an ICL 2900 memory module, the difference being that the DAP was an `active' memory, having the array of simple processors `distributed' throughout it. It was not a commercial success, with only six being sold (none outside the UK), in part because of this intrinsic connection to a particular mainframe computer.

Without involvement from outside ICL, the history of the DAP might well have ended in the early 1980s. RSRE however intervened to offer ICL a contract to redesign the DAP and make it suitable for military signal processing. With this Ministry of Defence contract, and design assistance from RSRE, ICL staff made use of advances in integrated circuit technology to shrink the DAP. The original production version of the DAP occupied 250 cubic feet and weighed two tons. The new militarised version (`MilDAP') is small and light enough to fit into a standard aircraft avionics box. It is `stand alone' (capable of autonomous operation) and `ruggedised'.

A follow-up project was begun under the VHPIC Applications Demonstrator programme (see case 3) to develop an even more highly miniaturised `VDAP'.

The Influence of Military Needs

The miniaturisation and ruggedisation of the DAP reflected military needs, and the greatly enhanced input-output capacity of the MilDAP, by comparison with its predecessor, was necessitated by the demands of its envisaged applications in military signal processing. However, neither RSRE nor military needs influenced the unchanged fundamental SIMD architecture of the DAP. The changes made were, rather, adaptations of an existing technology for the military environment. Furthermore, especially in respect to miniaturisation, they were changes valuable in almost any application of the DAP.

Commercialisation

In 1986, Active Memory Technologies (AMT: its name echoing the DAP's `processor within memory' architecture) was set up, with ICL transferring intellectual property rights in the DAP to the new company. ICL retained a 20 per cent stake in AMT (the remainder of the original capitalisation was £4 million raised from venture capitalists), but the VDAP project came to a halt at that point: it was no longer relevant to ICL, and AMT lacked the resources to pursue the development and production of a DAP by implementing the most advanced integrated circuit technology. Instead, AMT focused its early efforts on producing and marketing the DAP 510, essentially a production version of the MilDAP.

The DAP 510, and the larger, more powerful but similar DAP 610, have been remarkably successful machines. Between October 1987 when the first machine was delivered to a customer, and June 1990, over 80 DAPs had been sold. AMT's estimated 1990 sales total of $12 million is still modest, but is enough to make it the fifth largest participant worldwide in the small but growing market for massively parallel machines. Unusually for a British company, half AMT's total sales have been in the US.

However, this has been achieved in part by AMT transforming itself into an American company (although it is still owned primarily by UK venture capitalists). Its hardware development was, from the beginning, based in California, close to the world's largest concentration of silicon design skills. Production has also been based in America, while software development has remained in the UK. In November 1989, the company's headquarters was shifted from the UK to Irvine, California. The American identity has brought access to US Department of Defense development money: the Defense Advanced Research Projects Agency (DARPA) is funding AMT to develop, in conjunction with the Texas defence contractor, E Systems, a version of the DAP implemented in gallium arsenide (see case 3). The DAP is seen as a potential contender for a central computational role in some versions of the `Star Wars' Strategic Defense Initiative.

Though the military market remains crucial for the DAP, university and some other civil sector sales have developed. DNA sequencing and chemical modelling are among important applications. Apple Computer has bought a DAP for research on speech recognition, and Reuters has purchased one for database searching.

Case 6: MIMD Parallel Computing[34]

The Technology

In a SIMD computer, processors have to act in lockstep: one processor cannot, for example, be multiplying while another is adding. That constraint is relaxed in a multiple instruction stream, multiple data stream (MIMD) computer. Each different processor can follow its own `subprogram'. The price of this greater flexibility is a greater problem of interconnection and co-ordination. Processor/memory relations are a particular issue: if a single common memory is retained (`shared memory'), contention between processors for access to it can easily become a bottleneck, and the number of processors that can usefully be employed is limited. Separate, `distributed' memories permit more massive parallelism, but the consistency of their contents then becomes an issue.

RSRE's Work

As in its SIMD work and support, RSRE's MIMD development has concerned the central strand of British MIMD computing: massively parallel distributed memory architectures, built upon the transputer - a CMOS microprocessor designed specifically for parallel processing (as well as for stand-alone embedded computing) by Inmos, the company set up in 1978 by the then Labour government to try to end British exclusion from the commercial mainstream of the world microchip business. The change of government the following year, and the market power of large American and Japanese companies, ensured a chequered history for the new firm which was sold off to Thorn-EMI in 1984. Despite that, Inmos successfully brought the first transputer, the T414, onto the market in 1985. At that point, a group of Inmos designers and managers left the firm to set up Meiko with their own capital, a small company devoted to exploiting the potential for using transputers to build MIMD computers.

RSRE became involved not with Meiko, but in a European Community Esprit project christened Supernode and initiated by computational physicists at Southampton University, to build a transputer-based MIMD computer. RSRE, which had earlier worked with Thorn-EMI on emulators of the transputer, took on the role of project management for Supernode. Thorn-EMI, Grenoble University and the French electronics companies Apsis and Telmat were also involved in the project. As well as leading to a transputer-based MIMD parallel computer, the Supernode project provided much of the context and funding for the development of the second-generation transputer, the T800.

RSRE and Inmos now jointly lead a new European Community MIMD development project, Parallel Universal Message-passing Architectures (PUMA), which is supporting *inter alia* about half the elements in developments necessary for the next-generation transputer, the T9000.

The Influence of Military Needs

RSRE has developed a small, rugged version of Supernode ('Mousetrap') for military use. This apart, RSRE involvement did not lead to any specifically military influence on matters such as the choice of architecture for Supernode or the design of T800 transputer, nor has RSRE sought to exert any such influence.

Commercialisation

A new company, Parsys, was set up under the auspices of Thorn-EMI in April 1988 to develop the prototype Supernode into a commercial product (in France, the same task was undertaken by Telmat, one of the original collaborators). Within its first year, Parsys sold the very respectable total of 35 machines. By 1990, when Parsys became largely independent of Thorn-EMI following a partial management buy-out, its sales, while still lagging those of Meiko, had grown to 50. The T800 transputer, developed in part under the Supernode project, has been important for the success of Meiko as well as the Supernode companies, and indeed has been a major success for Inmos itself.

Alfonso Molina's study of the Supernode project shows that RSRE's role was pivotal in the project. Unlike the private firms, it had no financial vested interest and thus could be seen as 'objective' in the disputes that were inevitable in a large international project. Unlike the universities, however, RSRE had considerable experience in project management.

Again, though, there is irony, from a British point of view, in the success of the transputer and transputer-based MIMD computers. In April 1989 Thorn-EMI sold its share of Inmos. Though transputer development is still physically based in Britain, Inmos is now part of the Franco-Italian SGS-Thomson combine.

Case 7: Computer Security

The Technology

Recent publicity about hacking and viruses highlights the vulnerability of computer systems to unauthorised access and malicious acts. Computer security is concerned with protecting systems against such risks. It addresses how systems are used and - more importantly as far as the RSRE work is concerned - how they are designed.

A major (though not exclusive) concern has been developing secure operating systems for multi-user computers. Such operating systems control access to the computer (for example through a system of passwords) and prevent users from reading or modifying each other's data, unless authorised to do so. A particular problem is when data of different degrees of sensitivity (unclassified, restricted, secret, top secret, etc.) are being processed simultaneously and different users may have different levels of clearance. A secure operating system for these circumstances will be designed to ensure that information with a particular security classification can flow only to those with appropriate levels of clearance.

There are two (arguably distinct) types of characteristic to consider. One is **functionality**: the security services provided by a system. The other is **assurance**: the nature and extent of evidence that a given system does indeed possess the desired security properties.

RSRE's Work

RSRE has worked on computer security since the 1970s. One early project was developing a security package for a network linking computers in different Ministry of Defence research establishments. The network was never actually built, in part because of security concerns, and the project brought home to RSRE researchers that 'the problem is not just security but building a system so that the security claims are manifest'.

RSRE's work has been directed primarily at ensuring that the Ministry of Defence specifies security requirements intelligently and that industry has the awareness, techniques and components to meet them. RSRE has itself developed a series of SCP (Secure Communications Processor) computers. SCP2, involving new RSRE software running on existing hardware, has been evaluated as secure at level 5 of the UK computer security evaluation criteria. These criteria are administered by the Communications Electronic Security Group, an offshoot of the Government Communications Headquarters (GCHQ). RSRE's work on computer security, which predated that of GCHQ by several years, influenced the detail of the security criteria, but the primary influence on their creation was the earlier establishment, in 1983, by the US Department of Defence of its Trusted Computer System Evaluation Criteria, the so-called 'Orange Book'. US level A1 and UK level

6 are the highest levels of security assurance, and require formal mathematical proof of security properties. This requirement has encouraged formal methods research at RSRE, but to date only components, not entire systems, have successfully been evaluated at level 6. In the US, the Honeywell SCOMP operating system and the Unisys `Blacker' communications processor have both been evaluated A-1.[35]

Other RSRE developments have been an enhanced security version, developed in conjunction with ICL, of the latter's George 3 operating system. RSRE has also worked with DEC to encourage the development of secure operating systems for DEC computers. An SCP3 (now known as SMITE), which unlike the SCP2 is a brand-new machine with new chips and new microcode, as well as high security software, is under development, as is work on crucial components (access control; routing centre; cryptographic key distribution centre and logging centre) for a DSS (Distributed Secure Systems) network which can be shared by users and information at different security levels.

The Influence of Military Needs

Civil as well as military organisations have a need for secure computing. However, the forms taken by these needs typically differ.[36] These forms can indeed be seen as the technical expression of different typical pre-computer security concerns. The defence sector has been preoccupied above all with preventing unauthorised disclosure of information: for it, security thus primarily means confidentiality. The civil sector (especially financial institutions[37]) has been concerned above all with preventing improper transactions and unauthorised modification of data: for it, security thus primarily means integrity. There are also typical differences in the type of threat being considered. The defence sector has had to consider a threat from a determined, well-resourced, technically sophisticated hostile intelligence agency. A bank, on the other hand, is more concerned with relatively unsophisticated and opportunist fraud by its own employees.

RSRE's work has chiefly concerned security in the sense of confidentiality, and has posited a `high-level threat'. To that extent, its work on computer security reflects military needs.

Commercialisation

Because of this military emphasis, the commercial sector has not been interested in RSRE-designed secure systems. Even for defence-sector customers, the costs of an evaluated secure system are high. Evaluation is expensive and slow, and the need for evaluation makes it difficult to update components as improved versions become available. Demonstrating assurance of security can mean sacrificing security functionality and other desirable facilities. There is a vicious circle in secure computing, where high-cost low-functionality systems mean small markets, which in turn lead to small production runs and high costs.

This is not a problem unique to Britain. Indeed, it is fully manifest in the US, despite the US computer security market being at least ten times larger than that of the UK.[38] Nevertheless, it meant that the SCP2, marketed by GEC Computers, now GPT, was not a commercial success (although RSRE staff hope that component technologies from the SCP programme will be commercialised successfully).

Any eventual answer to the problems of the computer security market must involve harmonisation of different national computer security criteria - to expand the market - together with quicker evaluation and perhaps some reconciliation of military and civil security priorities. RSRE has taken a leading role in these efforts. A DTI Commercial Computer Security Centre was set up in 1986/87, originally at RSRE and headed by an RSRE staff member. The DTI centre worked with the defence-sector Communications Electronic Security Group to produce joint computer security criteria, and moves are being made to harmonise computer security criteria for Britain, France, Germany and the Netherlands. The evaluation of systems against UK (and eventually wider) security criteria is conducted within the private sector, and two software houses, Admiral and Logica, have been licensed to set up computer security CLEFS (Licensed Evaluation Facilities).

Case 8: Static Analysers

The Technology

A major difficulty in being able to trust computer software is that full empirical testing is generally impossible. The number of possible combinations of input conditions and internal states for a system of any complexity is astronomically large. Because of this, `bugs' are frequently discovered even in programs that have been subject to extensive testing. `Static analysis' of software - a name deliberately chosen to contrast with `dynamic' testing (running programs in order to check empirically for the presence of bugs) - involves automated examination of the structure of a program. Static analysers are computer programs that translate the structure of a program under examination into standard form, and search for anomalies in the structure that indicate badly-written or erroneous programs. In more sophisticated versions, static analysers support attempts to prove program correctness mathematically rather than empirically. The specification of a module of a program is expressed formally, and static analysis tools, which incorporate rules of logical inference, help a user construct a proof that the program module does indeed comply to specification.

RSRE's Work

RSRE has long been distinguished by a structured and rigorous, rather than `quick-and-dirty' empirical, approach to software. It is perhaps not accidental that the RSRE department housing most of its computer work was the Mathematics Division. In the archetypal split between the widely used FORTRAN and `purist' ALGOL programming languages,[39] RSRE was definitively on the latter side, in particular producing the standard ALGOL 68 compiler for ICL 1900 series mainframe computers. In the 1960s RSRE also devised CORAL 66, a high-level language designed specifically for programming the early mini-computers used for real-time and process control, and played a major role in its development and introduction as the Ministry of Defence's preferred high-level language in these applications, superseding the use of assembly code. Like ALGOL, CORAL is designed to support well-structured programming.

The static analysis work at RSRE was begun in the 1970s by Dr Bob Phillips, superintendent of one of the RSRE computing divisions. Phillips was seeking ways other than empirical testing of assessing the reliability of software, and RSRE's experience with ALGOL and CORAL may naturally have suggested the value of concentrating on program structure. A mutual acquaintance, realising the significance for Phillips' work of mathematical developments on the complexity of graphs, put him in touch with a specialist, Bernard Carré, of the University of Southampton. Together they worked on applying graph theory to the static analysis of computer programs. After Phillips' death, both Carré and other RSRE staff continued this work. The result was two (broadly similar) sets of static analysis tools: SPADE (Southampton Program Analysis and Development Environment) and MALPAS (Malvern Program Analysis Suite). The development of SPADE was a joint effort of RSRE and Southampton University, with the latter's work supported by RSRE funding; MALPAS was an in-house RSRE development.

The Influence of Military Needs

An early concern motivating Phillips' work was software problems in military systems: a particular issue in the period, and subject of some public discussion, was false alarms in nuclear attack early warning systems. Worries about computer security also provided some of the motivation for RSRE work on static analysers. Static analysis could help detect anomalies that might, say, have been deliberately introduced into a piece of software by a hostile agent; it might even permit proof that a piece of software had desired security properties. These security factors were used to justify further development work to create a classified `engineered version' of the static analysis tools (this is what became MALPAS).

Security considerations cannot, however, be said to have shaped the technical development of static analysers, and one RSRE staff member described the security connection as 'a good funding ploy'. Most of the application of static analysers seems to have been to safety-critical rather than security-critical software, and while it is true that much of the former work has been on military systems, a significant proportion has been civil. The techniques themselves are independent of whether it is a security property, a safety property, or, in principle, any other kind of desired property, of a program that is at issue.

Commercialisation

As well as supporting Carré's research, RSRE funded him to set up training courses in static analysis. The success of these, and the interest shown particularly by engineers from British Aerospace, encouraged the establishment by Carré in October 1983 of Program Validation Limited. As well as continuing to run courses, the firm put together existing static analysis tools into the SPADE package. It sells this package, paying 10 per cent royalties to the Ministry of Defence, of which half is returned to the University of Southampton and is there largely devoted to the support of closely related academic work. Program Validation Limited has continued to develop the tools, notably expanding them from structural analysis in the direction of support for proof. Although the firm is small, its mix of training services and tool development and marketing has made it modestly successful. Static analysers, it is worth noting, are a uniquely European product. No analogue exists in the US market, although the Ithaca-based Odyssey Research Associates may introduce competitors.

When Defence Technology Enterprises (DTE) was set up to transfer technology from defence research establishments to civil application, its RSRE 'ferret' discovered the classified 'engineered version' of the static analysis tools. Declassified and christened MALPAS, this version was licensed through DTE to a Surrey firm, Rex, Thompson and Partners, whose primary expertise had hitherto been in hardware reliability. This attempt at further commercialisation has also been successful, although there have reportedly been problems along the way, both financial and with the extent of the development work involved in making even the engineered version of MALPAS usable. Program Validation Ltd.'s established position in training may also have caused problems for MALPAS.

Case 9: Hardware Verification

The Technology

Hardware verification is another response to the general problem outlined in case 8, the perceived impossibility of exhaustive empirical testing of digital computer systems. The goal here is, again, mathematical proof: this time, proof that the design of a piece of computer hardware (for example a microprocessor) is indeed a correct implementation of its specification.

RSRE's Work

During the 1980s, a team within RSRE's Computing and Communications Group - the `High Integrity Computing' group - designed, and sought to verify the design of, a microprocessor called VIPER (Verifiable Integrated Processor for Enhanced Reliability). They drew on RSRE's experience with integrated circuits, and in particular on ELLA, an RSRE-developed language for the description of integrated circuits. They also drew on work at the University of Cambridge on LCF_LSM and HOL (Logic of Computable Functions_Logic of Sequential Machines; Higher Order Logic), both systems designed for the verification of computer hardware designs. Although a simple microprocessor by the standards of the chips found in personal computers, VIPER was an almost unprecedentedly ambitious attempt at the formal verification of a real system. The VIPER microprocessor was also subject to extensive conventional simulation and testing, and it has several features desirable in safety-critical situations. For example, two VIPER 1A chips can be run in parallel, each checking the output of the other, and stopping should a discrepancy be encountered. A VIPER 2 (faster, more sophisticated, and designed by deduction from specification, rather than proved by *post hoc* verification of design) is under development.

The Influence of Military Needs

The setting up of the High Integrity Computing group was influenced by both computer security concerns (case 7) and worries about computing in safety-critical military applications (those, in other words, where computer error threatens the lives of operators or by-standers): `Integrity' can indeed be seen as spanning both concerns. In practice, however, computer security remained primarily the province of others at RSRE, and to the extent that a specific concern shaped the VIPER work it was safety not security. Though safety is a pervasive issue in military software, it is in no sense exclusive or peculiar to it, and indeed the only actual application of VIPER to a safety-critical system has been civil.

Commercialisation

Though the basic VIPER design was by RSRE, both Ferranti Semiconductors and Marconi Electronic Devices Limited worked on implementations of it, under contract to RSRE and to some extent from their own resources (Marconi implementing VIPER in Alvey-supported radiation-hard silicon-on-sapphire). Both advertised it, but numbers sold have been modest. Following a competition run by

Marconi, a small Worcester-based firm, Charter Technologies Ltd., won the rights to sell and support the VIPER software toolset, a suite of software (linked to static analysers) for use in conjunction with VIPER. Charter also purchased from Defence Technology Enterprises the right to sell the VIPER prototyping system, essentially a cabinet with power supply, input-output facilities and a range of printed circuit boards. Supported by Charter, Teknis International Railroad Systems Pty. of Adelaide won a contract in 1988 which involves the use of VIPER to control signalling equipment for automatic crossings on the Trans-Australian and Central Australian rail routes. Aside from experimental and evaluation work, the only other adoption of VIPER has been for a classified secure communications project.

Initial expectations for the adoption of VIPER had been higher. Users seem to have been reluctant to abandon `tried and trusted' microprocessors, even though these did not claim formal verification of design (and even contain, in at least one case, a known design error). The range of suitable applications for VIPER was also limited by its relative slowness and (quite deliberately) restricted instruction set. In 1988-89, however, a further factor intruded: criticism, especially in a US report commissioned by NASA, of the claim that VIPER's design had been formally proven. From April 1990 onwards this criticism became the subject of considerable publicity. No design error has been discovered, and RSRE defends the chain of mathematical reasoning connecting VIPER's specification and its implementation as being stronger than that for any other commercially available microprocessor. However, in January 1991, Charter Technologies Ltd. began legal action against the Secretary of State for Defence seeking damages for alleged misrepresentation both in estimates of the market for VIPER and in its description as having a proven correct design. These allegations were contested vigorously by the Ministry, and Charter's legal action has been halted following the company's liquidation in June 1991.[40]

Case 10: Liquid Crystal Displays

The Technology

Liquid crystals have been known since 1888, and tens of thousands of different such materials have been synthesised since then. They combine the properties of a liquid with orientational order similar to that usually found in solid crystals. The optical and electrical properties associated with this molecular orientation give liquid crystals their potential for display technology. The typical liquid crystal display uses the `twisted nematic' effect, which utilises the polarising properties of the material. A thin layer of the liquid crystal is held between two glass plates whose inner surfaces are coated with a transparent conductor. In the absence of an electrical field the liquid crystal rotates the plane of polarised light. If the enclosing plates are crossed polarisers then light is transmitted. When an electric field is applied to the liquid crystal the polarising effect is removed and so light is not transmitted, giving the dark image which, for example, makes up the numerals on a digital watch display.[41]

RSRE's Work

RSRE's interest in liquid crystal displays stems from 1967, but, even before this, advances in semiconductor electronics had led to a perception that the standard cathode-ray tube (CRT) display constituted something of a bottleneck. However, while developments in electronics offered smaller size and lower power requirements which made the CRT look outdated, they also kept staff at RRE (as it was then) so busy as to rule out any speculative work on alternative display technologies. This changed in 1967, following a visit to RRE by the then Minister of State for Technology, John Stonehouse, in March. During his discussions with the Director, Dr. (now Sir) George MacFarlane, the issue of financial returns from inventions came up, and MacFarlane stated that the UK was paying royalties to the US firm RCA for CRT technology which amounted to more than the development costs of Concorde.[42] The next day the Minister telephoned MacFarlane to suggest that the UK should instigate a programme to develop a solid-state alternative to the CRT.

This was initially greeted with scepticism at RRE, but a working party was set up to investigate the possibilities. The first draft of the working party's report was ready in October 1969, and recommended work on eight main topics, not including liquid crystals. However, the final version, issued in December, was substantially altered by Cyril Hilsum, the head of RRE's Display Section, to emphasise liquid crystals, as he later recalled:

'... the original `final' version recommended a large programme on ferroelectric ceramics, and one small-scale exploratory contract on liquid crystals. I was uneasy as I read it, feeling that there was something wrong, and almost doodling, replaced the words `ferro-electric ceramics' everywhere by `liquid crystals'. In some curious way it now had the right feel, and I had the final version issued. Three years had passed since the Stonehouse visit, and at last we knew what we wanted to do'.[43]

Through the Ministry of Defence's Components, Valves and Devices (CVD) programme, RRE now arranged funding for a team at Hull University which was already looking at liquid crystals. This team continued its search for suitable materials that were stable and worked over the desired temperature range. Two years of eliminating unsuitable materials eventually led to the synthesis of cyano-biphenyls in August 1972. By mixing various of these compounds it was possible to get a reasonably wide range of operating temperatures, and the general performance and stability of the materials was good. Realising the commercial potential of this, RRE immediately started to mark consortium documents `Commercial-in-Confidence' and to use codewords to describe the materials.[44]

Demand for the materials now exceeded Hull's production capability and so an industrial supplier was chosen. Although lacking any previous experience with liquid crystals, BDH Chemicals was selected because of other successful work they had done for RRE.[45] In November 1973, about a year after accepting the liquid crystal work, BDH (by now actually owned by another liquid crystal producer, the German company E. Merck) announced the commercial availability of four liquid crystals. Of these, one known as E4, with an operating range of 4°C to 61°C, was thought to be the most useful for display devices.[46] Then, in August 1973, a mixture of biphenyls named E7 was created which had properties close to requirements which RRE had been given by watch manufacturers. These properties included an operating range of -9°C to 59°C.

The Influence of Military Needs

Apart from inspiring interest in low-power, compact displays and in keeping abreast of relevant technology in general, the Ministry of Defence's military requirements do not appear to have played a significant role in the detailed direction of the liquid crystal work. The search for mixtures of materials which provided wider operating temperatures was necessary for all potential applications, and was not stifled by the especially rigorous demands of Milspecs. Actual defence applications of liquid crystal display technology lagged behind their commercial uptake. For some years the technology still fell short of the stringent requirements for defence applications, though there may also have been an element of military conservatism involved. The first Ministry of Defence use was in a display for the Rapier air-defence system which became operational in the late 1970s. Although ruggedised, it was not `state of the art' due to the long procurement cycles involved, and it had been necessary to `freeze' component design at an earlier stage than would have occurred in the civil sector. As military use of liquid crystal displays expanded, the Ministry of Defence were, however, able to take to take advantage of the considerable development work that had been performed in the civil sector.

Commercialisation

Liquid crystal technology can be divided into two levels of commercial product: the liquid crystal materials themselves and devices which utilise them. Commercialisation of the materials developed under the aegis of CVD has been one of the Ministry of Defence's greatest, best publicised, success stories. Commercialisation of liquid crystal devices, on the other hand, has been undertaken outside the UK, mainly by Japanese companies.

Despite some initial resistance — due to device manufacturers having invested in processes specific to other materials, and rumours that biphenyls were carcinogenic — BDH had become the world's largest liquid crystal producer by 1977.[47] Biphenyls produced under licence to BDH, Merck and Hoffman La Roche earn the MOD royalties of about half a million pounds per year. In 1979 this success was marked by a Queen's Award for Technological Achievement which was conferred jointly on RSRE, BDH and Hull University. BDH currently accounts for about a third of world liquid crystals production.

In contrast to this success with the development and production of liquid crystal materials, UK exploitation of devices which utilised them failed to materialise. A typical instance of UK failure to exploit LCD devices is the `supertwist' display invented by Peter Raynes at RSRE in 1982 and now widely used in laptop computers. GEC were funded to develop prototypes of the technology, but despite this early advantage were unable to achieve the level of commercial success of LCD manufacturers in Japan.

Discussion

We do not claim to have presented a representative sample of cases of technological development at, or technology transfer from, the Royal Signals and Radar Establishment. Our self-imposed restriction to areas conventionally understood as falling within information technology is one obvious restriction: our cases would obviously have been different had we chosen, for example, to focus on radar development. We have, furthermore, had a quite conscious and deliberate bias towards what we (in the light of our more general background knowledge of information technology) felt to be significant technical developments. RSRE, like all research and development organisations, is home to research that does not bear fruit, and to research the fruits of which are only of limited and specific interest.

This bias in the selection of cases must be borne in mind when we conclude, as we do, that the overall impression we form of RSRE's work in information technology is of technical excellence. We have, after all, deliberately chosen to look at some of[48] the best of what RSRE has done in this field. We do not possess the data that would be needed to construct quantitative indicators of excellence - for example numbers of refereed publications, numbers of citations to RSRE publications, or numbers of patents granted[49] - but we would note that RSRE has won about 15 per cent of Queen's Awards in the area of electronics, and about 15 per cent of the Fellows of the Royal Society in the area of electronics come from RSRE.[50] Certainly, our chosen cases demonstrate the significance, scope and synergy of RSRE work. The last of these is perhaps worth a further remark. One of RSRE's great advantages in information technology has been the way that on a single compact site,[51] and with a staff small enough to allow much personal interaction, it spans the gamut of information technology from semiconductor materials to software and displays. That has allowed quite large collections of different skills economically to be brought to bear on complex projects. Though it has had its difficulties, the VIPER project - spanning integrated circuit design and fabrication, mathematical verification, and software development - is a good case in point.

This inventive excellence is not fully matched by a record of universal success in the commercial development of RSRE innovations by British industry. All the technologies we studied were taken up by industry, at least to some extent.[52] The outcomes ranged from dramatic commercial success in liquid crystal materials to much more modest success elsewhere. In itself, that is not surprising. Partial success in commercialisation is only to be expected: our overall experience of studying technical change suggests that most innovations do not enjoy dramatic commercial success, wherever they take place. `Pioneering don't pay', as Andrew Carnegie put it, and the exceptions to his rule, though striking, are greatly outnumbered by the cases that conform to it.[53]

However, RSRE staff themselves often felt that British industry was not taking full commercial advantage of RSRE's work in information technology. Furthermore, we could not help but be struck by two types of case within our data: (a) cases (such as systolic arrays, or the `supertwist' display) where British companies proved unable to capitalise on the technological lead that RSRE work had given them; and (b) cases where British companies which have developed technology successfully then pass into overseas ownership (such as Inmos or BDH) or move overseas (AMT).

So, alongside the many very real achievements in the commercialisation of technology developed at RSRE, there is also some evidence of the stereotyped British failing: inventive success followed by failure to reap its full commercial benefits. What might account for the latter? We can dismiss the explanation that either RSRE as an institution or its staff as individuals have not been interested in commercial exploitation. At least in the second part of the 1980s, attention to the latter has been great, and very considerable effort, strongly supported by the management of the Establishment, has gone into it. True, there are very strong constraints on the extent to which an RSRE staff member, as a civil servant, can profit financially from successful technology transfer, and greater generosity and flexibility in this regard might be worth experimenting with. But responsibility for successful commercial exploitation is highly regarded at RSRE, for example in the prominence given to the Establishment's success in the Queen's Award scheme, which requires such exploitation as well as technological excellence. While we have no systematic evidence on the point, we have no reason to doubt that promotion within the Establishment takes success in this respect into account. Furthermore, the plain satisfaction of seeing something one has helped develop put into practical use can be at least as important a motivator as either money or career.

The will to technology transfer has thus unquestionably been there. In no case have we found RSRE staff to have been anything other than enthusiasts for the commercial development of their inventive work. Indeed, the difficulties of the most troubled of the cases we examined, VIPER, can perhaps be attributed to overenthusiasm rather than inertia.

Another explanation that can be dismissed is that RSRE develops technologies that are only of military interest. There are cases amongst those we considered of specifically defence-sector needs shaping technological development at RSRE, but those cases are a minority. More often what was developed at RSRE was a technology with relevance to both the civil and military sectors, and the influence of defence needs was restricted to, for example, the development of specifically military variants of a generic technology (such as the military versions of the parallel computers discussed in cases 5 and 6).

Perhaps the difficulties lie in the mechanisms for technology transfer? It is, for example, sometimes asserted that defence research establishments can become isolated from industry and the wider technological community. Emphatically, this is not the case for RSRE. RSRE has enjoyed, and continues to enjoy, good links with academia and industry. Furthermore, specific mechanisms for technology transfer have been established: the late 1960s RSRE Commercial Department; Defence Technology Enterprises (DTE) in the late 1980s.

The latter mechanism had, however, an inherent handicap. The notion of technology transfer that underlay the setting up of DTE was that its `ferrets' would discover unexploited pieces of technology in defence research establishments. These would then be offered to outside firms, who could if they wished purchase a license from DTE to market these technologies, and proceed to exploit them commercially.

This is a naive view of technological change. A research establishment does not produce prototype technological `black boxes', which a firm then has simply to mass produce and offer to the market. Not only is further development always going to be necessary (which was acknowledged under the DTE scheme), but fundamental reshaping for success in different environments may often been needed. Market needs have often to be *created*, not just understood and met, and this requires committed product champions. Technologies are never isolated artefacts, but crystallisations, as it were, of technical knowledge. Some of this knowledge is written or verbal, and can thus readily be transferred; much of it is tacit, and can only be learnt through prolonged personal contact.

It is thus perhaps less a matter of technology transfer than of what we might call `technology translation'.[54] As with the translation of human languages, this is a delicate process, success typically requiring extensive contact with, even immersion in, both the culture from which a text is drawn and that into which is rendered. A large part of the success of Program Validation Ltd.'s SPADE, for example, was the firm's extensive involvement in the original development of static analysers, and commitment to, and experience of, education and training in their use. By contrast, in the case of VIPER there was a literal failure of translation, with different parties involved having different understandings of `proof'.[55]

If the preconditions for successful technology translation are there, the parties involved would almost certainly know of each other already, and (to switch metaphors) a `marriage broker' such as DTE is unnecessary. If the preconditions are not there, a broker is needed, but the chance of the marriage being successful are slim, at least without as much as five to ten years of `courtship' and mutual adjustment first. That seems, for example, to have been the experience of the British Technology Group, but the small number of years DTE was given to show success meant that this amount of time was not available to it.

Experienced RSRE staff knew that the model of technology transfer underlying the setting up of DTE was flawed. One such senior staff member told us that, therefore, `the only things I've put out to DTE are things I don't believe in'. That implies, of course, that there were other mechanisms for the translation of the technologies this staff member did believe in. Long-standing ties, often involving years of personal contact, joint work, and trust do exist between RSRE and many British firms. It is not surprising that it should be to these ties that RSRE staff have naturally turned when they have felt it really mattered.

That mechanisms for the translation of technology exist does not, of course, mean that they could not be improved on. The nature of RSRE's remit means that existing ties are primarily to defence sector firms. This, together with what we have found to be a variable (but not entirely negligible) degree of shaping of RSRE's research and development work by specifically defence needs, does imply that commercialisation for the defence market will often be easier than commercialisation for the civil market. Connections to the civil sector are, however, far from rare, and the more they are fostered the more likely successful translation to the civil market will become.

That is uncontroversial. The sharpest issues concerning translation mechanisms perhaps have to do with what is known from the literature on technological change to be the most effective means of technology transfer, the movement of people.[56] RSRE staff members do sometimes move to posts in large firms, and a significant number leave for university positions, particularly professorships. For them to leave to set up their own firm to exploit technology they have developed at RSRE is, however, virtually unknown. The latter move would involve sacrificing what has hitherto been the civil servant's security and (crucially) pension. Furthermore, while the Ministry of Defence has sometimes been generous in the transfer of intellectual property rights to outside bodies (see below), it would probably not have taken the same attitude to its own staff. The shadow of the Official Secrets Acts might even fall on former RSRE staff members seeking themselves to exploit commercially work done at RSRE.

That they should be permitted readily so to do is, of course, not self-evident. There clearly needs to be a balance between enhancing technology translation and preventing undue personal gain from publicly funded research. Those in outside industry might be aggrieved at unfair competition if, for example, RSRE staff were to set up their own firms while still employed there. On the other hand, university staff are permitted (with a variety of controls) to do this: sometimes continuing to work simultaneously for a firm and for their university; sometimes `testing the water' until they are reasonably sure a commercial venture will succeed. Again, this is an area where greater flexibility in arrangements might prove beneficial.

It is, however, important not naively to assume that a mechanism of technology translation, like the spin-off firm, that has been successful in other countries would be successful in Britain. Crucially, would such spin-offs be able to attract venture capital funding? What rate of interest would they have to pay on any borrowings? Would those involved have to mortgage their homes to raise capital?

Questions like these point to a difficulty deeper than improving translation mechanisms. It is simply that the wider culture and economy of late twentieth century Britain has not been in general supportive, in practice, of indigenous commercial exploitation of technological innovation. The litany of complaint is familiar enough: a society where the accountant is in practice more highly valued than the engineer, and which is said to employ 120,000 of the former, compared to 7,000 in Germany;[57] where interest rates have persistently been `twice those in Germany, three times those in Japan';[58] where companies have to pay great attention to the threat of takeover; where short-term profits are preferred to long-term returns on investment; where technical education and, especially, in-post training have not received sufficient priority.

RSRE staff themselves repeatedly diagnosed reluctance by the British information technology industry to commit itself to major investment as the ultimate cause of the commercialisation of RSRE work being less successful than it might have been. Some also detected a continuing attitude of dependency amongst defence electronics firms on Ministry of Defence development contracts. With respect to silicon-on-sapphire integrated circuits, for example, one RSRE staff member told us `we thumped the table more times than I remember' trying to persuade industry to take on further development, persistently receiving the reply `how much will you give us to do it'.

There tend, of course, always to be two sides to such stories - silicon-on-sapphire, for example, is regarded by some in the semiconductor business as a blind alley[59] - and without extensive interviewing in the information technology industry it is difficult to be sure of the reasons for particular cases of reluctance to invest. It is nevertheless striking that in the most dramatic commercial success amongst the cases we examined - liquid crystals - exploitation was in the hands of a company from a sector of British industry (chemicals and pharmaceuticals) that has avoided the malaise of much of the British information technology industry.

To summarise, then, there is at least some evidence for the diagnosis that the most important causes of failure of technology translation lie not in the genesis of the technology, nor primarily in the translation mechanisms, but in the economy and culture into which translation is attempted. That is a pessimistic conclusion, since these last are matters which are difficult to change, but it does seem to be a conclusion that is hard to avoid.

Finally, some comment on the changing situation of RSRE itself is needed. Over the years (in particular between 1975 and 1985), the different component establishments and then RSRE itself suffered a rapid decline in staff numbers, from a peak of around 4,500 to the current level of around 1,600. The prime reason for this is common to all the British defence research establishments with the partial exception of Aldermaston: the gradual transfer, to industrial prime contractors and to other parts of the Ministry of Defence, of responsibility first for oversight of production and then for system development, leaving the establishments with a consultancy role in procurement and responsibility for medium-term and long-term applied research.

Just as RSRE's role and numbers stabilised in the mid-1980s, another change began to have effect: the emergence of a more commercial ethos in British government, including (associated in particular with the names of Michael Heseltine and Peter Levene) defence. RSRE staff are highly conscious of this change, often contrasting the situation of the early 1980s and before with that now. In the earlier situation technology transfer from RSRE often lacked the commercial formalities of the present. Copies of RSRE's Algol 68 compiler were, for example, distributed for a nominal charge to British universities, and RSRE's arrangements for transfer of intellectual property rights to firms also sometimes seemed more like gifts than like sales: see, for example, RSRE's generous arrangement with Program Validation Ltd. It is worth pausing before we condemn this attitude, from the allegedly more hard-headed perspective of recent years, as lax. It is difficult to see how the British tax payer would have gained from one public institution paying to another a large sum for a compiler, and many cases of influential software developments (eg UNIX, LATEX) have begun with the effectively free distribution of source code. The Ministry of Defence may perhaps have had little financial return from its relations with the University of Southampton and Program Validation Limited, but 350 people, many working on defence projects, have to date passed through the courses organised by the university and firm on static analysis, program proof and formal methods. While this benefit is impossible to quantify, it has been considerable: certainly, from the Ministry of Defence's point of view, worth the cost of the original research agreements.[60] More generally, we have found the process of technology translation to be delicate enough even where firms' payments to the Ministry of Defence have been relatively token. Seeking greatly to increase such payments would make success even rarer, at least where small and financially vulnerable firms are concerned.

In the years to come, however, RSRE will have to move even further to a commercial ethos than it already has. As part of the Defence Research Agency, one of the many quasi-privatisations of the Thatcher Revolution in Whitehall, RSRE's links to the armed forces and Ministry of Defence will start to take on the form of customer-contractor relationships. In theory, the Ministry and armed forces will be able to buy as much (or as little) of RSRE's work as they wish, and there will be considerable pressure for RSRE to expand the current fifth of its intramural work which is performed for third parties such as the Department of Trade and Industry, Civil Aviation Authority and the European Esprit programme.

The establishment of the Defence Research Agency coincides with the introduction of 'package management' within the Ministry of Defence. Instead of defence research establishments receiving an annual budget, managers of defence programmes will be given funds to pay for research and development relevant to these programmes. RSRE staff worry that this change will lead to the prioritisation of research with a short term military pay-off. Paradoxically, the resultant closer shaping of RSRE's work by perceived military need could, in the long run, act to the detriment of the defence sector. As we have already noted, the majority of the cases examined above involved RSRE development of a generic technology that was a significant advance on the current state-of-the-art. Civil users benefited, but so did military ones. In some cases, such as liquid crystal displays, military users were able to take advantage of further development work conducted, at no expense to the defence budget, by civil sector firms.

More generally, the RSRE staff we spoke to nearly all viewed with some trepidation their transformation into a division of the Defence Research Agency. Their views ranged from plain dislike and regret to a sense that the new arrangements might (if they evolved in a satisfactory way) provide considerable opportunity for an enhanced role for the Establishment, particularly in civil technology.

We are not privy to the disputes that are reported to have raged in Whitehall over the detailed charter of the Defence Research Agency. What did, however, emerge clearly from our interviews was a sense that the Defence Research Agency arrangement could easily be, for RSRE, a most unsatisfactory half-way house, in which staff members carry the risks of self-management (an uncertain budget) without corresponding autonomy. Trivial (and presumably soon to be corrected) though the example is, we were struck by the remarkable complaint of one quite senior RSRE staff member that he needs to make a written case to his superintendent whenever he wishes to use first-class rather than second-class post. Even though he had the responsibility of seeking substantial external contracts, he was not granted even this petty autonomy.

In the Autumn of 1990, at least, even senior RSRE staff did not seem to know whether, under the Defence Research Agency, the Establishment would be able to make employees redundant should it make a loss; whether it would be able to raise funds on the capital market; whether their civil service pensions would in the long run be secure. This uncertainty was clearly not good for morale.

As experience is gained with the new arrangements, the uncertainty will vanish. Beyond administrative issues, however, we had a sense that a valued role had been lost, without a clear replacement being found. That role was captured in the phrase used by several interviewees: `UK Ltd.', a partnership between government and British industry, with the national well-being (including, but not exclusively, military security) as its goal. As one distinguished RSRE researcher put it: `We've always regarded ourselves as playing for UK Ltd. Now they've messed us around we don't know who we're playing for.'

UK Ltd. was not a successful firm, at least outside of its remarkable record, little remarked upon in the literature on British decline, in high-technology military endeavour.[61] Even in the latter, it has inevitably become something of a junior partner to the vastly wealthier conglomerate across the Atlantic. That dependence has long been clear in strategic nuclear weaponry, and in the areas considered here there are examples of British developments (VHPIC, the computer security evaluation criteria) which are clearly reactions to prior American initiatives (see Chapter 3). In infrared technology, where there was a British research lead, it took adoption by the Americans to prompt serious UK development work.

For all its shortcomings and potential ugly side,[62] the idea of `UK Ltd.' did provide a framework within which RSRE staff were able to make sense of their efforts. It implied that public good and moderate private gain were not in conflict, thus promoting relaxed and open relations between RSRE and industry. It may even (to be grandiose about it) have helped RSRE staff to find a reason - other than security and the pension - for foregoing the much higher salaries many could command in industry, especially in the United States. It helped create a sense of shared interest between RSRE and those outside it, especially in universities, who were not enthusiasts for the development of British military might. Collaboration with, and support from, RSRE has almost always been acceptable even in university departments where any other form of involvement with the defence effort would have been rejected.

The much touted alternative to UK Ltd.'s corporatism, and to the curious dialectic of deference and rivalry between the British and American defence efforts, is of course Europe Ltd. (Europa GmbH, some might comment). In some respects at least, corporatism is not dead, but has merely moved address from Whitehall to Brussels. RSRE is already heavily involved in European Community programmes, and, as we saw in case 6, there is a sense in which it has resources to bring to these which are unique not just in Britain but in Europe.

And yet, for all the pragmatic advantages of European involvement, `Europe' is still for most people in Britain not an emotionally meaningful term. Perhaps, though, out of all the doubt and confusion surrounding the move to the Defence Research Agency a renewed sense of mission for establishments such as RSRE will emerge. That may be so, but for ourselves we must say we cannot yet perceive even its outline.

Endnotes

1 In addition to funding from the Science Policy Support Group, the research on information technology drawn on here was supported by the Economic and Social Research Council under the Programme in Information and Communication Technologies (PICT). We are grateful to Stephen J. Robinson, OBE, FRS, Director of the Royal Signals and Radar Establishment, for his cooperation with this research, and for the help of many of his staff. We have not for practical reasons been able systematically to investigate technology transfer from the point of view of the 'receiving' firms, but have had useful discussions with members of several companies. The views expressed in this article are, of course, our own, not those of RSRE, nor (except where quoted explicitly) individuals on its staff. Nor are they those of the bodies who have supported this research financially.

2 For a discussion of work on the impact of the military on the development of science and technology, see MacKenzie, D., **Science and Technology Studies and the Question of the Military**, *Social Studies of Science*, Vol. 16, 1986, pp. 361-71. None of this academic work has systematically considered the role of the large defence research establishments, though there have been a number of studies, usually by current or retired staff of these establishments, of their work in particular technical areas.

3 This appears to be because data on the question has not been collected systematically, rather than because it exists but has not been released.

4 We are, however, also researching developments at other establishments. See MacKenzie, D., **The Influence of the Los Alamos and Livermore National Laboratories on the Development of Supercomputing**, *Annals of the History of Computing*, Vol. 13, 1991, pp. 179-201.

5 In 1953, the Royal Radar Establishment (RRE) was formed from the Radar Research and Development Establishment (working mainly for the Army) and Telecommunications Research Establishment (supporting the Royal Air Force). In 1976, the RRE merged with the Signals Research and Development Establishment (Army) and the Services Electronic Research Laboratory to form RSRE. For the history of RSRE and its predecessor organizations see: Tomlin, D.H., **The RSRE: A Brief History, from Earliest Times to the Present Day**, *IEE Review*, Vol. 34, 1988, pp. 403-407; and Putley, E.H., **The History of RSRE**, *Physics in Technology*, Vol. 16, 1985, pp. 5-12.

6 BBC, **Horizon**, 1984.

7 Putley, E.H., **Infrared Spin-off**, Vol. 17, 1986, 32-7 at 32-3.

8 Reprinted in Smith, D.A., **Thermal Imaging: A Transfer of Technology**, RSRE, Malvern, 1990, p. 5.

9 Putley, E.H., **History of the RSRE**, *RSRE 1985 Research Review*, RSRE, Malvern, 1985, pp. 165-174, at 170.

10 Smith, ***op. cit.***, p. 5.

11 We are very grateful for the declassified excerpts from this report which were supplied to us by the author, David Smith. This quotation is from Vol. I, 20.

12 Vol. I, 15.

13 Vol. I, 20.

14 Vol. I, 26.

15 Watton, R., **Thermal Imaging with the Pyroelectric Vidicon**, 1.

16 Brodsky, M.H., **Progress in Gallium Arsenide Semiconductors,** *Scientific American*, February 1990, pp. 56-63 at 56.

17 *Ibid*, 57-8.

18 *Ibid*, 61.

19 **Services Electronics Research Laboratory 1945-1976**, RSRE, Malvern, 1986, p. 10.

20 Hilsum was succeeded by Dr Brian Mullin of RRE in 1969, who in turn handed over to Dr Don Hurle in 1975.

21 Hurle, D.T.J., **National Collaborative Research into Gallium Arsenide**, *Electronic Engineering*, June 1985, pp. 149-53.

22 *Ibid.*, p. 150.

23 *Ibid.*, p. 150, p. 152.

24 *Ibid.*, p. 151.

25 Roberts, D.H., **Silicon Integrated Circuits: A Personal View of the first 25 Years**, *Electronics and Power*, Vol. 30 1984, pp. 282-84; Morris, P.R., **A History of the World Semiconductor Industry**, Peter Perigrinus, London, 1990.

26 See Oakley, B. and Owen, K., **Alvey: Britain's Strategic Computing Initiative**, MIT Press, Cambridge, Mass., 1990. Oakley had headed the RSRE Commercial Department, set up during the reign of the Ministry of Technology. Oakley's disagreement with what he calls (*ibid.*, p. 79) the `RSRE gang' seems primarily to have concerned the latter's alleged indifference to the potential contribution of university academics to VLSI research, although he also seems to have had a general worry about over-strong defence influence on the Alvey VLSI work. At one point Oakley instructed VLSI Director Fawcett to reduce RSRE/Ministry of Defence involvement in Alvey (*ibid.*, p. 135).

27 Hobday, M., **Strategies for the U.K. Semiconductor Industry: Lessons from the Alvey Program**, *Technovation*, Vol. 10, 1990. pp. 193-210.

28 Hoselitz, K., **VLSI: A Personal Appraisal. A Report to the Alvey Directorate**, Science Policy Research Unit, August 1985.

29 Hobday, **Strategies**, p. 203.

30 Kung, H.T. and Leiserson, C.E., **Systolic Arrays (for VLSI)**, *Sparse Matrix Proc. 1978*, Academic Press, Orlando, Florida, 1979.

31 See McCanny, J.V. and McWhirter, J.G., **Some Systolic Array Developments in the United Kingdom**, *Computer*, July 1987, pp. 51-63.

32 This section draws heavily on a report commissioned by Edinburgh PICT: Trew, A. and Wilson, G., eds., **Past, Present, Parallel: A Survey of Available Parallel Computing Systems**, Springer, London, 1991.

33 Flynn, M.J., **Some Computer Organizations and their Effectiveness**, *IEEE Trans. Comput.*, Vol. C-21 1972, pp. 948-60.

34 This section again draw heavily on Edinburgh PICT work, this time that of Alfonso Molina. The fullest version of this is Molina, **The Transputer Constituency: Building up UK/European Capabilities in Information Technology**, University of Edinburgh: Edinburgh PICT Research Report No. 1, 1989. Sales data are drawn from Trew and Wilson, **Past, Present, Parallel**.

35 Pfleeger, C.P., **Security in Computing**, Prentice Hall, Englewood Cliffs, NJ, 1989, p. 290; Munro, N., **NSA Plan may Stymie Improved Computer Security**, *Defense News*, 10 September 1990, 3 and 36.

36 Chalmers, L.S., **An Analysis of the Differences between the Computer Security Practices in the Military and Private Sectors**, IEEE Symposium on Security and Privacy, Oakland, Calif., 7-9 April 1986, pp. 71-76; Clark, D.D. and Wilson, D.R., **A Comparison of Commercial and Military Computer Security Policies**, IEEE Symposium on Security and Privacy, Oakland, Calif., 27-29 April 1987, pp. 184-94.

37 It seems likely that in their perceived security needs civil departments of government such as the Department of Social Security or Inland Revenue will be closer to financial institutions than they are to defence. It is conceivable that fear of industrial espionage might drive industrial firms to a more military attitude to computer security, but we know of no evidence of this.

38 System Security Study Committee, **Computers at Risk: Safe Computing in the Information Age**, National Academy Press, Washington D.C., 1990. For example, according to Munro, **NSA Plan**, purchase of 500 Blacker systems is being contemplated, although Blacker is being opposed by the NSA, which prefers an alternative system, still under development, known as Caneware.

39 For the history of this, see Peláez Valdez, M.E., **A Gift from Pandora's Box: The Software Crisis**, PhD thesis, University of Edinburgh, 1988.

40 Further details of the dispute of the VIPER proof can be found in MacKenzie, D., **The Fangs of the VIPER**, *Nature*, Vol. 352, 8 August 1991, pp. 467-68.

41 This description is drawn from Raynes, E.P., **Cyanobiphenyl Liquid Crystals—An MOD Success Story**, *J.N.S.*, Vol. 7, No. 1, pp. 40-46.

42 Hilsum, C., **The Anatomy of a Discovery—Biphenyl Liquid Crystals**, (typescript, hand-written date, 6/3/84), p. 2.

43 *Ibid.*, 5.

44 *Ibid.*, 11.

45 *Ibid.*

46 *Ibid.*, 13.

47 *Ibid.*, 15.

48 There are other important cases we could have chosen to focus on, for example RSRE's development of ELLA. We were prevented from doing so by considerations of time, of the length of this report, and of our limited understanding of some areas.

49 It would be instructive to construct time series of indicators such as patents, publications and citations, and to compare them (bearing in mind differences in focus and in number of qualified scientists and engineers employed) with those for both university science and engineering departments and industrial research and development laboratories. Any such indicators of course need to be treated with caution. Quite different attitudes are taken to patenting in different areas of technology. There are, for example, notorious difficulties in the patenting of software, and yet programming languages and software methodology have been amongst RSRE's most important activities.

50 Robinson, S.J., interview by authors.

51 Strictly speaking, RSRE still occupies two sites separated by several miles, but all the activities we have examined are located on the South site, and preparations are in hand to abandon the underused North site.

52 Again, this finding is the result of our selection of `significant' technical developments, and would be unlikely to be replicated in a random sample of technical developments at RSRE, or indeed at any other research and development organisation.

53 Quoted by George Wise, **West Orange Works** [review of Millard, Edison and the Business of Invention], *Science*, Vol. 251, 25 January 1991, pp. 457-458, at 457.

54 For the usage of `translation' in the social studies of science and technology, see Latour, B., **Science in Action: How to follow Scientists and Engineers through Society**, Open University Press, Milton Keynes, 1987.

55 See Kershaw, J., **The Meaning of Proof**, *SafetyNet*, Vol. 4, 1989, p. 4.

56 See, for example, Barnes, B. and Edge, D., **Science in Context: Readings in the Sociology of Science**, Open University Press, Milton Keynes, 1982, part three.

57 Peter Lilley, as interviewed by Ian Hargreaves in the **Financial Times**, 11 March 1991, p. 30.

58 Oakley, B., **Look Back in Alvey: Why Support for R&D is not Enough**, Edinburgh University: Programme on Information and Communication Technologies, Working Paper 18, 1990, section 6.1.

59 Hoselitz, **VLSI**.

60 This body of expertise also helped make the UK competitive in bidding for software work for the European Fighter Aircraft.

61 Edgerton, D., **Liberal Militarism and the British State**, *New Left Review*, No. 185 January/February 1991, pp. 138-69.

62 One long-term collaborator with RSRE recalls being upbraided for lack of patriotism by an RSRE staff member (not one of the immediate VIPER team, it should be added) for raising doubts about the extent to which VIPER's design could be described as `proven', even though he did not do so in any public context.

Chapter 6

British Helicopter Developments 1945-1960: Government Technology Policy in a Changing Defence Environment

Matthew Uttley

Introduction

This chapter is a case study of aviation technology and government decision making, and assesses the issues raised by British Government attempts to foster an indigenous helicopter manufacturing capacity between 1945 and 1960. The text is divided into two sections: the first analyses British experience in helicopter research, development and production; and the second tentatively considers the lessons of British helicopter developments for Government policy towards new and changing defence environments.

By 1944, with the end to hostilities in sight, the British Government had formulated its policy towards post-war helicopter research, development and production. In the transition to peacetime the Government's objective was "to stimulate the interest of aircraft firms on Helicopters" as it was perceived that there would be "potential fields, civil and military, for this type of aircraft"[1]. Implementating the policy was to be through research and development (R&D) contracts with the aircraft industry on the assumption that Government support was essential to foster and maintain the capability to meet future domestic and export civil and military helicopter requirements.

Direct Government intervention in stimulating indigenous helicopter developments was subsumed under a broader strategy for converting the aircraft industry to a peacetime role. First, with the anticipated post-war decline in orders for military aircraft, Government-sponsored R&D across a range of aviation technologies was seen as a mechanism for keeping the industry in being at a time of declining output. Second, the pace of wartime aircraft production had precluded extensive research and development, and Government support was considered essential if British firms were to compete in future state-of-the-art aircraft manufacture. Third, virtually all Allied transport aircraft production had been centred in the United States. Consequently, "compared to American firms, the industry was not prepared for commercial production" and "...a vigorous commercial producer - a goal desired by both government and industry - demanded extensive government support"[2].

A Case Study of British Helicopter Research, Development and Production, 1945-1960

An overview of the research, development and production activities of the British helicopter industry between 1945 and 1960 indicates *prima facie* success in Government attempts to foster an indigenous capacity. The industry as a whole was responsible for the manufacture of a series of commercially successful helicopters for the domestic and export civil and military markets (Table 6.1). Significantly, however, R&D during the same period is characterised by a catalogue of cancelled and unfinished projects (Table 6.2).

Table 6.1: British Helicopter Production, 1945-1960

Manufacturer/ Helicopter	*First Service*	*Role*	*Total Built or Ordered*		
			Home Use Military	*Home Use Civil*	*Export*
Westland Dragonfly[1]	April 1950	Rescue	88	8	41
Bristol Sycamore	Feb 1953	Rescue	109	2	66
Westland Whirlwind[2]	June 1954	Rescue/ ASW	308	20	90
Saunders-Roe Skeeter	Jan 1957	Army Light	66	2	10
Westland Widgeon	Sept 1957	Civil	-	6	6
Westland Wessex[3]	April 1960	ASW/ Assault	c.200		
Total			1022		
Total Westland			767		

Notes:
(1) Westland licence variant of the Sikorsky S-51 helicopter.
(2) Westland licence variant of the Sikorsky S-55 helicopter.
(3) Westland licence variant of the Sikorsky S-58 helicopter. 1960 order figures for the Wessex are based on 1960 estimates.

Source: Figures taken from **Report of the Committee of Inquiry into the Aircraft Industry, 1964-65**, HMSO, *Cmnd 2853*, pages 121-122; and R Hafner, **British Rotorcraft**, *Journal of the Royal Aeronautical Society*, 70, Part I, 1966, page 241.

Table 6.2: Ministry of Supply Sponsored Helicopter R&D Projects, 1945-1960

Project	*Company*	*Project Initiation*	*Approx Date of Cancellation*
Sycamore (B171)	Bristol	1946	n/a; entered UK service in February 1953
W9	Cierva	1944	1946
Air Horse	Cierva	1946	1951
B173	Bristol	1946	n/a(1)
Gyrodyne	Fairey	1946	1949
Rotodyne	Fairey	1947	1962
Ultra-Light	Fairey	1954	1956
Small Ramjet	Bevan	1948	1953
Gas Turbine	Percival	1952	1956
Crop Sprayer	Cierva	1948	1952
Skeeter	Saunders-Roe	1948	n/a; entered UK military service in January 1957

Notes: (1) The tandem rotor B173 was the precursor to the Bristol B191, B192 and Belvedere helicopters: the latter entered service with the Royal Air Force in July 1960.

Source: AVIA 65/6, **Statement of Expenditure on Rotary Wing Aircraft**., 10 May 1954.

This pattern of helicopter developments can be explained by two factors. On the one hand, seventy-four per cent of production is attributable to one firm - Westland Aircraft Limited. In contrast to its British competitors, with Ministry of Supply (MoS) approval Westland concentrated on the licence production of helicopter technology developed in the United States by Sikorsky, but received no Ministry R&D contracts. On the other hand, whilst Westland dominated the market, Bristol, Fairey and other companies in receipt of MoS R&D funding failed to enter significant helicopter production. Despite the relative failure of MoS R&D during this period, as subsequent sections illustrate, the success of Westland did enable the UK to maintain an indigenous development and production capability after 1960.

Westland dominated production for two reasons. First, by circumventing in-house R&D and relying on US Sikorsky design expertise, Westland was able to compete against customer-specific indigenous helicopter R&D projects. Indeed, ninety-eight per cent of Westland's production was based on orders for three licence helicopter types: the Dragonfly (Sikorsky S-51), Whirlwind (Sikorsky S-55) and Wessex (Sikorsky S-58). In each case, Westland was able to outcompete comparable British projects within the MoS helicopter programme. Second, despite Ministry of Supply funding, other UK firms were unsuccessful in commercially developing a series of prototypes to fulfil civil and military requirements against which Westland did not compete. Consequently, therefore, British research, development and production projects indicate a serious inability of MoS policy to develop commercially-viable indigenous helicopter technology with the consequent reliance on overseas (American) design.

What then, were the specific reasons why Westland was able to win the majority of U.K. service and civil production contracts, despite MoS funding and support for a range of R&D projects? And correspondingly, what factors explain the failure of MoS policy initiatives to produce competitive alternatives?

Westland Licence Production and Market Dominance

The primary factor dictating the pattern of post-war helicopter production was that by producing Sikorsky helicopters under licence, Westland gained a clear advantage in the UK helicopter market. This advantage had its origins early in the Second World War when the US aircraft industry built up a significant lead in helicopter production technology.

Before the outbreak of wartime hostilities the helicopter was in its infancy as a practical vehicle for civil and military duties. Nevertheless, British firms were at the forefront of rotorcraft development, principally with work at the Cierva Autogiro Company, G&J Weir's and the ARIII Construction (Hafner Gyroplane) organisation[3]. After 1937, promising experimental work in Germany by the Focke and Flettner companies had stimulated limited Air Ministry financial support for British firms[4] as:

"...it had become clear that, like every important project in aviation, it [helicopter development] could not be run as a commercial undertaking and that Air Ministry control was essential if this country were to retain its position in relation to other countries."[5]

In 1939, Air Ministry policy towards helicopters remained unchanged. After the fall of France in 1940, however, two factors led to the abandoning of all British development work, and by tacit agreement between the US and British Governments, helicopter R&D was left to the Americans. First, Government policy was to concentrate qualified manpower on the more urgent wartime need for large scale fighter and bomber production[6]. In the interim at least, the priority assigned to other projects meant that helicopter work could only be resumed when funds permitted. Second, in an attempt to rationalise Allied aircraft production, intergovernmental agreement was reached to concentrate transport aircraft types - a category into which helicopters were defined - within American industry[7]. At this stage, the Ministry's assumptions were that:

"If a helicopter is likely to be required for any special duty, it might be possible to interest an American firm and get them to develop it for us."[8]

and:

"...we should be able to take up the [development] threads again without difficulty and doubtless we should learn a lot from the practical difficulties encountered by [the Americans]".[9]

The direct effect, however, was to allow the U.S. firms to build a lead in helicopter production by 1945. With either direct U.S. Government backing or tacit support, seventeen firms had been engaged in helicopter R&D[10]. A major breakthrough came with the Sikorsky R-4 helicopter which was procured by the British government for naval duties[11]. Despite MAP recognition after 1943 that Sikorsky's success may place British firms "in an inferior position to the Americans commercially" when British developments resumed, this was accepted as "the price we pay for placing the war first and post war commerce second"[12].

After 1944 as the MAP began reestablishing an indigenous helicopter industry, attention was focused on the "possible needs of (future) civil users"[13]. Policy was implemented by the placing of Experimental Contracts with the reformed Cierva company (1944), and the newly-established Helicopter Division of Bristol Aircraft (1946)[14]. By 1946, however, the comprehensive design, development and production lead established by the Americans was clearly of concern to MoS, highlighted by the observation that:

"...we [in Britain] are far behind the Americans in this branch of Aeronautical Engineering, as is borne out by the fact that only two British prototypes at present under construction are likely to have any production future, whereas the Americans have about 16 types flying and at least 2 in limited production."[15]

An illustration of the relatively advanced position of U.S. firms was that by 1946 Sikorsky, building from experimental work and unininterupted technical development began S-51 manufacture, which had established the viability of the helicopter for civil and military transport operations[16].

Then in 1946, when Bristol and Cierva were embarking on basic helicopter research, Westland obtained the S-51 licence from Sikorsky[17]. Within two years, Westland had completed initial modification and `anglicisation' of the original S-51 design, and forwarded a pre-production batch to the Admiralty for evaluation[18]. Impressed by the performance of the helicopter, the Royal Navy immediately placed an initial order for 24 aircraft. Air Ministry contracts soon followed[19].

Admiralty preference for the Westland S-51 (renamed the Dragonfly) over the `all-British' alternative, the Bristol B171 was pragmatic. On the one hand, Dragonfly evaluations in 1948 demonstrated superior performance over the Sikorsky R-4 helicopters purchased during the war and then in RN service[20]. On the other hand, this performance was in contrast to the Bristol project which was at the prototype testing stage and the "future of which was then very uncertain"[21].

The S-51 licence had provided Westland with a technological lead over firms in receipt of MoS helicopter R&D funding. In addition, however, it enabled Westland to circumvent constraints affecting MoS initiatives in the late 1940s, identified in 1950 as the `priority problem'. Confronting MoS-sponsored helicopter programmes was that:

"On the one hand neither MoS nor the British industry has had sufficient support from the Services (and civil) Corporations...to make the helicopter sufficiently attractive to give it priority; on the other hand, the Services, dissappointed at the slow rate of development progress have been unwilling to give us such support"[22].

As a result:

"The Users have little confidence in our ability to meet their requirements in a reasonable time... (and) look elsewhere for alternative equipment that exists, and can be produced quickly. This has already happened in the case of the Dragonfly...".[23]

The priority problem had two sources. First, the Air Ministry was ambivalent about the operational usefulness of the helicopter *per se*; and second, the armed service were unwilling to commit themselves to firm helicopter requirements on which production projections could be based[24].

Consequently, the Bristol and Cierva projects were denied large-scale funding to "force the pace of developments" that Service interest and specifications would have generated. In contrast, Westland as a licence producer was the recipient of helicopter production experience from the considerable financial investment Sikorsky had received from the American armed services[25].

Looking to maintain its technological lead, Westland obtained a second licence in 1950 for the Sikorsky S-55: an eight-seat helicopter which had recently entered production in the United States[26]. In contrast, British developments were falling further behind as immediate military requirements were met by the

Dragonfly, and lacking service orders, other British programmes were either on the drawing-board or in receipt of limited MoS funds for prototype testing[27].

By 1952, Westland had received Admiralty orders for anglicised versions of the S-55 (renamed Whirlwind in its Westland form). Its selection was based on two factors: first, the urgency of requirements for larger lift helicopters in the Malayan campaign[28]; and second, the absence of an `all-British' alternative helicopter.

Westland did not simply benefit from the US design and production experience of Sikorsky. Westland's competitive position was also enhanced by changes in the Ministry of Supply's strategy towards helicopter research and development. After 1949, the MoS had the option of concentrating resources on piston-engined helicopter designs which could compete with the Whirlwind. Instead of focusing effort on the most promising piston-engine design - the Bristol B173 - the Ministry elected:

> "In an effort to get ahead of the Americans...[to] broaden our programme to include two projects for turbine engined helicopters...".[29]

Though the objective was to meet "the long term future demand for a very large and fast helicopter"[30] which would compete with American developments, it carried the penalty of retarding the move to production of UK piston-engined helicopters in the interim.

Commercial success with the Whirlwind prompted the Westland Board to seek a further manufacturing agreement with Sikorsky in 1955 for the larger S-58. A year later Westland commenced design modifications of the S-58, including replacing the engine with the Napier Gazelle turbine[31]. Despite MoS assurances to Westland that there was no service interest in purchasing the helicopter for military duties[32], the S-58 Wessex was to further the company's domination of British helicopter production.

When Westland began work on the Sikorsky design, the company received assurances that existing Admiralty ASW requirements were to be fulfilled by the tandem rotor Bristol B191 which was at the prototype phase of development[33]. After 1956, however, service evaluation of the Wessex, and technical failure on the B191 led the Admiralty to cancel orders with Bristol and procure the Wessex.

Westland's production success with the Wessex is again attributable to its relationship with Sikorsky. On the one hand, Westland again benefited from Sikorsky's incremental improvements to the tried and tested S-55 design. On the other hand, the development of the B191 had been retarded by the MoS supporting too many helicopter projects after 1950, and time slippages caused by under-investment in R&D[34].

in 1945 was composed of 22 major aircraft design groups and nine major aero-engine groups, and had produced over 26,000 aircraft in 1943 and 1944, including an average of 5,000 heavy bombers in each of these years[49]. Clearly, the anticipated decline in post-war output seemed to require industrial rationalisation and the concentration of design expertise in smaller industrial groupings.

On the other hand, the pace of wartime production had excluded extensive aircraft research and development, and work was necessary on neglected lines if Britain was to retain its position in future civil and military aircraft production. At this stage, however, the potential future civil and military markets for these experimental technologies was far from clear to government.

As Wood points out:-

"It was clear that the Labour government which came to power in 1945 should have tackled the problem of [the] multiplicity of companies, many of them lacking the financial resources to carry on a realistic separate existence."[50]

Instead of industrial restructuring, however, government policy was to spread research and development contracts throughout the industry and keep a fragmented group of firms in being. Rationales assigned to this extensive and often duplicating development work were the concepts of `prototyping' and `reinsurance': developing prototype aircraft of various configurations and propulsion methods for similar operational requirements allowing a choice of aircraft to enter production, thus providing insurance against the failure of a specific programme[51]. The ability to conduct this prototype approach was dependent on the low cost and "relative simplicity of contemporary aircraft which were engine/airframe combinations, with little avionic equipment"[52].

Ministry of Supply attempts to create an indigenous helicopter industry appear to confirm Wood's observation that effective post-war conversion required the questions of industrial structure and the concentration of design efforts to be addressed[53]. In addition to the specific problems resulting from the Ministry's policy of developing a large number of helicopter types on an extremely limited R&D budget, the fragmented nature of the industry clearly precluded the focus of design expertise and funding on helicopter types for which production was likely[54].

MoS Policy and the Domestic Military Helicopter Market

Ministry of Supply attempts to foster an `all-British' helicopter development and production capacity provides insight into government policy and `technology markets'. Clearly, Westland, as a licence producer of Sikorsky technology was able to exploit emerging domestic British and export helicopter markets. Conversely, MoS-sponsored helicopter efforts were largely unable either to compete with Westland, or to exploit potential markets for which Westland was not a direct competitor.

Part of the problem for indigenous efforts was the specific nature of the domestic British military helicopter market throughout the 1940s and 1950s. As the case study demonstrates, a number of projects were conducted with trickle MoS R&D funding because of the unwillingness of the Air Ministry to place production contracts and "[force] the pace of developments"[55]. The result was that when urgent military helicopter requirements did arise, the only available option in the necessary timescale was from Westland. To illustrate this point, during the Malayan campaign in 1952 there was "complete agreement at all levels on the immense value of the helicopter for a variety of tasks" and "the supply of helicopters as a matter of the greatest urgency [was] well appreciated at the highest levels"[56]. This urgency of requirement contrasted with the `priority problem' affecting indigenous developments, and highlighted the fact that the military market for helicopters was based on production availability.

The Whirlwind case highlights the mismatch between MoS helicopter industrial policy on the one hand, and the actual market for helicopters on the other. That is, the MoS was implementing what it considered to be "a logically planned development of the gear driven helicopter to provide a reliable twin engined aircraft"[57], whereas the actual market was not for long-term development projects; rather for production helicopters to fulfil immediate service requirements.

Licence Production and Indigenous Capability

The analysis of the British helicopter industry between 1945 and 1960 demonstrates that despite a series of indigenous R&D projects, the British armed services and civil operators relied predominantly on production technology of US Sikorsky origin. Furthermore, by 1960 Westland had emerged as the UK's sole manufacturer, having merged with or taken over the helicopter interests of its UK competitors: in 1959 it acquired the helicopter interests of Saunders-Roe, and a year later took over Bristol and Fairey Aviation[58]. In this context, it seems pertinent to assess the issue of whether, or to what extent, the commercial failure of the MoS helicopter R&D programme affected Britain's indigenous helicopter design capacity. That is, did the combination of Westland's production success and the relative failure of MoS-sponsored R&D programmes mark a fundamental loss of an indigenous British helicopter technology capability?

Indications are that despite the failure of Ministry of Supply policy to foster `all-British' helicopter projects, Britain did not lose an indigenous capacity *per se*. Instead, it appears that by 1960, Britain had established an independent national design and production expertise. First, technology transfer from Sikorsky provided Westland with an in-house R&D capacity. As a result, Westland were able to absorb and extend technologies originally developed in the United States. Westland had, in effect, unilaterally acted in keeping with the British Government's wartime approach of opting out of helicopter development and re-entering on the basis of U.S. work. Second, the long-needed reorganisation of the British helicopter industry by 1960 concentrated indigenous British design expertise under one roof; expertise which had previously been dissipated on a range of underfunded programmes. Collectively, this capability was carried forward to a series of commercially successful collaborative projects with the French in the mid-1960[59], and the Scout and Wasp helicopters.

An indication of Westland's ability to absorb know-how from its relationship with Sikorsky is provided by Westland improvements to technology provided by the American firm. To illustrate this point, in 1945 Westland was a company specialising in the manufacture of fixed-wing naval aircraft. Its decision to obtain a helicopter manufacturing agreement with Sikorsky rather than conduct in-house development was based on the fact that "they did not have the staff or facilities to do anything else"[60]. Westland's early achievement in `anglicising' the S-51 during the late 1940s was to re-engine and reproduce components of essentially American specification.

With successive generations of Sikorsky designs, however, Westland was accumulating in-house design expertise. In the case of the Wessex, for example, Westland's achievement was to combine its in-house rotor and airframe developments with the proven Sikorsky design[61]. With the incorporation of the Napier Gazelle gas-turbine engine, Westland produced a helicopter of superior performance to the parent American version.

Other evidence of Westland design capability from technology transfer was the companies capacity to develop helicopter systems in-house. By 1953, for example, Westland had developed the five-seat Widgeon helicopter[62], incorporating Sikorsky rotor head technology and a Westland-developed fuselage[63]. Later, in the mid-1950s, Westland commenced the Westminster project on a private venture basis: a large helicopter designed in civil and military variant, with a lift capacity of 15,000lb, or provision for 45 passengers[64]. By late 1959, the Westminster had completed flight trials and established Westland's credentials as a capable helicopter design company.

In addition to the process of technology transfer which enabled Westland to accumulate in-house design expertise, the rationalisation of the industry as a whole in the late 1950s concentrated British design expertise. This reorganisation focused development effort under one roof and financial resources on fewer helicopter types for which production was likely.

This experience indicates a number of potential approaches to creating an maintaining an indigenous technological capability. After 1945, the British government policy towards helicopters was to equate indigenous capacity with a programme of government-sponsored research, development and production. At this stage the Government's position was to consider licence production of foreign helicopter technology as undesirable on the grounds that this would undermine an indigenous helicopter capacity[65]. Clearly, however, Westland licence production of Sikorsky technology was not incompatible with a future indigenous helicopter research, development and production capacity; rather, it indicates an alternative strategy of selectively encouraging technology transfer from overseas industry to stimulate domestic technological know-how.

Conclusion

Between 1945 and 1960, British helicopter production was dominated by Westland, a licenced producer of overseas technology. Westland's pre-eminence in the helicopter field was due to the technological lead that the company acquired from Sikorsky, and the commercial failure of a series of British helicopter programmes.

As this case study demonstrates, a number of factors accounted for the relative commercial failure of 'all-British' helicopter projects. First, the failure of British Governments to reorganise the aircraft industry, and remove organisational constraints which were to hinder indigenous development efforts. Second, an inadequate assessment of the nature of the British helicopter market by the Ministry of Supply, and the availability of Westland licence helicopter variants further undermined the commercial viability of Government-sponsored R&D. Despite the reliance on Westland for manufacturing output, indications are that Britain did not lose an indigenous research and development capacity. Rather, the process of technology transfer to Westland and the rationalisation of the industry in 1960 provided the basis for a viable indigenous helicopter research, development and production capability. The British experience with helicopters raises a 'moral for the future': a policy of ceasing domestic work and relying on the technology of others can work, but the optimum method to pick up may be licence production rather than redesigning.

Endnotes

1. AVIA 15/954, **Minute from Director of Research**., 1 May, 1945.

2. Snyder, W.P., **The Politics of British Defence Policy, 1951-1961**, Princeton University Press, 1963, p.331.

3. AVIA 15/954, **Minute by Director General of Research and Development**, 6 February 1941. For an account of Cierva's prewar activities, see for example, Hafner, R., **Four Decades of Rotating Wing Activity, 1928-1965**, in Brie, R.A.C. (ed.), *A History of British Rotorcraft, 1866-1965*, Westland Helicopter Ltd., August, 1968.

4. AVIA 15/954, **Rotary Wing Aircraft Development**, 23 December 1940, p.1.

5. *Ibid.*

6. **The Supply of Military Aircraft**, H.M.S.O., February 1955, Cmd. 9388, p.3.

7. Reader, J., **The Weir Group: A Centenary History**, London, 1971, p.142. Reader's observation is confirmed in AVIA 15/954, **Minute by Director of Research**, 2 January 1943.

8. AVIA 65/6, **Wing Aircraft Development**, 23 December 1940, p.5.

9. AVIA 15/954, **Minute from Chief Executive**, 14 February, 1943.

10. War Production Board 314.2.42, **Inspection of Helicopter Projects in the United States**, by Grover Loening (Consultant on Aircraft War Production Board).", 29 April 1944, (War Production Board Collection, National Archive, Washington D.C.).

11. See Bryson, L.B., **Helicopters in the Royal Navy**, *Journal of the Royal Aeronautical Society*, 76, 1972, p. 471; and Everett-Heath, J., **British Military Helicopters**, Arms and Armour Press, London, 1986, p.27.

12. AVIA 15/954, **Minute from Director of Scientific Research**, 2 January 1943.

13. AVIA 65/6, **The Helicopter and its Potential**, 6 February 1953, p.3.

14. *Ibid.* For more details on these projects, see Taylor, J.W.R., and Allward, M.F., **Westland 50.**, Ian Allen, London, 1965, p.158.

15. McClements, A., **Review of British Rotorcraft Activities, 1943-46**, in Brie, R.A.C., *op. cit.*, p.103.

16. Prouty, R., **Military Helicopter Design Technology**, Jane's, London, 1989, p.6.

17. For more detail, see Taylor and Allward, *op. cit.*, p. 107.

18. *Ibid.*, p.109.

19. *Ibid.*

20. Bryson, L.B., **Helicopters in the Royal Navy**, *Journal of the Royal Aeronautical Society*, 76, 1972, p.471.

21. AVIA 65/6, **The Helicopter and its Potential**, 6 February 1953, p.4.

22. *Ibid.*

23. *Ibid.*

24. *Ibid.*

25. See Hafner, *op. cit.*, p.240.

26. Mensforth, E., **Family Engineers**, Ward Lock Ltd, London, 1981, p.118.

27. AVIA 65/6, **The Helicopter and its Potential**, 6 February 1953.

28. AVIA 65/6, **Memorandum extract on Helicopters and Light Aircraft, DRP&P (52)**, 15 December, 1952, p.1.

29. AVIA 65/6, **Meeting to Discuss Development and Production of the Helicopter in the U.K.**, 30 June 1953.

30. AVIA 65/6, **Note on the MoS Helicopter R&D Programme with Special Emphasis on the Civil Transport Role**, 17 October 1953.

31. Barnes, C.H., **Bristol Aircraft Since 1910**, Putnam, London, 1988, pp.368-9.

32. Cheeseman, I., Edmonds, M., & Simpson, J., **The Procurement of Military Aircraft 1945-1970**, in Gregory, F., Imber, J., & Simpson, J., *Perspectives Upon British Defence Policy, 1945-1970*, Southampton University Press, 1978, p.197.

33. See Barnes, *op. cit.*

34. See, for example, Walker, G.E., **Activities of Weir, Hafner and Bristol, 1933-1960**, in Brie, R.A.C., *op. cit.*, p.76.

35. See, for example, Wood, D., **Project Cancelled**, MacDonald & Jane's, London, 1976, Chapter 8.

36. Worcester, R., **Roots of British Air Policy**, Hodder & Stoughton, London, 1966, p.180.

37. Second Report from the Select Committee on Estimates, Session 1956-1957, **The Supply of Military Aircraft**, p.vii.

38. See, for example, Snyder, *op. cit.*

39. Second Report from the Select Committee on Estimates, *op. cit.*

40. *Ibid.*

41. See, for example, AVIA 55/90, **A Study of the Potential Applications of the Helicopter to Army Roles**, 11 August, 1945.

42. Towle, P.A., **Pilots and Rebels: The Use of Aircraft in Unconventional Warfare, 1918-1988**, Brasseys, London, 1989, p.126.

43. Second Report from the Select Committee on Estimates, *op. cit.*, p.237.

44. *Ibid.*

45. AVIA 65/6, **The Helicopter and its Potential**, 6 February 1953.

46. See, for example, Taylor, H.A., **Fairey Aircraft Since 1915**, Putnam, London, 1974, pp. 420-411.

47. AVIA 65/6, **Meeting to Discuss Development and Production of Helicopters in the U.K.**, 30 June 1953.

48. Second Report from the Select Committee on Estimates, *op. cit.*, p.351.

49. Snyder, *op. cit.*

50. See Wood, *op. cit.*, p.16.

51. Second Report from the Select Committee on Estimates, *op. cit.*, p.viii.

52. Gregory, F., and Simpson, J., **The Acquisition of Military Aircraft in Great Britain and West Germany**, in Horton, F.B. (ed.), *Comparative Defence Policy*, Johns Hopkins University Press, London, 1974, p. 459.

53. See for example Wood, *op. cit.*

54. See for example Uttley, M.R.H., **British Helicopter Production, 1945-1960: A Case Study of Technology Transfer and Market Dominance**, *Science and Public Policy*, Volume 18, Number 4, 1991, pp. 239-240.

55. AVIA 65/6, **The Helicopter and Its Potential**., 6 February 1953, p.2.

56. AVIA 65/6, **Memorandum Extract on Helicopters and Light Aircraft: Extract DRP&P (52)**, 15 December 1952.

57. AVIA 65/6, **Note on the MoS Helicopter R&D Programme with Special Emphasis on the Civil Transport Role**, 17 October 1953.

58. See, for example, Hartley, K., **The Mergers of the Aircraft Industry, 1957-60.**, *Journal of the Royal Aeronautical Society*, December 1965, pp.848-851.

59. See **Jane's All the Worlds Aircraft, 1974-75**, Jane's, London, 1975, p.236.

60. Fitzwilliams, O., **Westland Helicopter Activities, 1946-60**, in Brie, R.A.C. (ed.), *A History of British Rotorcraft, 1866-1965*, Westland Helicopters Ltd., August 1968, p. 127.

61. *Ibid.*

62. See, for example, Wragg, D.W., **Helicopters at War: A Pictorial History**, Robert Hale, London, 1983, p.51.

63. See Taylor and Allward, *op. cit.*, p. 114.

64. For more details on the Westminster project, see Wood, *op. cit.*, p. 126.

65. Evidence that the MoS considered licence production as detrimental to a comprehensive indigenous British helicopter design and production capacity is contained in: AVIA 65/6, **Ministry of Defence DRPC: Ultra-Light Reconnaissance Helicopter, Memorandum by Ministry of Supply**, 27 November 1952; and AVIA 65/6, **Note on the Ministry of Supply Helicopter R&D Programme with Special Emphasis on the Civil Transport Role, MoS Air 2 (a)**, 17 October 1953, p.3.

Part 3

Industry, Procurement and Conversion

Chapter 7

Changes in Defence Procurement and the European Technology Base

Philip Gummett and William Walker

Introduction

The size and shape of the European defence sector has, until very recently, reflected the specific geopolitical circumstances of the Cold War. As the East-West conflict dissipated during the latter 1980s, and the Warsaw Pact was wound up, the defence sector suffered not just a loss of demand, but a tremendous loss of coherence in consumption patterns and technology policies. The military strategies and force structures pertinent to defending territories against massed attacks from the East lost their relevance, and it was no longer clear how to organise military forces in response to the more diffuse set of risks that emerged.

Even had Mr Gorbachev not appeared on the scene, profound changes would in any case have occurred at the defence industrial level. These were arising from a general over-capacity of production, a shifting balance of leadership as between defence and civil technologies, the indirect effects of the Single European Act, and a concern within defence ministries about the competitiveness of European defence firms vis-a-vis their United States counterparts.

The significance of these changed circumstances arises from the fact that the defence industries have been central to much of European high technology and industrial performance. They have been flagships for national technological prowess. Considerable proportions of public spending on research and development (R&D) have gone to the defence sector, especially in France and the United Kingdom. Even where these percentages have been smaller, as in Germany or Italy, their significance for the support of advanced technologies should not be underestimated.

After decades of relative stability, the defence sector now faces profound change. Companies are engaged in major restructuring, within and across borders, which is likely to accelerate as defence budgets are cut. These changes are extremely important for the future shape and capabilities of key parts of European high technology, in aerospace and elsewhere. Yet they are largely excluded from both the promotional and the regulatory provisions of the Treaty of Rome, and are only questionably covered by the Single European Act.

The exclusion of a field of such technological and industrial importance is increasingly being questioned. At the highest level of European politics, it raises the issue of how far the technological and industrial changes serve European security interests, and how far they are autonomous from those interests. A second reason for the questioning is that one important effect of the move towards the

Single European Market (and beyond that, to political and monetary union) has been to increase the tendency towards integration of science and technology policies between European states. Since, at the same time, but for independent reasons, the distinction between the defence and civil sectors is also weakening, this debate can be expected to intensify.

To set the scene, a few remarks on the changes in the defence markets and on the effects of the Single European Market (SEM) on science and technology policy in general may be helpful.

Changes in Defence Markets

Defence markets in the larger European countries were, until very recently, largely closed to each other's products. Although still heavily protected, trade was often freer across the Atlantic than within Europe. Moreover, the defence and civil markets developed separate regulatory structures. Both these characteristics began to break down in the 1980s, for several reasons, all of which are significant for European technological capabilities[1]:

1. Against a background of pressures to reduce defence budgets (even before the autumn of 1989), the growing cost of sustaining defence industrial capabilities encouraged national procurement agencies to seek a division of labour among the numerous European defence suppliers (see Chapter 8).
2. The perceived competitive threat from the much larger, and increasingly hungry, US defence industry brought calls, notably in the Vredeling report of 1986, for a greater integration of European defence markets and industries.[2]
3. The pressure to integrate defence markets was reinforced, particularly from the mid-1980s, by a perceived need to increase Europe's self-reliance in defence. It could no longer count on the USA maintaining such a large military presence in Europe, for budgetary and other reasons.
4. The defence industries found themselves having to respond to the indirect effects of the Single European Market (SEM), and the economic pressures that lay behind it. Most defence contractors had large civil interests, and were thus pressed to restructure on a European scale. Moreover, the greater dynamism of civil technology in a number of areas, and the greater scale of civil markets for high technology products, was forcing firms and governments to reconsider the relationship between civil and military R&D.[3]

In response, governments have tried to liberalise defence markets, in both national and European contexts. They are also having to adjust to the changed security context since the autumn of 1989. Contraction of defence markets will add to the complexity of the issues, as competing tendencies to concentrate, to internationalise, and to protect national firms, are played out.

Precisely how these processes will relate to science and technology policy more generally within the countries of the European Community is a complex issue, partly because policies on science and technology are so diverse within Europe. Analysis is eased by the fact that only two countries, France and the United Kingdom, have very high commitments in the defence sector, followed, but at a distance, by Germany and Italy. Nevertheless, the significance of the defence sector for some of the other European countries should not be under estimated. Thus, for Spain, defence is important as a source of new technology through such routes as collaboration on the European Fighter Aircraft (EFA) and active participation in the EUCLID (European Cooperation for the Longer-term In Defence) programme of the Independent European Programme Group of NATO members. Greece and Portugal also place considerable emphasis on international cooperative programmes, not least through NATO's (civil) scientific programmes.

European Science and Technology Policy and the SEM

In addition to the changes in the defence markets, the other important current influence on European science and technology is the Single European Market. What specific effects might arise from the SEM that might be important in assessing the future of the defence sector?

A study by Collins and Stein[4] on science and technology and the SEM offers helpful guidance.

Among the areas of competence opened up for the Commission by the Single European Act are, first, the funding of science and technology through the Community's Framework Programme and through the Social and Regional Structural Funds. An important question here is the scope for compensating for the effects of cuts in defence R&D, if it were felt that without such compensation weaknesses might be introduced into the general European science and technology base. In respect of the Regional and Structural funds, of which it is expected that some 10-15 per cent will go to technology development and human science and technology resources (making a total expenditure that is roughly equivalent to the budget for the R&D Framework Programme), the high geographical concentration of the defence industries in most of the European countries could lead to regional development arguments for support for new enterprises that might absorb displaced defence scientists and engineers.

Second, the intention behind the SEM of gradually replacing competing national standards by a Europe-wide system raises the question of how far standards for defence equipment might be brought within this system - particularly in relation to components and software.

Third, one of the most difficult problems under the SEM concerns `State Aids' for R&D. These take many forms, including partial State ownership, State-financed training schemes, soft loans and export credits, favourable tax regimes, preferential access to technology developed in national laboratories, and outright grants. Such activity is controversial within the SEM context because the strengthening of local R&D capability may distort competition within the Community. The area is complex and has been the subject of a Commission-originated survey of State Aids for R&D and innovation, which has served to highlight the definitional difficulties.

An important issue will be the degree to which support for defence R&D, to the extent that it is excluded from the SEM, can be used as a means of State Aid for industry in a way that might be regarded as unfair by others. This issue, and the wider question of state intervention in industry through defence firms, was aired to some extent in the UK in the enquiry by the Monopolies and Mergers Commission[5] in 1991 on the proposed (and since abandoned) merger between the missile interests of British Aerospace and Thomson-CSF, where the question of the effects of State ownership of Thomson was discussed.

Fourthly, public procurement is an important instrument of industrial and technology policy in many countries, nowhere more so than in the defence sector. In the UK, for example, the Ministry of Defence is the largest single customer of British industry. Collins and Stein deal with a particular aspect of procurement, namely, that relating to the purchase of R&D services. They observe that where R&D is treated as a separately identifiable marketable commodity (eg, through contract research), then it can in principle be regulated; but this is harder to do when, as in some Member States, it is embedded in national purchasing schemes. Moreover, although in principle the Commission will have the authority to enforce a public procurement regime that includes R&D, it is thought unlikely that it would do more than require greater transparency with respect to the R&D elements on public procurement contracts.

We may add that a particular difficulty in this area is the variety of national practices and institutions for the funding of R&D. This applies equally to the defence sector, where practice varies (even within a country) as to whether R&D contracts are awarded separately from production contracts (see Chapter 2). The Commission's difficulties over intervention in the general case suggest that the defence case will be even harder to deal with. Nevertheless, in respect of both this question and the issue of State Aids, a stronger line may be taken after the Maastricht Summit. It was in any case reported in November 1991 that the EC Competition Commissioner, Sir Leon Brittan, would henceforth be scrutinising defence contract awards to see whether the national security exemption was being used as `a device to protect so-called dual-use production with primarily civil applications'.[6]

Summing up, Collins and Stein suggest that the Single Market `is creating an environment for science and technology that is progressively changing the expectations and plans of individuals, institutions and industry alike.' They also conclude that a `single market for science and technology is gradually developing as a natural by-product of the Single Market proper', and that the changes taking place make it more likely that the Community's role in science and technology will grow substantially. This claim should be put into perspective: at present the Community R&D budget is only about 4 per cent of total public expenditure on R&D within the Twelve. However, as Findlay[7] has observed, it is nevertheless bigger than some member states' own R&D budgets, and it has had a disproportionate effect on European attitudes.

Against this background, then, what can be said about the effects of changes in the defence environment, both on defence science and technology and on the wider European scene in science and technology? Let us begin to answer this question by briefly reviewing the statistical position.

Funding of R&D

A detailed discussion of data on defence R&D, and of its analytical value, is given in Chapter 2. For now, it suffices to note that any discussion that relies on international comparative data on R&D is obliged to begin with a *caveat* about the quality of the data. This is especially true when the data relate to defence R&D. In Britain, for example, there are numerous difficulties with the official statistics on defence R&D which may mean that they exaggerate true expenditure on defence R&D (as defined by the Frascati convention) by up to 50 per cent.[8]

Levels of general support for science and technology vary widely among the EC countries, as can be seen from Table 7.1. (Note that the Table uses data from 1988 and 1987: more recent data sets are less complete, but the relativities that they show do not differ significantly from those for 1987-88). Thus, gross domestic expenditure on R&D (GERD), from all sources, in millions of US dollars (at purchasing power parities) for 1988 ranged from $24 billion for Germany to $255 million for Portugal. For comparison, the Japanese and US figures, and the total for the EC, are also given. These figures give a sense of the absolute scale of activity, which is important for an area of economic activity in which, in many fields, an inability to pay the entry costs may greatly reduce access to certain technologies.

Expressed as percentages of GDP, these figures range from 2.83 for Germany to 0.33 for Greece. The percentage of this figure that is financed by government also varies considerably, from Portugal's 63 per cent and Italy's 54, to Germany's 34 per cent and Belgium's 27.

These figures suggest that the impact of government cutbacks, such as may follow from defence cuts, is likely to vary considerably between countries. However, a better representation of the effects of such defence R&D cuts is given in the final two rows in the table, which show the decomposition of GERD, expressed as a percentage of GDP, into its civil and defence components. Here we see that in Italy (and even more so Portugal), despite the large percentage of GERD that is government-financed, defence cuts will not be highly significant, at least in quantitative terms. The same is true in Germany, despite recently reported figures showing that the area of defence research has been growing as a percentage of Federal spending on R&D, from 16 per cent in 1980 to 22 per cent in 1990.[9]

Table 7.1: Statistics on R&D, EC, USA JAPAN

	Military R&D as Percent of GDP, 1987	Civil R&D as Percent of GDP, 1987	Gerd as Percent of GDP, 1987	Percent Government Finance 1987	Gerd, millions US $, PPP, 1988
Germany	0.1	2.7[(3)]	2.83	34.7	24,626
France	0.4	1.9	2.29	51.7	17,528
UK	0.5	1.8[(4)]	2.27	38.7	16,184[(1)]
Italy	0.1	1.1[(3)]	1.19	54.0	10,004
Netherlands	0	2.3	2.33	44.3	4,365
Belgium	0	1.6	1.65	27.6	2,056
Denmark	0	1.4	1.43	45.9	973[(1)]
Spain	0	0.6	0.62	48.5	2,437
Ireland	0	0.9	0.94	43.8	270
Portugal	0	0.4	0.45[(2)]	63.5	255[(2)]
Greece	0	0.4[(3)]	0.33[(2)]	74.4	252
EC12	-	-	1.95	-	78,950
USA	0.8	2.1	2.90	48.7	137,816
Japan	0	2.7	2.67	19.6	47,649

Notes: (1) 1987
(2) 1986
(3) value estimated as the share in GDP of GERD less government appropriations for defence R&D
(4) 1985

Source: CNR-ISRDS elaboration of OECD data, as presented in tables 3.2, 3.3 and 3.5 of D Archibugi and M Pianta (1990), **The European Technological Specialisation : An EEC report on the science & technology activities of advanced countries** (Rome : CNR, 1990).

But in France and the UK, (and even more so in the USA), defence R&D cuts would clearly have more profound effects. The effect on Spain, although small in quantitative terms, might be higher in qualitative terms because of the Spanish commitment to collaborative defence projects in high technology, it being a deliberate aspect of Spanish technology policy to develop high technology capabilities through the defence sector.[10]

It is worth adding, although not shown in these figures, that not only Spain, but also Germany and Italy, have a higher proportion of their defence R&D committed to international collaborative projects than do France and the UK. This increases their vulnerability to decisions made elsewhere though, by the same token, it gives them some influence over those decisions.

Table 7.2 offers another view of the statistical position. It shows the weight of France and the UK in European defence procurement (together amounting to more than half the total), and the high proportion of those countries' government-funded R&D that is devoted to defence. The table also shows the high degree of self-sufficiency in arms production of the top four European defence spenders, and Spain's efforts to move into the same category, though it should be noted that figures at this level of aggregation do not fully reflect dependence on other countries for components or for licence agreements. The higher import penetration figures for some countries also conceal the existence of small but significant specialised defence industries, such as small arms in Belgium and naval communications in the Netherlands.

The Future of Defence R&D in Europe

Against this complex background, then, let us consider the future of defence R&D in Europe, and its implications for civil science and technology. Four questions arise:

1. Are we wise to assume that defence R&D will be cut substantially?
2. If we are, in what sectors would the impact be most felt?
3. What is the likelihood that defence R&D cuts would result in a transfer of funds to civil R&D?
4. What, in any case, is the scope for using civil R&D to compensate for defence R&D cuts?

This section discusses these questions, and the next examines some indirect effects on the civil sector of an opening up of EC defence procurement markets, including such questions as the extent to which military R&D is in any case benefiting the civil sector, and the significance of military programmes as technology drivers.

Table 7.2: European defence production, trade and R&D, 1988[a]

	Defence spending (% GDP)	Equipment[b] procurement ($bn)	Defence R&D/ total govt R&D (%)	Defence trade ($m)[c] Imports	Defence trade ($m)[c] Exports	Import penetration (%)[c]
UK	5.6	8.8	47.3	681	1,722	8
France	3.8	7.2	37.0	173	4,234	2
Germany	2.9	5.1	13.3	463	1,739	9
Italy	2.4	3.9	10.3	203	880	5
Spain	2.2	1.5	19.1	350	453	23
Belgium	2.8	0.51	0.6	321	254	63
Denmark	2.2	0.34	0.4	110	4	33
Netherlands	3.0	1.4	3.2	584	124	42
Greece	6.7	0.81	1.9	295	38	36
Ireland	1.2	0.04	n.a.	13	-	33
Luxemburg	1.3	0.02	n.a.	6	-	30
Portugal	3.7	0.14	n.a.	75	138	52
EC Total	3.6	30.4		3,501	9,604	11
Norway	3.2	0.62	6.8	227	18	37
Sweden	2.7	0.96	n.a.	90	185	9
Switzerland	1.8	0.65	n.a.	522	287	80
United States	5.9	70.0	65.4	557	11,698	1

Notes: a Defence expenditure according to NATO definitions to give comparability. Note that they usually differ from expenditure figures recorded in national accounts. Trade statistics are taken from the United States Arms Control and Disarmament Agency (ACDA)

b Figures for France, Ireland, Luxemburg, Sweden and Switzerland are estimates

c Average 1983-87, constant 1987 prices

d Imports divided by procurement expenditure

Souces: IISS, 1990; ACDA, 1989; NATO's Sixteen Nations, 1990: OECD R&D statistics from unpublished sources

Taken from W Walker, 'Defence' in C Freeman, M Sharp and W Walker (eds), *Technology and the Future of Europe* (London: Pinter, 1991), p 368.

1. Will defence R&D be cut?

A prior question concerns the projections for defence spending as a whole where, at least for Britain and France, the nature and extent of overall reductions, despite the cancellation of a number of projects and expected reductions in equipment budgets, remains unclear. But even when the picture clarifies, as the costs of the 1991 Gulf War and the transitional costs of radical reductions in the armed forces work through,[11] it does not follow that defence *R&D* will necessarily be cut, or cut by much. In a speech in September 1991, the British Minister of State for Defence Procurement, referring to the importance of developing a `reconstitution capability' as an element of defence strategy, suggested that "we might also consider whether to give R&D greater priority within the defence budget".[12] He added that he was not proposing a flood of new money, but rather was wondering "whether we should not be researching new technologies and demonstrating them, while not automatically taking them into Full Development as before. We would therefore be thinking in terms of giving pure research, and technology demonstration, greater priority".

Leaving aside the difficult question of whether the existing pricing structure for defence contracts would make such a proposition attractive to industry, the ministerial voicing of such ideas, even if speculative, should at least give pause for thought about the inevitability of substantial reductions in defence R&D expenditure. Moreover, given the traditional French concern about maintaining high technology capabilities, and current discussions about maintaining and upgrading defence equipment, especially after the Gulf War exposed a number of deficiencies in European capabilities, it would be surprising if similar thoughts were not occurring in Paris and Bonn.

Thus far, in Britain and France (just as in the United States), there is little clear evidence of defence R&D cutbacks. On the one hand it has been British policy since 1987 to cap defence R&D spending, and the 1991 Statement on the Defence Estimates[13] reiterated the Government's "aim to achieve a gradual reduction in Government-funded defence research and development over the next decade". But neither the projections in that Statement, nor those by the Cabinet Office[14] showed any sign of such a reduction. Indeed, the Cabinet Office figures showed planned expenditure for 1992-93 and 1993-94 that is higher in real terms than for 1991-92, and this against a background of steady decline in provision for government funded civil R&D. On the other hand, the working assumption in the Defence Research Agency (formed in April 1991 from the four main non-nuclear research establishments of MOD) is that its budget will fall. Thus at the Royal Signals and Radar Establishment it is being assumed that it will be necessary to generate £15 million of additional non-MOD business by 1997 (a doubling of the present level) in order to remain at its present size.[15] Part of the increase shown in the Cabinet Office figures may be accounted for by higher expenditure on the nuclear deterrent, some production as well as R&D costs being charged to the budget of the Atomic Weapons Establishment.

In France, the civil context is brighter than the British. It was announced in September 1991 that civil R&D is a `priorité majeure' within the 1992 budget projections: it is set to grow by 7 per cent against growth in the overall public sector budget of 3 per cent.[16] On the defence side, and again unlike Britain, it has been announced that 400 posts are to go over the next 18 months at the main nuclear weapons research unit, which represents a slight acceleration in already planned reductions. Even here, however, the cuts appear to be concentrated in administration and production rather than research.[17] As for conventional defence R&D, so far there is no clear evidence of cuts.

2. Which areas would be cut?

This question is even more difficult to answer, as it depends upon the outcome of rethinking that is going on in European national capitals, and in NATO, about equipment needs following the collapse of the Soviet empire, and also in the aftermath of the Gulf War.

The difficulty that all countries face is that of identifying requirements in a coherent fashion, and then of finding the necessary funds at a time of public pressure for cuts. Statements abound to the effect that, when `the threat' came clearly from the Soviet Union, it was possible to plan fairly straightforwardly. Moreover, because of the scale of forces assembled to deal with that threat, lesser defence problems could be managed with some configuration of forces drawn from the large total. But the single large threat has now been replaced by a multiplicity of smaller, but less clearcut, `risks'. Not only is it difficult to know what to plan for, but the force totals available will be much smaller than in the past, thus reducing the scope for cobbling together elements of the total to meet particular eventualities. If it could be confidently assumed by each country that it would meet all conceivable eventualities in the company of the same fixed set of allies, then a division of labour might be agreed. But even this seems implausible at present. Hence the profound uncertainty that grips defence planners and, by extension, those responsible for planning defence R&D.

The emphasis in NATO's London Declaration of July 1990 upon smaller, more versatile and mobile forces does, however, suggest that within a reduced total, a premium will be placed on maintaining a variety of technologies capable of providing battlefield mobility and rapid deployment of reserves and their equipment. This suggests a combination of helicopters and transport aircraft, as well as appropriate ground transport, together with the means of acquiring air superiority. Associated with this concept will probably be a renewed emphasis upon surveillance, including signals intelligence and communications, all functioning within integrated command, control and communications systems. The forces will be well equipped, and will depend upon highly accurate weapons and high survivability under attack. The latter requirement might imply further development of stealth technologies, and further application of electronic warfare - especially electronic counter-measures against detection and attack. Some of these requirements might call for wholly new weapons platforms and supporting systems. But budgetary pressure might also increase interest in upgrading existing platforms and stretching their working lives, especially if there seemed less likelihood of their being used against an equally sophisticated enemy. The proposed reduction in training and exercises will increase demand for simulators. Protection against chemical and biological weapons will continue to be a priority and Britain and France will have to consider the future of their nuclear forces. Verification technologies will also be important, particularly if there is further progress with all types of arms control.

The experience of the Gulf War, with the problems of long range transport and other logistic support, surveillance, anti-missile defence, and (especially for France, among the larger forces) of night-fighting equipment, confirmed these trends, and has also put a premium on weapons that reduce civilian casualties - that it, on precision guided munitions. For example, as a direct result of the Gulf War, France has relaunched a project to develop a helicopter capable of radar detection of mobile targets at ranges up to 150 kilomètres.[18]

On these assumptions, the requirements for R&D will favour electronics and information technology - especially the software side - and the means of providing rapid and reliable local and long-range transport. Emphasis will be given in this regard to materials R&D for lightness, strength and stealth characteristics - all areas with scope for synergy between defence and civil technological programmes. In contrast, more traditional areas such as shipbuilding and tank construction will decline.

It remains to be seen how correct these assumptions will prove. Interestingly, however, the speech referred to earlier by the British Defence Procurement Minister speaks of the likelihood that high technologies will become widely distributed, so that, in the light of this possibility and the prospect from time to time of facing adversaries who are deploying numerically greatly superior forces,

"the `good guys' are going to need a *quantum* superiority in high technology - stealth, terminal guidance, electronic countermeasures, communications, and target acquisition."[19]

3. Likelihood of transfer of funds from defence R&D to civil R&D

Is any peace dividend likely to lead to a shift of resources in science and technology from defence to civil? The answer to this question depends on individual governments and their conception of science and technology policy. Countries that take a view of a national science and technology budget, which can then be divided among the various claimants, or which consciously integrate defence and civil science and technology, are likely to respond differently from those in which decisions about defence and civil science and technology are taken separately by separate ministries.

Britain falls firmly into the latter camp, even though in recent years the Cabinet Office machinery for coordinating departmental decisions in respect of science and technology has been considerably strengthened. Although a decision has been made recently to increase funding for certain categories of civil science, there is no reason to suppose that this has anything to do with compensation for defence cuts. Similarly in *France*, although the national Plan reviews overall spending on science and technology, the defence sector has traditionally been kept largely outside the planning process. However, in 1989, the Intergroupe Recherche et Développement Technologique, in a report on *La Science, la Technologie, l'Innovation: une Politique Globale pour le Commissariat Général du Plan* (1989), did devote two pages to defence R&D, to discuss the effects of this expenditure on the armaments industry itself, and upon the civil sector via diffusion of technologies. But there is so far no suggestion that any cuts in defence R&D would automatically transfer into increases on the civil side, although, as we have seen, it does so happen that France is at present increasing its civil science budget quite sharply.

The scope for transferring funds may be greater in some other European countries, mainly because defence and civil science and technology are on the whole not so firmly separated. Thus, in *Germany* defence related research is not monopolised by the Defence ministry, nor is it exclusively carried out in government research establishments or the laboratories of major defence contractors. The government's policy is to encourage the performance of civil and military R&D in the same establishments, whether private or state, thereby facilitating a more ready transfer of ideas between the two types of research. In institutes such as the Deutsche Forschungs und Versuchsanstalt fur Luft und Raumfahrt, civil and military research are given comparable priority, and funding by the Defence Ministry amounts in any case to only about one-fifth of the total budget. In the *Netherlands* approximately three quarters of defence R&D is conducted by a civil agency, the Netherlands Organisation for Applied Scientific Research. It is incumbent upon this agency to make its results available for use by civilian industry. The *Spanish* government's defence research is organised by several departments: the Ministries of Defence, Education and Industry and Energy. This joint responsibility is particularly important in the area of enabling technologies such as information technology and electronics. Military R&D in *Italy* is overseen by a Defence Industry Committee which includes representatives of the non-defence ministries as well as private industry, but there are no clear indications as to whether this increases the possibility of transferring funds from military to civil R&D. The tradition of a lack of strong central control of the R&D activities of the different armed services in Italy[20] would, however, suggest that such transfers are unlikely.

4. Scope for civil technology to substitute for military

Whether or not funds are directly transferred in any country from military to civil R&D budgets, there is another, possibly more important, potential linkage between the two areas. This derives from the growing importance of certain areas of technology of civil origin for defence applications, the possibility of making more use of such technologies, and of deliberately developing technologies aimed at both civil and military markets (so-called `dual-use' technologies). As an editorial in the French defence journal *L'Armement*[21] put it, in introducing a special issue on `Les Technologies Duales',

"Le temps n'est plus où les contraintes de secret et de spécificité conduisaient la Défense à mener des recherches isolément, en espérant, peut-être, des "retombées" civiles. Les conditions économiques et techniques d'aujourd'hui imposent de mener recherches et développements en pensant dualité: ce que je cherche n'existe-t-il pas ailleurs? Ce que je trouverai ne sera-t-il pas utile ailleurs?"

It is from such considerations that the concept of `*dual-use*', or `*dual-market*', technologies arises.[22] Such technologies are more likely to be found within governmental and industrial organisations that are concerned with the development of manufacturing and process technologies, with generic materials, electronic and information technologies, and with component manufacture, than in the higher realms of sub-system manufacturers and prime contractors.

Historically, the 1990s may come to be seen as the decade in which there finally ended the post-1945 presumption that defence technology is necessarily more advanced than civil. Associated with it, at least in the USA, Britain and France, was an assumption that the generic underpinnings of defence technology should be developed through extensive dedicated defence research programmes.

A number of factors are now operating to change this assumption. First, in Britain at least, industry's role in the setting of defence requirements is increasing as the result of government policy to reduce the role of its own defence research establishments. This in itself says nothing about the relative standing of defence- and civil-originated technologies, but taken in the context of the generally more competitive environment in which companies find themselves, it suggests that they will be anxious not to keep separate and expensive defence technological facilities unless this is really necessary or government provides appropriate incentives.

Second, in some fields civil technology is already outstripping defence, and even where it is not, industry is anticipating this development. For example, the European space programme is beginning to assume this role (just as the NASA moon programme did in the USA in an earlier decade), and there is even talk in the aerospace industry of trans-atmospheric vehicles becoming key technology drivers of the early Twenty-First Century, not to mention international discussions about a second generation supersonic transport and other attempts to generate new, advanced, civil demand.[23]

In several areas of electronics and new materials (for example, semiconductors - especially VLSI - and some thermoplastics) the technical lead already lies in the civil sector, or honours are shared between the two. (For example, the performance requirements for military communications software are not markedly different, in terms of security and reliability criteria, from those for the analogous communications networks of international financial centres). This development lay behind the various US expressions of concern about their loss of leadership in a variety of military and civil technologies to Japan.[24]

This point assumes greater importance when we consider the structure of defence production. Increasingly, the prime contractor, at the top of a hierarchy of subcontractors, functions as design and management authority, systems integrator and final assembler. The complexity of the technologies that make up sub-assemblies means that the fraction of value-added by the suppliers is growing - Edmonds, Hayhurst and Uttley estimate it to be generally more than 50 per cent[25] - increasing the dependence of the prime on its suppliers and squeezing its profit margins. Just such a concern was voiced by the chairman of Vickers Defence Systems (the British tank manufacturer) who, at a conference on manufacturing strategies in May 1990, reportedly warned that companies faced a range of threats, "not only from their direct competitors but also from suppliers developing technologies that form the core of the final product".[26] This is particularly an issue in electronics, where economies of scale give an increasing advantage to the major civil suppliers over small defence suppliers, and where it has already been accepted for some years that, in the field of Very Large Scale Integration, military electronics must use civil components, albeit in modified form. As budgetary pressures grow, the appeal of defence equipment that is developed on the back of civil technologies will also grow. So too will the risk to defence firms that civilian holders of technology will move sideways into defence markets. To a degree this is already happening, as shown recently by IBM's success in winning the contract to manage the electronics package in the EH101 helicopter project.

Another factor encouraging this trend arises from the lead time for major defence projects, which can be ten or more years. In some fields of civil technology, especially electronic systems, the rate of generational change is far higher than that. Hence there is a great danger that specifications set down today may be woefully out-of-date by the time the equipment comes into operation, requiring `mid-life' up-dating to begin almost at once. A modern frigate, such as the British Type 23, which carries more than 200 computers linked into a single network, therefore presents a major procurement problem. Bespoke computers risk being obsolete before they come into use.

French concern about these trends is evident in the October 1991 issue of *L'Armement* devoted to the question of dual-use technology, as referred to above.

In Britain, the Defence Procurement Minister has voiced his concern, in relation to the supply of high speed integrated circuits, that:

"There is only one country in the West which can supply this equipment in its most sophisticated form. Is it prudent that over the long term future both the US and the Community should be dependent on one monopoly national supplier?"[27]

He went on directly to observe that:

"In the future I see the MOD making increased use of commercial off-the-shelf technology wherever we can. Our R&D will be increasingly targeted on producing military derivatives of basically civil technology, and on those areas where civil technology is not suitable or simply does not exist. In the constantly extending border area between military and civil technology there will be scope for MOD to become a more eclectic - though discriminating - patron and customer of work with potential for civil application."

Such talk, while fairly novel for the UK, will seem quite familiar in, say, Germany or the Netherlands, and indicates the extent to which perception of the scope for more attention to dual-use technologies has taken root throughout Europe, as well as in the United States and, of course, Japan.

In this respect, too, there is clearly scope for more action by the European Community. Within the Third Framework Programme for Community Research and Technological Development (1990-1994), the adopted programmes on Enabling Technologies provided a natural locus for dual-use work, in respect both of information and communication, and industrial and materials, technologies. The precursor ESPRIT and BRITE/EURAM programmes were already drawn upon by defence research laboratories and defence firms. The new programmes seem to offer equal potential. The element within the industrial and materials technologies programme for aeronautics research also appears to offer a way of responding to specific concerns about this sector. These concerns include, for example, arguments from within the Commission that aerospace R&D is unusual in that it is the only industry where the state provides more than 50 per cent of R&D expenditure, and that:

"Taking account of the consequences of the reduction in defense budgets on research in the military area and the technology transfer within dual undertakings, it could be useful for the sector as a whole, if the Community, while respecting the principle of subsidiarity, were to support increased research in those areas common to both the military and the civil."[28]

Particular appeals for help have also been voiced by representatives of the aerospace industry in the UK and France.[29]

Indirect Effects on Civil Industry of Open Defence Markets

The discussion of dual-use technologies leads naturally to the issue of the consequences for civil industry of the changes that are underway in defence markets. If the defence sector in the past has been important to the civil sector as a `technology driver', with benefits flowing to the civil sector either through spin-off, or through the development of dual-use technology, then the reduction in scale of the defence sector that is in train could have wider significance.

The concept of *spin-off* is problematic.[30] Suffice it here to note that much weight has been put on this concept in the past whenever it has been felt politically necessary to justify expenditure on defence R&D on other than purely defence grounds. The problem is that much of the evidence relating to spin-off is anecdotal, based on individual cases. Where it is based on surveys, these generally do not withstand much scrutiny. Where it is based on econometric attempts to demonstrate relationships (positive or negative) between levels of spending on defence R&D and wider economic performance, the data rarely turn out to be capable of supporting the weight of econometric analysis.

A widely held view among students of this subject is that while a number of well-known technologies (nuclear power, jet engines, computers, for example) did spin-off from developments made around the time of the Second World War, and while electronics received a considerable boost from demand for components arising from US defence and space programmes in the 1950s and 1960s, the paths followed by most civil and military technologies, at least at the level of major systems, have diverged considerably since then, reducing the scope for spin-off. In addition, as we have seen, in some areas the leading edge no longer lies in the military sector.[31]

In assessing, therefore, the impact of defence R&D cuts on the civil technology base of companies that operate in dual markets, these conclusions give some guidance. But they do not tell the whole story. Also important is the internal structure of the company, which varies widely. The crucial point is that many large companies operate as multi-divisional firms, with very little cooperation (and sometimes even direct competition) between divisions. Others, particularly smaller firms, may manage to work with more internal cohesion, but even here the different accounting requirements of defence work, and other differences in work practice, may mean that defence and civil tasks are kept largely separate, thus reducing the possibility for spin-off.

There is, however, one other significant consideration in this equation, and its effect is to increase the significance for the civil sector of defence cuts. This factor is the degree to which defence funds dominate a sector of technology within a country. Where the prime source of research funding is the defence ministry, then even if the rate of spin-off is low, the loss of the funding could nevertheless be serious. Unfortunately, data at this level of disaggregation are simply not available on a systematic basis. Impressionistic evidence suggests, however, that in some countries and some fields (for example, new materials research, which is notoriously long term and therefore difficult to pursue on any other than defence project-like timescales and funding), reductions in defence R&D would have significant effects on the national technology base.

These effects are more likely to be experienced in countries whose technology policy is organised in terms of what Ergas[32] has called a `mission-oriented' approach. In Europe, France would be the best example, with much of its government expenditure on science and technology, even in the civil field, going to `grands projets'. The thinking behind this approach is that demanding technological projects of a kind that catch the popular imagination (thus assisting the maintenance of long term political support) create demand for a variety of new technologies which then diffuse through the rest of the economy. In contrast, Ergas refers to `diffusion-oriented' technology policies, such as in Germany, where the emphasis is more on raising general levels of competence and on providing means for rapid diffusion of new technologies. Although `grands projets' can be in the civil sector (Concorde; the TGV), they have tended to be found more in the defence sector, so that any decline now will again hit harder in the countries with the bigger defence R&D expenditures.

Some Concluding Questions

1. Towards a Japanese model?

We have seen that the expected decline in defence spending within Europe is not occurring uniformly or at the speed that some had hoped for. Nor is it yet clear what its implications will be for the development and production of defence equipment, and therefore for the defence industrial base. Assuming, however, that the future will see significant reductions in demand for defence equipment, admittedly falling more heavily in some areas than others, then a problem arises about how to maintain a technologically dynamic defence sector, whether conceived in national or European or, indeed, in trans-Atlantic, terms.[33]

A potentially attractive response is to seek to adopt the `Japanese model'. Granting that Japanese efforts to build a capability in civil aircraft owe a lot to work on defence aircraft, it may be that the model for the future is nevertheless the general Japanese one of having what Drifte[34] has called defence production without a defence industry. That is, defence production is managed as a small part of the work of large, technologically dynamic companies, whose main competences and markets lie elsewhere. To a considerable extent, this was the position in Europe, especially Britain and Germany, in the second half of the Nineteenth century. The `high technology' of the day took the form of railways and similar civil engineering projects, from which technology base the great armourers, such as William Armstrong, emerged in response to favourable defence market conditions.

Whether European firms are capable organisationally of working in this way remains to be seen. One clue arises from their `defence dependence', that is, the percentage of total sale that arise from defence products. As Table 7.3 shows, there is considerable variation in this respect among the leading European defence contractors (although these data should be taken as only broadly indicative, not least because they are probably changing quite fast at present). Despite thc very different structures of the German and Italian defence industries, it is interesting that, in the firms Daimler-Benz and Siemens, on the one hand, and IRI and Fiat, on the other, they exemplify at least statistically the Japanese model.

But the statistical picture may be misleading. More often than not, the main European defence contractors organise defence production separately from the rest of their business, thus compartmentalising their technological assets. This trend is apparently to be continued by the new French high technology giant, Thomson CEA Industrie, with the defence arm of Thomson (Thomson-CSF) being kept separate, possibly to be merged with other defence concerns.[35] Whether this position can be changed is a key question for the years ahead. Opportunities may arise under the rubric of defence conversion, or as part of more general programmes aimed at technological regeneration. There may also be scope for studies of the possibilities for, and problems of, such change. Possibly the best place to start such studies would be in Germany, where the pressures to cut defence R&D spending will be among the greatest in Europe, and where the industrial strength in high technologies is closer than anywhere else in Europe to the Japanese. As Walker[36] has observed, not only is German high technology industry, in particular Daimler-Benz and Siemens, larger and more robust than its European counterparts, but it also has greater underlying strength in the supply of materials, components and sub-systems. It may thus be better prepared both politically and industrially for the technological shifts that the decline in defence spending may entail.

2. Danger of too much concentration?

The last few years have seen considerable concentration within the defence sector, both within and across national borders. Moves towards a single European market for armaments can only further encourage this tendency. The advantage of this process is that it creates larger and stronger firms, capable of maintaining the necessary technological and financial resources, and thus of competing internationally, particularly with US firms, in what is expected to be an increasingly tough market.

Following Porter[37], however, it can be argued that successful industries tend to revolve around a `cluster' of firms that spur each other on. Because of their geographical proximity, they generate local demand for appropriate training schemes, create work for a network of high quality suppliers, and provide the conditions for a sufficient labour force, and one that is mobile between firms, thus helping to diffuse best practice.

Table 7.3: 20 Largest defence contractors in Europe, 1988

Company	Country	Industry*	Arms Sales ($m)	% Total sales
British Aerospace	UK	AC EL MI	5,470	54
Daimler Benz[a]	Germany	AC EL MI ENG MV	5,410	12
Thomson SA[b]	France	A EL	5,370	47
GEC[c]	UK	EL SH	5,090	41
Aerospatiale	France	AC	2,300	49
DCN[d]	France	SH	2,210	100
IRI	Italy	AC ENG EL SH	2,100	6
Dassault	France	AC EL	2,080	70
EIFM	Italy	AC MV EL	1,520	43
Fiat	Italy	ENG MV A	1,500	4
Rolls-Royce	UK	ENG	1,410	40
Siemens[c]	Germany	EL	1,240	4
Thorn-EMI	UK	EL	1,200	20
GIAT	France	A MV	1,150	100
CASA	Spain	AC	980	65
Oerlikon	Switzerland	AC A EL	930	32
Vickers SEL	UK	SH MV	830	100
Nobel	Sweden	A EL MI	810	23
SNECMA	France	AC	770	45
Hawker Siddeley	UK	AL ENG	680	20

Notes
[a]Includes MBB acquired in 1989
[b]Includes Philips defence electronics, acquired in 1989
[c]Plessey, acquired by GEC and Siemens in 1988, divided equally between them
[d]Direction des Constructions Navales

*Industry Code: A = artillery, AC = aircraft, EL = electronics, ENG = engines, MI = missiles, MV = military vehicles, SH = ships

Source: Extracted from Table 7.2 in Anthony *et al.*, 1990a, with adjustments where there are obvious inaccuracies; the figures for arms sales should be treated as estimates.

To the extent that we accept this argument, and might wish to transpose it to the European level (Porter's own thinking being confined to national frameworks), two questions arise:

i) Do the geographical requirements of successful clusters, particularly their labour force needs, mean that the future European defence industry will need to achieve a higher degree of geographical proximity than at present? If so, would this coincide with centres of gravity of technological capability (the emerging European `technopoles') more generally? What would be the consequences for `outlying' regions?

ii) Is the process of mergers, acquisitions and other forms of inter-firm teaming that has characterised the European defence industry in recent years, moving beyond the point where realistic prospects of intra-European competition for major defence contracts can be maintained anyway, especially in the face of the reduced demand for defence equipment that may be expected? Put the other way around, is there a danger that, unless adequate regulatory steps are taken, the European defence industry may concentrate itself in such a way as to reduce competitive possibilities, unless that competition be imported from outside Europe? If, on the other hand, the `Japanese model' could be followed, then the risk of excessive concentration would be much reduced because a wider range of essentially civil firms would be involved in defence production.

3. An integrated (military/civil) science and technology base?

We have tried in this chapter to set in context the consequences of cuts in defence R&D for European technological capabilities. We have suggested that the consequences will not, on the whole, be as great as proponents of the defence industries have sometimes suggested.

At the same time, we accept that considerable technological advances will continue to arise from spending on defence R&D. Some, particularly perhaps in the aerospace sector, will from time to time have wider applicability. It therefore behoves us to think in terms of structures that will maximise the gain from these possibilities. Moreover, it remains the case that in some countries, and for some technologies, the defence sector is still *a* (if not *the*) prime source of R&D funds, though our detailed information on this point is inadequate at the level of specific technologies.

In addition, during the period of transition that we are now in, skilled people are being displaced from their jobs, and there is a considerable risk that they will find little comparable work to go to. A recent SIPRI estimate suggests that between 350,000 and 500,000 jobs in the defence and related industries could be lost in the European NATO countries between 1990-1995.[38]

This could result in a reduction in the scientific and technological labour pool available in Europe. While there would clearly be little point in maintaining capabilities for which there is no demand, the abruptness and (often) geographical concentration of defence cuts can mean that there is little chance of any alternative demand manifesting itself within a short time period.

Dealing with both these problems would be easier if governments (especially those for whom this represents a major change) began urgently to consider ways of developing defence and civil technologies out of a common technology base. There are limits to the extent to which this will be possible: some requirements will continue to be highly specific, or to need especially high security. But the scope for more action across the traditional military-civil divide is considerable. It is, in any case, likely to be increasingly in the interests of defence ministries to pursue this possibility in order to be able to cover the desired technological ground with budgets that may increasingly force them to focus their own resources on those things that have to be done within a defence context. This applies not only to technologies related to new products but also, and at least equally importantly, to new manufacturing technologies: developments in flexible manufacturing could be of great importance for the problem of seeking cost-effective production of small batches of sophisticated defence products.

The scope for such action will vary by country and by sector. Thus, in *aerospace*, where demand for civil aircraft is strong, and where military demand for helicopters is likely to persist whatever happens to demand for fixed wing aircraft, there is clearly scope to ease the transition for the relevant firms, which happen to lie mainly in France, Germany, Italy and the UK, and to an increasing extent in Spain. Similarly in *electronics*, there is great scope for using defence-originated capabilities as a springboard for entry into new markets, and for drawing upon the growing civil base, but in this sector the European firms (located mainly in France, Germany, Italy, Netherlands and the UK) will face the full force of Japanese and US competition. *Armoured vehicles* present fewer opportunities, although the expanding need for investment in rail transport and other infrastructures requiring heavy engineering may offer some prospects. *Shipbuilding* presents similar problems, though these are less than those faced by the *munitions* sector.

At the European level, there may also be scope for closer integration between EUCLID (the cooperative research programme of the IEPG countries) and the EC Framework Programme, not to mention EUREKA (bearing in mind the closer association now of the non-EC EUREKA partners in the European Economic Area). Much here will turn on the extent to which the Commission feels able to move into the defence area after the Maastricht Summit, and on how the debate about a European `defence identity' affects the possibilities for cooperation over technological programmes between the IEPG and the EC.[39]

4. Might the indirect effects of other policies matter more?

Finally, we should reflect on the possibility that, whatever steps might be taken along the lines outlined above, they may in the end be less significant than other measures associated with the Single Market, and with other forces at work on industry. As we have already seen, EC funding for science and technology is only a small fraction of total public spending in this field. In any case, decisions made by companies, according to the logic of their own individual circumstances and strategies, may be a stronger influence on Europe's technology base than the actions of governments, except perhaps in areas dominated by government rather than company R&D funding, such as aerospace. Action by the EC over procurement policy in general, over standards, and over competition and regulatory policy, as well as through the use of the Structural Funds, might also have a greater effect than any explicitly science and technology policy measures, whether civil or military.

To conclude, it is increasingly being appreciated that the capacity of countries and regions to act autonomously in future will depend more on economic than on military power. The question for Europe, therefore, is how to manage the present historic transition without losing the skills that lie in the defence sector, and while maintaining such dynamism as continues to be required in respect of defence technology. Governments are proving slow to adjust to the post-Cold War conditions - perhaps inevitably so, for the issues are profound and complex. As agreement is gradually reached over such matters as the details of NATO's new Strategic Concept, and the defence identity of Europe, so greater clarity may be expected over defence requirements, and hence over defence technologies also.

In the meantime, the firms that constitute the technological base for meeting those requirements have to formulate their own strategies for survival. Faced with declining markets and the threat of financial losses, they are having to respond to the new conditions faster than governments. They may in the process be foreclosing options that governments might, in time, wish had been kept open. The key requirement for firms at present is some sense of what governments will want from them. But this is precisely what governments are still having such difficulty in defining.

Endnotes

1. See Walker W., and Gummett, P., **Britain and the European Armaments Market**, *International Affairs*, 65, 1989, pp. 419-442; Taylor, T. and Hayward, K., **The UK Defence Industrial Base: Development and Future Policy Options**, London, Brassey's, 1989; Taylor, T., **Defence Industries in International Relations**, *Review of International Studies*, 16, 1990, pp. 59-73; and Moravcsik, A., **The European Armaments Industry at the Cross-Roads**, *Survival*, 32, 1990, pp. 65-85.

2. Vredeling Report, **Towards a Stronger Europe**, Report by an Independent Study Team established by Defence Ministers of Nations of the IEPG. Brussels, Independent European Programme Group, 1986.

3. Gummett, P. and Reppy, J. (eds.), **The Relations Between Defence and Civil Technologies**, Dordrecht, Klewer, 1988.

4. Collins, P. and Stein, J.A., **Science and Technology and the Single European Market**. Submitted to *Science and Public Policy* 1991.

5. Monopolies and Mergers Commission, **British Aerospace plc and Thomson-CSF SA: A Report on the Proposed Merger**, London, HMSO, Cm. 1416, 1991.

6. Reed, C., **EC Awards to Meet Fair Trade Rules**, *Jane's Defence Weekly*, 914, 9 November, 1991.

7. Findlay, G., **International Collaboration**. In *Science and Technology in the United Kingdom*, edited by Sir Robin Nicholson, C. Cunningham and P. Gummett, Harlow, Longman, 1991, p. 278.

8. Gummett, P. (ed), **Future Relations Between Defence and Civil Science and Technology**, A Report for the (UK) Parliamentary Office of Science and Technology Review Paper No. 2, Science Policy Support Group, London, 1991, appendix 1; National Audit Office, **Classification of Defence Research and Development Expenditure**, HMSO, London, HC 105, 1991.

9. Peel, Q., **Time to Spread the Wealth**, *Financial Times*, 24 September 1991.

10. Molas-Gallart, J., **Spanish Participation in the International Development and Production of Arms Systems**, *Defense Analysis*, 6, 1990, pp. 351-65.

11. Britain is planning to cut the Royal Navy by 13%, the Army by 28% and the Royal Air Force by 16% over the next few years. The effect on the equipment budget is expected to be of the order of 6% in real terms over three to four years (Ministry of Defence, **Statement on the Defence Estimates 1991**, London, HMSO, 1991, Cm. 1559). France is planning to cut its army by 20% by 1997 (Isnard, J., **L'Armée de Terre Perdra le Cinqième de ses Effectifs**, *Le Monde*, 14 November 1991). All France's major non-nuclear programmes are to be preserved (Lewis, J., **Joxe Preserves Major French Programmes**, *Jane's Defence Weekly*, 987, 23 November 1991). The biggest cuts in Europe so far announced are those in Germany, where force levels are to be reduced by 40% over the next four years, and the equipment budget is to be reduced by 2.3 billion ecu annually by the mid-1990s (Inglewood, Lord, and Huxham, Q., **The Defence Industry after the IGC's**, The Bow Group, London, 1991, pp. 7-8).

12. Clark, A., Speech on **Defence and High Technology Industries**, London, World Economic Forum, 4 September 1991. Available from the Ministry of Defence as News Release 106/91.

13. Ministry of Defence 1991, *op. cit.*, para. 622.

14. Cabinet Office, **Annual Review of Government Funded Research and Development 1991**, HMSO, London, 1991, Table 1.2.2.

15. Mears, A.L., **Serving the Customer**, *RSRE Bulletin*, 1990.

16. Vincent, C., **La Recherche est Confirmée comme une "Priorité Majeure"**, *Le Monde*, 26 September 1991.

17. Dawkin, W., **French N-Research to Shed 4,000 (sic) Jobs**, *Financial Times*, 9 November 1991. The 4,000 must be a misprint, and would make no sense given the scale of the military applications division of the CEA; the figure of 400 is given in the body of the article.

18. Insard, J., **La France Relance un Projet d'Hélicoptère Radar**, *Le Monde*, 29 October, 1991.

19. One test of whether such policies are actually being pursued will be to monitor the percentage of defence budgets that are allocated to equipment, as opposed to personnel. In Britain, this has fallen from 46 per cent in 1985-86 to 39 per cent in 1991-92.

20. Graziola, G., and Nones, M., **Recent Trends in R&D in Italy and in Military R&D in Particular**, in Gummett, P. and Reppy, J. (eds.), *op. cit.*, 1988, pp. 213-226.

21. **L'Armement: Revue de la Délégation Générale pour l'Armement**, No. 29, Paris, October 1991, p. 3.

22. These terms are themselves inadequate. They suggest too sharp a dichotomy between the defence and civil sectors, missing, for example, the shading between defence and `quasi-defence customers' like the nuclear industry or PTTs which resemble defence ministries in being expert and monopsonistic customers with high technical requirements. However, possible alternative terms have other difficulties. For example, `generic technologies', which captures part of the sense intended here, is sometimes used to refer to too narrow a set of technologies for our purposes. Because of its widespread currency, we will use the term `dual-use' technologies.

23. McLain, L., **Concorde Heirs Fly to the Future**, *Financial Times*, 1 August 1990.

24. Gummett, P., 1991, *op. cit.*, especially section 4.3.3. and appendix 6.

25. Edmonds, M., Hayhurst, G. and Uttley, M.R.H., **Defence-Critical Technology, Dependence and Civil Conversion: the Challenge to the UK Technological Base**, University of Lancaster Mimeo, 1990, p. 9.

26. Leadbeater, C., **Industry Urged to Speed Up R&D**, *Financial Times*, 24 may 1990.

27. Clark, *op. cit.*

28. Commission of the European Communities, **A Competitive European Aeronautical Industry (Communication from the Commission)**, SEC(90) 1456 final, Brussels, July 1990, para. 5.2 and Annex 6.

29. See the letter of 17 June 1991 from Sir Roland Smith, then chairman of British Aerospace, to the leader of the UK Opposition, Mr Neil Kinnock, as published in **The Guardian**, 4 October 1991, in which he complained of the damage that MOD policies were doing to British manufacturing industry; and the call by M. Henri Martre, chairman of Aerospatiale, for greater EC support for the aerospace industry through research and technology contracts (Betts, P., Allebeck, A. and Wulf, H., **Western European Arms Production: Structural Changes in the New Political Environment**, SIPRI, Stockholm, 1990).

30. For more details see Chapter 1; and various chapters in Gummett and Reppy, 1988, *op. cit.*; and Hartley, K., and Singleton, J., **Defence R&D and Crowding-Out**, *Science and Public Policy*, Vol. 17, No. 3, June 1990, pp. 152-157.

31. See Gummett, 1991, *op. cit.*, section 4.2.2 and Appendix 7 for a more complete discussion.

32. Ergas, H., **Does Technology Matter?**, OECD, Paris, 1986, mimeo.

33. US-CREST, **Cooperative Strategies: High Technology Security Cooperation - A Transatlantic Industrial Perspective**, US-CREST/Hudson Institute, Arlington Va., 1991.

34. Drifte, R., **Arms Production in Japan: The Military Application of Civilian Technology**, Westview, Boulder Colorado, 1986.

35. Dawkins, W., **Cresson's Champions**, *Financial Times*, 19 December 1992; and leading article on 18 December.

36. Walker, W., **Defence**, in Freeman, C., Sharp, M. and Walker, W., *Technology and the Future of Europe*, Pinter, London, 1991, pp. 365-82, at 379.

Chapter 8

The Political Economy of International Collaboration

Keith Hartley and Stephen Martin

Introduction

Purchasing defence equipment is costly and the trends are towards rising costs in real terms. A modern combat aircraft such as the European Fighter Aircraft might cost £8 billion to develop and its unit production costs might be some £30 million per aircraft. Moreover, new equipment is more expensive than the generation which it replaces (although the new equipment is more effective): typically, the real unit production costs of defence equipment (aircraft, helicopters, missiles, warships, submarines) increases by about 10 per cent a year implying a doubling in cost every 7.25 years[1]. Because defence budgets usually fail to match equipment cost increases, there are inevitable downward pressures on the size and formation of the armed forces, and associated imperatives to re-structure the defence industries which supply the forces. Since the signing of the 1990 CFE Treaty, European nations are reducing defence expenditure and will be seeking to increase the efficiency with which they use their limited and declining budgets. Inevitably, there will be a search for lower cost methods of acquiring expensive weapons systems.

Defence procurement can take a number of forms, each with different cost implications. The options range from national development and manufacture (self-sufficiency), through collaborative ventures, co-production, licensed production and offsets, to off-the-shelf purchase (imports). Each procurement strategy offers the purchaser varying degrees of indigenous involvement in the development and production of the equipment, and hence a different degree of support and protection for the national defence industrial base (DIB).

Protecting the DIB, however, is not costless. Compared with importing, independence is an expensive option: as Michael Heseltine, the former British Minister for Defence, has pointed out, there are few things you cannot buy cheaper from the USA[2]. Faced with constant or declining real defence budgets and an ever-increasing cost of the latest technology hardware, the leading European nations have increasingly forsaken national development programmes. Rather than buy off-the-shelf from American manufacturers, European governments have attempted to retain some domestic capability by pursuing collaborative development and production schemes for a range of equipment procurement programmes. Declining defence budgets and the trend towards greater economic and political union in the EC is likely to give a renewed emphasis to collaboration. Collaboration offers states the opportunity of retaining a defence industrial capability by sharing high technology work and it is likely to become more important as defence cuts deepen. As a result, it is likely to become a preferred policy between the extremes of independence and importing.

This chapter examines the characteristics, extent and results of collaboration. The first section analyses the rationale behind collaboration and presents the stylised facts of previous and current collaborative ventures. There follows a comparative evaluation of the performance of collaborative programmes and national ventures using three performance indicators: development times, production runs and cost. Third, the results are then assessed from a different perspective: a public choice analysis is employed to consider how and why collaboration and the creation of a European DIB might impact upon demands for reduced defence spending and the opportunities for conversion. Finally, the chapter concludes with various policy recommendations.

Trends in Collaboration

This section presents the stylised facts about international collaboration in the European defence industries, and civil aerospace sector (where the motives for such civilian ventures have been similar to those behind military undertakings and the same nations and firms have been involved with both joint civil and military programmes). To provide an overview of characteristics, the analysis considers: how much collaboration there has been; which nations have been involved; the type of products which have been developed collaboratively; and the organisational arrangements for these joint ventures.

Rationales for Collaboration

Table 8.1 provides details of current collaborative ventures in aerospace. Joint ventures in the three sectors of the aerospace industry (aircraft, aero-engine, and missiles) were commenced at the beginning of the 1960s. Previously, there had been several examples of European production of US-designed aircraft, but the first European projects involving two or more nations sharing *development* work were the Breguet Atlantic, an anti-submarine aircraft (including Belgium, France, Germany and the Netherlands), and the Transall C-160 military transport aircraft (involving France and Germany). Enthusiasm for these early joint ventures came largely from France which saw collaboration as a means of developing its own national aerospace industry[3]. Political motives also lay behind the UK's entry into the collaborative club with the project to develop a civil supersonic airliner (Concorde, 1962). The British government envisaged that the Anglo-French venture would convince France of Britain's commitment to Europe and enhance the UK's chances of being admitted to the EEC, hitherto blocked by the French government[4].

For military goods an added attraction of collaborative development was in improving NATO equipment standardisation and inter-operability. Theoretically, collaboration offered both economic and operational benefits: reducing the number of combat aircraft types within the NATO inventory, for example, would reduce stocks of spares; pilots of one nationality could fly aircraft of other NATO members; and aircraft could be serviced and repaired at bases throughout the Alliance.

Collaboration in the civil and military aero-engine sectors and missile development and production was also initiated in the early 1960s. Like France, Germany (formerly FGR) saw collaboration as a way of improving its domestic aerospace capability: the first collaborative aero-engine project was the Rolls Royce/MAN RB 153 engine (Germany-UK) developed for the (later abandoned) EWR-Sud VJ101D supersonic VTOL aircraft. The first civil aero-engine development was the Rolls-Royce/SNECMA Olympus 593 engine for Concorde. Amongst the earliest of collaborative missile projects were ventures involving Nord (France) and MBB (FRG) to develop two surface-to-surface missiles (HOT and Milan) and one surface-to-air missile (Roland). Britain's involvement commenced in the mid-1960s with the Martel air-to-surface missile (France-UK). Finally, the European Space Agency (ESA) started operations in 1975 and combined the activities previously undertaken by the European Space Research Organisation and the European Launcher Development Organisation. ESA aims to promote co-operation between European states in the peaceful pursuit of space research and technology.

Economic factors can be added to the list of military and political reasons for collaboration in aerospace. In particular, the aerospace industry exhibits a number of characteristics which, when taken together, encourage nations to share the development and production of new products. First, R&D is extremely costly and risky; second, production is often subject to substantial learning and scale economies; and third, significant development and production costs often have to be recovered over a relatively small domestic market. Together these factors imply that unit R&D costs can be a relatively high proportion of total unit costs and that unit production costs depend, to a large extent, on the often related issues of the length and speed of the production run. Collaboration offers the opportunity to ameliorate the effect on costs of both a high R&D burden and short production runs inherent in a European state manufacturing for a small domestic market[5].

Consider R&D first. International collaboration saves on duplication of R&D and offers the opportunity to spread risks and costs between more than one nation. If collaboration does not add to a project's total R&D costs, then with three equal partners only one R&D budget is required with each nation paying one-third of what a national project would have cost. So, for an R&D project costing £3 billion, aggregate R&D expenditure is reduced from £9 billion for three independent ventures to £3 billion for a joint programme, with each nation paying only £1 billion.

Table 8.1: Current Joint Ventures in Aerospace

Project	**Year**	**Joint Company**	**Owners and shareholding or Participants and workshares**		**Project type**
(a) **Aircraft**					
Jaguar	1966	SEPECAT	British Aerospace Dassault	50% 50%	Strike aircraft
Gazelle	1967	N/A	Aerospatiale Westland	60% 40%	Multi-purpose helicopter
Lynx	1967	N/A	Aerospatiale Westland	30% 70%	Multi-purpose helicopter
Puma	1967	N/A	Aerospatiale Westland	90% 10%	Multi-purpose helicopter
Airbus	1969	Airbus Industrie GIE	Aerospatiale British Aerospace Deutsche Aerospace CASA	37.9% 20% 37.9% 4.2%	Family of civil transports
Alpha-Jet	1969	N/A	Dassault Dornier	50% 50%	Trainer/ light attack
Harrier	1973	N/A	British Aerospace McDonnell Douglas	50% 50%	V/STOL close support aircraft
BK 117	1977	N/A	Deutsche Aerospace Kawasaki	50% 50%	Multi-purpose helicopter
CN-235	1980	Aircraft Technology Industries	CASA IPTN	50% 50%	Turboprop utility transport
AMX	1980	AMX International Ltd	Aeritalia Aermacchi Embraer	46.5% 23.8% 29.7%	Fighter/strike

Table 8.1 continued

EH 101	1980	EH Industries Ltd	Agusta Westland	50% 50%	Multi-purpose helicopter
ATR 42/72	1981	ATR GIE	Aerospatiale Aeritalia	50% 50%	Turboprop utility transport
European Fighter Aircraft	1983	Eurofighter GmbH	Aeritalia British Aerospace CASA Deutsche Aerospace	21% 33% 13% 33%	Combat aircraft
X-31A EFM	1984	N/A	Rockwell Deutsche Aerospace	75% 25%	Experimental fighter aircraft
Euro-copter	1984	Eurocopter GIE	Aerospatiale Deutsche Aerospace	50% 50%	Anti-tank helicopter
MPC 75	1985	MPC Aircraft GmbH	Deutsche Aerospace CATIC	50% 50%	Turbofan regional transport
NH 90	1985	N/A	Aerospatiale Agusta Deutsche Aerospace Fokker	36.5% 36.5% 22% 5%	Multi-purpose helicopter
CBA-123	1987	N/A	Embraer FAMA	70% 30%	Turboprop transport
K-8	1987	N/A	NAMC PAC	50% 50%	Jet trainer/ light attack aircraft
TBM 700	1987	TBM SA	Socata (Aerospatiale) Mooney	70% 30%	Turboprop passenger transport
S-21/ Gulfstream VI	1989	N/A	Sukhoi Gulfstream	50% 50%	Supersonic business transport

Table 8.1 continued

European US SST	1990	N/A	Aerospatiale Boeing British Aerospace Deutsche Aerospace McDonnell Douglas		New generation supersonic passenger transport
(b) **Aero-engines**					
Adour	1966	Rolls- Royce Turbomeca Ltd	Rolls-Royce Turbomeca	50% 50%	For Jaguar aircraft
RB 199	1969	Turbo Union Ltd	Fiat MTU Rolls-Royce	20% 40% 40%	For Tornado aircraft
CFM 56	1971	CFM Inter- national	General Electric SNECMA	50% 50%	Family of engines
V2500	1983	Inter- national Aero Engines AG	Fiat Japanese Aero-Engines MTU Pratt & Whitney Rolls-Royce	6% 23% 11% 30% 30%	Family of engines
MTR 390	1986	MTU- Turbomeca- RR GmbH	MTU Rolls-Royce Turbomeca	33% 33% 33%	For Eurocopter helicopter
EJ 2000	1986	Eurojet Turbo GmbH	Fiat MTU Rolls-Royce Sener	21% 33% 33% 13%	For European Fighter Aircraft
New SST	1990	N/A	Lyulka Rolls-Royce	50% 50%	For S-12/ engine Gulfstream VI
(c) **Missiles**					
Milan	1962	Euromissile	Aerospatiale Deutsche Aerospace	50% 50%	Medium range anti-tank
HOT	1964	Euromissile	Aerospatiale Deutsche Aerospace	50% 50%	Long range anti-tank

Table 8.1 continued

Roland	1964	Euromissile	Aerospatiale Deutsche Aerospace	50% 50%	Surface-to-air
Martel	1964	N/A	British Aerospace Engins Matra	50% 50%	Air-to-surface
Otomat	1969	N/A	Engins Matra OTO Melara	50% 50%	Anti-ship
TRIGAT	1979	Euromissile	Aerospatiale British Aerospace Deutsche Aerospace	33% 33% 33%	Anti-tank (replace HOT and Milan)
ADATS	1979	N/A	Oerlikon-Buhrle Martin Marietta	50% 50%	Air defence, anti-tank system
ASRAAM	1982	N/A	British Aerospace Raufoss (Norway)	50% 50%	Air-to-air
Apache/ CWS 50	1983	N/A	Engins Matra Deutsche Aerospace	50% 50%	Air-to-surface
MSS 1.1	1986	N/A	OTO Melara Orbita Sistemas	50% 50%	Anti-tank
MSOW	1987	N/A	Two competing international consortia		Two medium range, one long range
ANS	1987	N/A	Aerospatiale Deutsche Aerospace	50% 50%	Anti-ship; also air-to-surface
(d) **Space**					
ESA	1975	ESA	13 nations		Civil space research and satellites

Source: **Jane's All The World's Aircraft**, **Jane's Weapon Systems**, various issues

More likely is that a collaborative R&D project will cost more than a comparable national one[6]. This collaborative premium may result from:

(i) increased administration costs associated with co-ordinating a project involving scientists and engineers from several countries;
(ii) the duplication of some R&D work, through, for example, each participant wanting its own flight test centre and/or development aircraft; and
(iii) the need to harmonize different operational requirements and national standards.

Even with a 50 per cent collaboration premium, however, each nation's R&D contribution on a tri-lateral venture will still be one-half of that for a comparable national project. One frequently cited rule of thumb is that the R&D costs for a collaborative project will exceed those for a comparable national venture by a factor of the square root of the number of partner nations. Thus in the case of a bi-national project, total R&D costs will exceed those for a comparable national venture by about 40 per cent although each participant will save about one-third of the cost of national development.

Reduced duplication and the spreading of R&D costs between partner nations is only one source of potential cost savings. International collaboration also offers the opportunity to exploit more fully any learning and scale economies in the production process by pooling the participants orders and thus increasing the rate and length of the production run. Economies of scale relate the unit cost of production to the level of output per time period. Supporters of collaboration point out that individual national European orders for, say, a fighter aircraft are too small to permit each domestic supplier to produce at the minimum efficient scale where most worthwhile scale economies have been achieved. In marked contrast, American fighter aircraft are typically ordered in much larger quantities. This means that their unit production cost can be far below those for a comparable European design. For combat aircraft, US production runs for their national forces of 1,000-2,000 units are typical at a rate of 12.5-15 units per month. In France and the UK, combat aircraft production runs for their domestic requirements might be 200-400 units, at a rate of two to five per month[7].

United States firms are also said to benefit from longer production runs through the existence of substantial and continuous learning economies, particularly in the production of aircraft. Learning economies relate the unit cost of production to the level of **cumulative** output, and there is a substantial body of evidence which suggests that these economies can make a significant contribution to the reduction of unit production costs. Labour learning curves of 75 per cent to 80 per cent are not uncommon in the aircraft industry[8]. In other words, man-hours per aircraft fall by about 20 per cent to 25 per cent for each doubling of cumulative output, which means that unit production costs fall by about 10 per cent. Supporters of collaboration argue that by pooling their national orders for, say, a fighter aircraft, European production runs can approach those of US manufacture. For example,

Britain intended to procure 385 Tornado aircraft but by collaborating with Germany and Italy, initial planned production was increased to 809 aircraft - similar to the number of F15 fighter aircraft purchased by the Americans. Consequently, international collaboration with lengthened production runs, learning and scale economies can reduce European unit procurement costs. In addition, European products are also at less of a cost disadvantage in comparison to rival US firms for export markets.

From the late-1950s the cost of independently developing state of the art aerospace systems began to exceed what a number of European countries were willing to pay. International collaboration promised the opportunity to reduce financial constraints and simultaneously retain and/or develop some independent industrial capability. Because the development and production costs of aerospace systems continue to increase[9], it can be expected that collaboration will continue to increase in significance.

The Organisation of Collaborative Projects

Table 8.1 provides details of current and previous joint ventures in aerospace. In some cases the project was overseen by a committee composed of representatives drawn from the participating firms and governments (eg Concorde). In others a new jointly-owned company was formed by the prime contractors (eg EH Industries Ltd.). A third type of organisation is where a company acts as the project leader and prime contractor and other partners as sub-contractors (eg the Aerospatiale-Westland helicopter package). The organisation and delegation of responsibility for a joint venture may have important consequences for project performance (eg cost escalation, delays, exports). On most performance indicators, for example, the Concorde project fell far short of the Anglo-French helicopter package. This might in part reflect the fact that Concorde was overseen by committee with responsibility shared between the partners, whereas on all three Aerospatiale-Westland ventures there was a single project leader with the other partner acting as a sub-contractor.

Related to the issue of project organisation is the issue of how project costs and work are shared between participants. Typically, work shares reflect cost shares and, in the case of military products, a country's work share is usually based on the percentage of total production which its government plans to buy. However, problems arise from exchange rate variations, or where governments reduce their planned orders.

The variety of organisational arrangements reflect experimentation and/or the benefits of learning and experience from previous projects. For example, Concorde relied on committee organisation with joint committees representing the purchasing governments and the partner airframe and engine companies. A few years later the Tornado project was organised quite differently: single international companies were responsible for airframe (Panavia) and engine contracts

(Turbo-Union), together with a single organisation to represent the governments of the partner nations (NAMMA). Organisational arrangements are likely to change through time as different firms and nations learn how to do business with each other. Learning effects might lead these arrangements to become more efficient as experience of joint ventures increases.

How Much Collaboration in Aerospace?

One indicator of the importance of collaborative ventures in aerospace is a measure of the defence resources allocated to them. For the UK and France, collaborative defence projects account for 15 per cent of defence equipment expenditure, and for Germany the corresponding figure is 25 per cent with a further 20 per cent on co-production[10]. Moreover, for the UK, air systems accounted for 95 per cent of all UK collaborative expenditure, reflecting technical complexity and the relatively high proportion of development costs in total procurement costs[11]. However, because of the difficulty of obtaining cost data (particularly for military equipment), and of ensuring the accuracy and comparability across nations of available figures, three more readily calculable measures of the level of collaborative activity have been used. These are:

(i) the absolute number of collaborative projects;
(ii) the percentage of all projects which are collaborative; and
(iii) the number of partners per collaborative project.

Absolute trends in the number of collaborative projects

Table 8.2 reports the number of civil and military collaborative projects in the aircraft, aero-engine and missiles industries, classified by start date to one of three ten-year periods. Though determining collaboration commencement accurately can prove difficult, the date employed is that when participants first signed a contract. Importantly, only projects which have not been subsequently cancelled are included so the recent data may tend to overstate project numbers because of the risk of future cancellation (eg EFA).

Table 8.2 reveals that international collaboration in aerospace in the 1960s was largely intra-European. Most projects involved exclusively European partners whilst the remainder had at least one European partner. In the following decade two trends are noticeable. First, there is a decline in the absolute number of new collaborative projects (from 27 to 14) in all three sectors. Various reasons can be put forward to account for this. First, because of the long life-cycle of aerospace systems, projects initiated in the 1960s would not require replacement in the following decade. Second, many European economies in the 1970s suffered recession, uncertainty and structural change following the substantial increase in the price of oil in 1973. Governments may have been more reluctant and less able to embark upon costly aerospace projects than they had been in the previous decade.

Table 8.2: Number of Collaborative Projects

Period	**Aircraft**				**Aero-Engines**				**Missiles**				**All Projects**			
	a	b	c	d	a	b	c	d	a	b	c	d	a	b	c	d
1960s	9	0	0	9	7	1	0	8	8	2	0	10	24	3	0	27
1970s	4	1	1	6	1	2	0	3	1	4	0	5	6	7	1	14
1980s	9	10	2	21	2	2	0	4	7	4	0	11	18	16	2	36
Whole period	22	11	3	36	10	5	0	15	16	10	0	26	48	26	3	77

Notes: Column a lists the number of projects with European only participants; Column b lists the number of projects with at least one European participant; Column c lists the number of projects without a European participant; and Column d = Column a + Column b + Column c.
Data based on date of start of collaboration.

Source: **Jane's All The World's Aircraft**, **Jane's Weapon Systems**, Janes Publishing Company, London, various issues

The second trend during the 1970s was the increase in the proportion of projects with a non-European partner (50 per cent rather than 11 per cent in the 1960s). This partially reflected the fact that as aerospace became more costly fewer nations could afford independent development, and began viewing collaboration as a way of maintaining some independent national development and production capability. In addition, developing countries (eg Brazil, Argentina, Pakistan) entered the aerospace sector and collaboration offered the least-cost route to market entry. It is also noticeable that the decline in new projects was not spread evenly across all sectors of the industry: the number of aircraft ventures, for example, fell by one third whereas aero-engines declined at twice this level.

During the 1980s the proportion of non-European partners remained at about 50 per cent. In addition, the trend towards fewer collaborative projects was reversed, most notably for aircraft. This pattern reflected the replacement of systems developed during the 1960s and increasing development costs.

Relative trends in the number of collaborative projects

Does this analysis of the absolute number of collaborative projects accurately reflect the importance of collaborative activity? That is, though the number of collaborative ventures may be declining, have the number of independent national projects declined more quickly, implying an increase in the relative importance of joint ventures. To examine this possibility the percentage of new projects which are collaborative has been calculated for the leading collaborative nations (Table 8.3).

Table 8.3: Collaborative Projects and All Projects

Collaborative projects as a percentage of all projects

	1960s	1970s	1980s	whole period
(a) **Aircraft**				
France	36%	18%	73%	38%
Germany	44%	56%	83%	63%
Italy	10%	0%	73%	35%
Spain	100%	33%	100%	82%
UK	27%	17%	53%	35%
All five nations	17%	14%	55%	26%
(b) **Aero-engines**				
France	25%	50%	25%	30%
Germany	57%	*	100%	73%
UK	57%	33%	43%	50%
All three nations	31%	33%	36%	33%
(c) **Missiles**				
France	43%	0%	47%	37%
Germany	80%	20%	91%	71%
Italy	50%	50%	75%	56%
All three nations	33%	20%	48%	36%

Notes 1) Key: * = no projects, collaborative or otherwise
2) the figure for *all three (five) nations* is the number of collaborative projects involving at least one of the three (five) nations as a percentage of all projects involving at least one of the three (five) nations

Source: As Table 8.2

At the aggregate level a pattern emerges for all three sectors: the percentage of all projects which are collaborative was higher in the 1980s than in the 1960s (when the first collaborative projects commenced). Nevertheless, the increase in the proportion of new joint projects varied between five percentage points for aero-engines and a 38 percentage point increase for aircraft. In addition, whereas the level of collaboration remained largely unchanged in the 1970s for aircraft and for aero-engines, it declined markedly for missiles - a decline which was more than reversed in the 1980s.

A number of reasons for the lull in collaborative activity in the 1970s can be identified. As we have already noted many high technology projects have a long (twenty-year) life-cycle and projects initiated in the 1960s were not replaced until the 1980s (eg the Tornado aircraft and the EFA). There may also have been some initial disappointment with the performance of early joint ventures (eg Concorde, Airbus) making governments reluctant to fund new projects until the successful performance of existing programmes was established.

Table 8.4: Partner Nations per Collaborative Project

Aircraft			
Period	Mean	Median	Mode
1960s	2.4	2	2
1970s	2.3	2	2
1980s	2.9	2	2
whole period	2.7	2	2
Aero-engines			
1960s	2.1	2	2
1970s	2.0	2	2
1980s	3.5	4	4
whole period	2.5	2	2
Missiles			
1960s	2.5	2	2
1970s	4.0	4	4
1980s	3.4	2	2
whole period	3.2	2	2

Source: As Table 8.2

Number of partner nations per project

Another indicator of the level of collaborative activity is the number of partners per joint venture (Table 8.4). The results for all three sectors are similar for the whole period: the median and the mode yield a figure of two partner nations per project, while the mean number of partners varies from 2.5 for aero-engines to 3.2 for missiles. Similarly, the upward trend in the mean number of partners between the 1960s and the 1980s is also common to the three product groups.

Who Collaborates With Whom?

To complete the picture of collaborative activity in aerospace, Table 8.5 shows which nations have been involved with collaborative aircraft ventures, and with which international partners. As expected the larger European economies have been most active in collaborative projects and, not surprisingly, these nations have largely collaborated with each other. The same analysis for missiles and aero-engines reveals a similar picture, though France and the FRG have collaborated significantly less on aero-engines than aircraft. Further, both countries have worked with the UK on aero-engines rather than with each other, reflecting the fact that the French and German aero-engine industries were less advanced than the UK industry. Collaborating with the British enabled both France and Germany to acquire technology which would have otherwise been more costly to develop indigenously.

Table 8.5: Nations in Collaborative Aircraft Projects

	France	**FRG**	**UK**	**Italy**	**Spain**	**Netherlands**	**USA**	**Others**
France	-							
Germany	12	-						
UK	9	7	-					
Italy	4	4	6	-				
Spain	6	6	6	4	-			
Netherlands	2	3	1	2	1	-		
USA	2	3	3	1	1	0	-	
Others	2	3	0	1	1	0	1	-
Total projects	19	19	16	9	9	4	7	3

Notes: i) For separate identification in this table a nation must have collaborated on more than two projects
ii) Sample period 1959-90

Source: Calculated from **Jane's All The World's Aircraft**, various issues

Collaboration on Other Military Equipment

Hitherto, the focus has been on collaborative ventures in aircraft, aero-engines and missiles. These are the sectors in which most of the resources devoted to collaboration have been spent, and where data are available. However, other equipment has been developed and produced collaboratively (Table 8.6). Missiles are included in Table 8.6 for comparative purposes, but aircraft, helicopters and aero-engines are omitted.

Table 8.6: Number of Collaborative Projects by Equipment Type, 1960-89

Type of military equipment	Number of projects
a) *Electronics-based projects*	
Airborne radar	4
Army fire control	3
Electronic warfare equipment (air)	1
Electronic warfare equipment (land)	1
Electronic warfare equipment (sea)	1
Electro-optical systems (land)	3
Ground radar (electronics)	2
Land based air defence	2
Naval fire control	5
Naval radar	2
Sonar and underwater detection	2
Underwater warfare	5
(b) *Missile-based projects*	
Anti-tank/assault	5
Coastal defence systems	1
Missiles not elsewhere specified	10
Mobile guided SAMs	3
Shipborne surface-to-air weapons	5
Shipborne weapons	2
(c) *Other weapons systems*	
Aircraft armaments	1
Army ordnance	1
Drones and RPVs	2
Total number of collaborative projects	61

Source: **Jane's Weapons Systems**, various issues.

Table 8.6 also disaggregates military equipment into three broad classes: missiles, electronics and other. Table 8.7 reports the number and percentage of the collaborative projects identified in Table 8.6 when allocated to the three broad headings. Table 8.7 shows that over the period as a whole there has been a broadly similar division between the number of electronics-based projects and the number of missile-based projects. However, this aggregation over the entire sample period masks a marked trend away from missiles and towards electronics in the population of all collaborative projects in the 1970s and 1980s. In line with the overall growth in collaborative activity, this relative increase in collaboration in electronics probably reflects the increasing real cost of sophisticated electronic systems.

Table 8.7: Trends in Collaboration

	Broad Type of Weapon System Hardware			
Period	Missiles	Electronics	Other	Total
1960s	10 (77%)	3 (23%)	0 (0%)	13 (100%)
1970s	5 (42%)	5 (42%)	2 (16%)	12 (100%)
1980s	11 (31%)	23 (64%)	2 (6%)	36 (100%)
Whole period	26 (43%)	31 (51%)	4 (7%)	61 (100%)

Note: Table shows the number and percentage of collaborative weapons systems by broad type for the 1960s to 1980s
Source: Calculated from Table 8.6

Table 8.8 provides further details on the other collaborative weapons systems as shown in Table 8.6 by reporting the number of such collaborative projects each nation has been involved in over three ten-year periods. For each period two figures are given: column (a) refers to all weapons systems; column (b) refers to missile-based projects only. At the aggregate level the quantitative pattern of collaboration in the development of other weapons systems mirrors aircraft and aero-engine industries: increases in activity during the 1960s, a sharp decline in the 1970s and increases, of varying degrees, in the 1980s. In absolute terms, the recovery was greatest in the weapons systems sector with almost three times as many collaborative projects in the 1980s as in the 1960s.

Table 8.8: Collaboration by Nations and Equipment

	1960s		**1970s**		**1980s**		**Whole period**	
	(a)	(b)	(a)	(b)	(a)	(b)	(a)	(b)
France	9	8	2	0	18	9	29	17
Germany	7	5	5	1	20	10	32	16
UK	2	1	2	0	18	5	22	6
Italy	7	4	2	1	8	2	17	7
USA	3	1	5	2	15	3	23	6
Netherlands	3	1	2	2	2	1	7	4
Norway	2	1	2	1	1	1	5	3
Canada	0		2	0	6	2	8	2
Spain	0		0		4	2	4	2
Denmark	2	1	2	1	1	0	5	2
Belgium	2	1	1	1	0		3	2
Greece	0		0		1	0	1	0
Australia	0		0		1	0	1	0
Total projects	13	10	7	2	34	10	53	22

Key: Column a refers to all weapons systems; column b refers to missile-based projects only.
Note: Sample for all weapons systems excludes privately-funded projects (n=8); sample for missile-based projects excludes privately-funded projects (n=4).
Source: As for Table 8.6

In summary, the analysis of the pattern of international collaboration in the aerospace and other military equipment industries has identified five features. *First*, that there has been a movement away from national projects towards collaboration, whilst the tendency has been for the number of partners per collaborative project to increase. *Second*, in aerospace collaboration was almost entirely intra-European in the 1960s. In the last two decades, however, other nations, particularly the USA, have participated in joint ventures though it is unusual for a collaborative venture not to include a European partner. *Third*, collaboration is not restricted to aerospace: a wide variety of military products have been developed and produced collaboratively. In absolute terms these projects are approximately equally divided between missiles and electronics. During the 1980s, however, collaborative electronic systems have outnumbered missile-based projects by more than two to one. *Fourth*, the leading collaborative nations are France, Germany and the UK, in both the aerospace industry and for all military equipment, though Italy, the Netherlands and the USA have also been involved. *Finally*, a variety of organisational arrangements have been devised for the administration and co-ordination of joint projects. How these arrangements might affect the performance of a collaborative venture is analysed in the next section.

Evaluating Collaborative Projects

Numerous problems confront an assessment of the performance of collaborative projects including identifying an alternative to which joint ventures can be compared. Ideally, a counter-factual approach would be adopted: what would have happened if a national venture had been undertaken? Because this is not possible, actual collaborative ventures have been compared with an ideal model and similar national projects. Here, questions arise as to whether European collaborative ventures should be compared with European national ventures or with American projects. Which is the relevant alternative?

Another complication is the necessity of comparing like with like. There are never two identical projects, let alone one a national and the other a collaborative venture. Thus when comparing the performance of two or larger groups of projects it is important to establish that they are sufficiently similar for comparisons to be meaningful. Problems also arise when we seek to extrapolate the performance of future collaborative ventures from past ones. As joint projects are a relatively new form of industrial organisation learning effects may mean that recent projects (eg Tornado; Airbus A310) are performing better than their predecessors (eg Jaguar; Airbus A300B).

Finally, how is the performance of any project to be measured? Profitability, the usual indicator of market efficiency, has a number of limitations. Accounts for joint ventures are usually submerged within the accounts for the participating firms so identifying costs and revenues in a particular project can rarely be isolated. Also, there are often hidden subsidies and preferential purchasing arrangements for domestic manufacturers, particularly in the aerospace industry. Furthermore, profits from the sale of equipment to defence ministries can be subject to government regulation and control. Nevertheless, the alternative indicators reviewed below can be employed as potential measures of the performance of collaborative projects[12].

Cost Savings

A frequent argument for collaborative ventures is that they are cheaper for participants than national projects, leading to savings in both development and production costs. If the development costs on a joint project are the same as for a comparable national venture, then on a bilateral programme each partner saves one-half of the cost of a national scheme. However, experience demonstrates that collaboration adds to total development costs through additional administrative costs, the need to harmonize different national standards and operational requirements, and duplication of activity (eg in the case of aircraft, each partner may want to build a prototype). The square root rule suggests that the development costs for a joint venture will exceed those for a national project by a factor equal to the square root of the number of partners[13]. Despite additional costs for three equal partners, each nation would save one third of the development cost associated with a comparable national project.

A review of published papers on high technology collaboration costs, concluded that "the general picture for aircraft R&D projects is one of increases ranging from 15-20 per cent for a bilateral programme to 50 per cent depending upon the number of partners, decision-sharing and multi-role compromise"[14]. Another study suggests that the collaborative Alpha-Jet cost at most 10 per cent more than a national West German programme[15]. Proceeding collaboratively with the EH101 helicopter rather than the nearest national alternative, the WG 34, was estimated to have saved the UK 40 per cent of development costs[16]. Others have concluded that where the square root rule applies, junior partners should count as a fraction, say one-half, of a full partner[17].

A structured interview survey of 18 executives and officials in the European aerospace industry focused on joint European projects and sought to compare them with national ventures. Seventeen respondents affirmed that joint projects have higher R&D costs than national ventures. Four replies said that this additional cost was very little, three put it at 10-20 per cent, six put the relevant figure at 30-50 per cent, and there was one vote each for 50-70 per cent and 70+ per cent[18].

Supporters of collaboration also argue that joint projects reduce unit production costs. By combining their orders, production runs are longer than they would have been for separate national ventures. Learning and scale economies are increased, leading to unit production costs below those for a national venture. Collaboration, however, is again not costless. Often, each partner nation wants its own final assembly line, so production costs may be greater than if one country had undertaken all of the work.

One survey found that of fifteen respondents, four stated that joint projects involved higher unit production costs than if all the manufacture had been done in one country; three thought such costs would be the same and eight assessed that they would be lower[19]. Estimates of how much higher or lower such costs would be ranged from +10 per cent to -30 per cent. A more recent study suggests that expected economies of scale are not always achieved in practice, and that the unit production costs of a collaborative programme might be higher than a national equivalent. For example, on the NFR 90 frigate, additional production costs for the UK were estimated at some £36 million compared with a national venture, though there was an offsetting saving in development costs of £160 million[20].

A closely related performance indicator is whether collaborative projects are prone to larger cost over-runs than national projects. Farrar and Balthazor found no evidence that collaborative project cost predictions were any more variable than national ones[21]. Hartley's survey evidence was more encouraging for joint ventures: five respondents thought that cost escalation on joint ventures was lower than on national projects, though four thought that it was the same and one respondent thought that it is higher[22]. In contrast, a National Audit Office Report[23], found evidence to suggest that cost escalation on collaborative ventures was greater than that for national projects. The weighted average development cost growth on national projects was 14 per cent, compared with 24 per cent, for collaborative programmes[24]. However, the collaborative projects in the sample comprised a heterogeneous group (aircraft, helicopter, missiles and land systems), whilst no details were provided of the national ventures.

Development Times

Critics argue that development times are longer for collaborative ventures than for comparable national projects. These differences arise from the need to harmonize different operational requirements and national standards; inter-governmental disputes over project leadership and over the allocation of costs and work; different national procurement practices which have to be reconciled; national approval and funding procedures; negotiations with industry on contract terms; and language difficulties. One rule of thumb is that the development period for a joint venture will exceed that for a national project by a factor equal to the cube root of the number of partners, although empirical evidence is rarely cited to support this claim.

On the one hand, a review of the evidence reported that "the timescales of collaborative European projects have been broadly comparable with those of national projects", although it was noted that timescales for the development of European projects (whether collaborative or national) have typically been twice as long as those in the USA[25]. A similar conclusion was reached in a study which compared six European multinational ventures with a sample of US aircraft[26]. Although the results were sensitive to the inclusion or exclusion of the Tornado programme from the sample of collaborative projects, it was found that "the evidence that collaborative European programmes tend to take more time than national European programs is far from conclusive"[27]. On the other hand, Taylor[28] suggests that there is a widespread belief that bilateral projects take 40 per cent longer and that trilateral projects take 70 per cent longer than national projects.

A survey of 18 executives and officials in the Western European aerospace industry addressed development times for joint projects[29]. Eight respondents replied that joint European projects take longer than national projects: three thought 1-2 years extra, one suggested 3+ years, three did not specify a figure and one said +20 per cent. However, a UK econometric study which sought to hold constant the influence of other factors on development times found no support for the hypothesis that collaborative projects take longer to develop than European national ones[30]. Martin[31] reports the results of a comprehensive statistical analysis comparing the development time (go-ahead to first delivery) for collaborative projects with that for all national projects involving civil aircraft seating 20 or more passengers whose first flight occurred after 1945. It was found that the mean development time for collaborative projects was greater than that for single-nation ventures but that with the exception of US projects this difference was not statistically significant. For military aircraft, though, the data indicated that collaborative projects take longer than both American and European national ventures, and that these differences are statistically significant.

Similar results were obtained when the population was reduced to those aircraft whose first flight occurred after 1960. For civil aircraft, collaborative projects took longer than both national European and American ventures but this difference was only significant in the latter case. For military aircraft both national European and American projects took significantly less time than collaborative ventures[32]. A related performance indicator is whether collaborative projects are more prone to time slippage than national ventures. In their review, Farrar and Balthazor[33] found no evidence that collaborative project time-scale predictions were any more variable than national ones. In Hartley's survey, however, three executives thought that the time escalation on joint ventures was greater than that for typical national projects, although three other respondents thought that it was the same and one thought it less than that for single-nation projects[34]! To complete this somewhat contradictory evidence, Rich *et al*[35], in a comparison of six collaborative European ventures with a sample of US aircraft, found that the median schedule overun of actual to planned first deliveries was 1.46 for the former and 1.03 for the latter.

Output

One of the arguments in favour of collaboration is that by pooling their orders, the European aerospace industry will be able to achieve production runs comparable with those of their American rivals[36]. In this way the Europeans will be more competitive in world markets as the greater learning and scale economies, from longer production runs, mean that their unit production costs and hence prices, can be lower than would be the case for a national venture. In addition, there is little prospect of amortising development costs for any aircraft unless at least 200 units are produced[37]. With a joint venture the Europeans improve their chances of recovering development costs by simultaneously pooling their orders and reducing potential competitors in world markets.

Martin's[38] statistical analysis compared aircraft production output for collaborative projects with independent national programmes whose first flight occurred after 1945. It found that for civil aircraft, US scales of output significantly exceeded those for joint ventures. However, collaborative projects had longer production runs than did national non-US ventures. Moreover, when the sample is restricted to post-1960 aircraft this difference between collaborative and national European output levels is significant[39]. For post-1945 military aircraft, US output levels significantly exceeded those for collaborative projects which in turn were similar to those for national non-US ventures. However, when the military sample is restricted to post-1960 aircraft, collaborative ventures perform better. Although US output levels still exceeded those of joint ventures this was not statistically significant, and collaborative output levels now exceed production runs for national European projects[40].

A related performance indicator is the proportion of output which is exported. This provides an indicator of international competitiveness, although hidden subsidies can obviously distort trade patterns. Pairwise comparisons are often made, comparing the export performance of similar collaborative and national aircraft (eg the Alpha-Jet with the Hawk, and the Tornado with the F-14). Hartley[41] concluded that "there are examples of both collaborative and national aerospace projects which are competitive in world markets".

Table 8.9: Summary of Evidence

Performance indicator	
1. Savings in R & D costs per nation compared with a national project	Yes
2. Savings in production costs per nation compared with a national project	Probably not
3. Longer development times compared with:	
i. a national European project	Probably not
ii. an American project	Yes
4. Increased output compared with:	
i. a national European project	Yes
ii. an American project	No

Summary of the Evidence on the Performance of Collaborative Projects

To summarise, much of the evidence on the performance of collaborative projects is contradictory, even when focusing on the same indicator. Consequently, both critics and supporters of joint projects will be able to find empirical support for their respective cases. Nevertheless, three broad conclusions emerge. First, R&D costs on a joint venture exceed those which would be incurred on an identical national venture. However, because total development costs are shared between participants, each partner incurs less expense than on a comparable national venture. Second, development time-scales for European aircraft, whether national or collaborative, are greater than those of their American rivals. But, when all other factors are taken into account, collaboration *per se* does not add to development time. Finally, for civil aircraft, collaborative output levels have been greater than those for national European ventures. There is some evidence that this is also true for military aircraft. Nonetheless, joint projects have not, as yet, approached US scales of output for either civil or military aircraft. The evidence on performance is summarized in Table 8.9.

Collaboration: A Public Choice Analysis

The diversity of benefits from collaboration makes it difficult to evaluate their efficiency and performance. Each partner nation is likely to have different policy objectives and differ in its "willingness to pay" for various benefits (end-outputs). For example, was the UK's involvement in the Tornado project the least-cost solution to providing the RAF with a modern combat aircraft, or was it designed to contribute to European unity, or to protect jobs in British Aerospace and Rolls-Royce, or to save dollar expenditure on the import of US equipment? In addition, where policy objectives are vague and ambiguous, there are opportunities for discretionary behaviour by governments, bureaucracies and weapons contractors, each pursuing their own ends. Indeed, the political market place creates considerable potential for inefficiency in collaborative projects.

International collaboration involves governments in a set of choices about what to build, with which partner countries, with which firms, how to organize the project and the criteria for allocating (sharing) the total work. These choices will be made in the political market place of voters, parties, bureaucracies and interest groups within the partner nations. The typical election arrangements mean that voters are usually unable to express their preferences between alternative procurement policies (eg nationalism, buy abroad, joint projects or licensed production); nor are they provided with information on the costs and benefits of different policies because of the alleged need to "protect national security". As a result, a government has discretion in interpreting the "national interest" and it will be influenced by the views of specialists in the form of bureaucracies and interest groups of producers and scientists. A defence ministry and the armed forces aiming to maximize their budget and the opportunities for power, prestige and personal satisfaction, will stress and exaggerate the apparently substantial cost savings from international collaboration and its major social benefits through protecting jobs, the balance of payments and promoting high technology. Bureaucrats will welcome the opportunities for regular international travel and the prestige involved in negotiating an international treaty, protecting the national interest, allocating contracts and "policing" the programme. They have an incentive to negotiate international contracts which make it costly for any partner nation to withdraw unilaterally, and to devise a set of monitoring arrangements which maximise their involvement in project decision-making (eg under the guise of public accountability and protecting the national taxpayer).

Similarly, the case for collaboration is likely to be supported by producer groups of management and unions seeking new contracts, and by the scientific lobby with its desire to expand the frontiers of knowledge - all at the taxpayers expense. As a result, the armed forces, bureaucracies, producers and scientists within each partner nation will insist upon imposing *their* requirements, ideas and technical aspirations. Bargaining will predominate. During the initial negotiations, each partner nation's armed forces will insist upon its operational requirements; firms will compete for project leadership and each country's scientists will demand to be involved in the most exciting technical advances. International rivalry will dominate the early stages of negotiations, as each national interest group submits its claims, exercises its bargaining skills, exaggerates its orders and threatens to withdraw (compare the process of collective bargaining between employers and trade unions). Ultimately, any international agreement will be a compromise between the maximum bids of each partner and the minimum terms required to persuade it to join and remain a member of the club. Such compromises are likely to reflect bargaining behaviour between the partners rather than efficiency criteria: behaviour within committees will determine outcomes rather than commercial considerations of efficiency and profitability. In its desire to obtain a preferred part of the project, a nation might be willing to sacrifice to its partners a major share in a less preferred part of the programme, or even offer compensation in other unrelated policy areas (eg support in a vital vote on EC agricultural policy).

Once started, collaborative projects are difficult to stop. International collusion replaces rivalry, and national governments will be confronted by a combined interest group of scientists, producers and bureaucrats in the partner nations. Such international groups of experts are likely to be influential in persuading vote-conscious governments of the technological, military, diplomatic and other social benefits of continuing with a collaborative venture. Their views on technology and estimates of development costs and time-scales are likely to be decisive, although optimistic. And, in the last resort, the costs of optimism are borne by each nation's numerous tax-payers. In other words, budget-sensitive bureaucracies in partner nations, supported by scientists and producer groups (defence contractors) will tend to exaggerate the social benefits and cost savings of joint programmes in order to persuade vote-conscious governments to undertake and continue the work. Collaborative European ventures will be attractive to governments seeking re-election. Each partner government can be seen to be promoting European unity, avoiding dependence on US technology and weapons, protecting the balance of payments, providing employment for its voters and creating the next generation of highly-paid jobs both directly and through "spin-off" to the civil sector.

A public choice analysis predicts that joint European ventures will be characterized by inefficiency and a departure from the ideal model. The political bargaining process creates constraints on the choice of the most efficient organisational arrangements and contractors. On collaborative aerospace ventures, this inefficiency is reflected in:

a) *The administrative and organisational costs* resulting from excessive government bureaucracy and duplicate organisations for procurement and supply. For example, a prime contractor - sub-contractor relationship might be the most efficient organisational form for managing a project, but such an arrangement might be unacceptable to two equal partner nations. Similarly, governments are likely to select the major contractors on political, rather than commercial, criteria (eg awarding work to marginal constituencies and to their national champions).

b) *Work-sharing.* Typically, some of the high technology development work has to be allocated to a partner country lacking the necessary technical knowledge and expertise. For example, a nation might join the club as a means of entering a new field of high technology.

c) *The duplication of R & D and production work* with each partner requiring a flight testing centre and a final assembly line.

d) *Each nation requiring modifications* on its military projects, so raising R & D costs and possibly reducing the economies from a long-run of one type (compared with the ideal model) as well as reducing standardisation.

e) *Delays* due to design by committee using unanimity rules and pursuing "over-elaborate" specifications reflecting the technical aspirations of the military and scientists in each partner nation. Delays also result from frequent meetings and paperwork, the need to consult all the partner nations before a decision can be taken, and the slow decision-making process by "over-involved" governments. Further problems arise from differences in language, culture, national pride, and managerial philosophy and practices. In other words, there are costs of creating new international organisations and doing business with strangers selected on political criteria.

f) *The substantial costs of controlling joint programmes.* They require a complex set of international transactions and contracts between governments and firms, embracing high technology projects which cannot be clearly-defined *ex ante.* The resulting contracts are costly to monitor and cancel. For example, on the Concorde project it was stated that "...the inherent difficulty of the multiplicity of contracts, the number of interested parties and the participation of two sovereign states... meant that the project had acquired a life of its own and was out of control"[42].

Collaboration and the European Defence Industrial Base

In aerospace, collaboration has brought together the major European companies into new international organisations embracing military and civil aircraft, helicopters, engines, missiles and space systems. The result has been the creation of larger European groups which could be the basis for the future development of a European aerospace industry, more able to compete with the USA. Table 8.10 shows the size of the major European aerospace companies and their US rivals. Mention of a *European* aerospace industry raises wider issues of a European defence industrial base. To date, European collaboration has been most extensive in aerospace, with some limited initiatives of varying degrees of success in land and sea systems (see Table 8.6). However, the Single European Market, moves towards monetary and political union in the EC, continued debates about future European security arrangements and pressures from cuts in defence budgets will give a renewed impetus to debates about creating a European defence industrial base (DIB). The impetus will come from both the demand and supply sides of the market reflecting strategic, political and economic pressures. National defence ministries and their armed forces will stress the military, strategic and independence benefits of a European DIB. Vote-conscious governments will be attracted by the apparent budget savings, together with the employment, high technology and balance of payments benefits, and their desire not to be "unduly dependent" on the United States. And defence contractors will see the opportunity of creating a protected European market with guaranteed business (Fortress Europe).

Attractive though a European DIB appears, the concept is not without problems. The following questions need to be answered:-

(i) What is meant by a European DIB? Does it, for example, refer to some minimum core of key strategic assets; if so what are the key assets[43]?

(ii) Is there an "ideal" model for a European defence market and DIB? Consideration needs to be given to the ideal size, structure, industrial composition and geographical location of the DIB. At one extreme, the EC might aim for a common market in defence equipment, allowing firms of all Member States free entry into national markets for defence contracts (the liberalised market scenario). Or, at the other extreme, a single centralised European procurement agency could be created with the agency pooling national orders and allocating work to European suppliers. With such an agency, there would be worries about the creation of an inefficient protected cartel resembling all the worst features of the Common Agricultural Policy! Or, a centralised European procurement agency could replace national defence ministries purchasing common equipment for a single EC army, navy and air force.

Figure 8.10: The Ten Largest American and European Aerospace Firms, 1990

Company	**Military Sales (1)**	**Total Sales (2)**	**(1) as a % of (2) (3)**	**Employment (4)**
(a) *American*				
General Motors	14080	137740	10	857400
McDonnell Douglas	9020	16225	55	121200
General Dynamics	8300	10182	82	98100
Lockheed	7500	9958	75	73000
United Technologies	6600	28742	23	233900
General Electric	6450	58414	117	298000
Raytheon	5500	9632	57	76700
Boeing	5100	27595	18	161700
Northrop	4700	5493	86	38200
Martin Marietta	4600	6143	75	62000
Total American	71850	310154	23	2020000
(b) *European*				
Daimler-Benz	11450	68584	17	499132
Thomson	11190	21685	52	161498
British Aerospace	7520	18818	40	127900
GEC	6450	58414	11	298000
IRI	4510	10482	43	388678
Direction des Constructions Navales	3830	3831	100	30500
Aerospatiale	3060	7024	44	42267
EFIM	3050	3888	79	47459
INI	2800	19592	14	166288
Dassault	2260	3454	52	14900
Total European	56120	215772	26	1776622

Note: Figures in columns 1 and 2 are in US $ million
Source: SIPRI 1992.

(iii) What are the likely costs of supporting a European DIB; will the member states be willing to bear such costs and how will the burden be shared?

(iv) Who are the likely gainers and losers from creating a European DIB? Which firms, regions and towns will benefit and which will lose, and will the potential losers be compensated?

Some of the difficulties inherent in creating and supporting a DIB emerged in the UK debate over the future of the Westland helicopter company in 1986[44]. Over the single issue of Westland, members of the same Government had different views as to whether the company was an "essential, key national asset". Imagine the potential for debate, controversy and bargaining over the possible creation of a European DIB, where national interests will dominate the policy choices. Nor should the alleged benefits of a European DIB be accepted uncritically.

Support for a European DIB would be based on its military, strategic and economic benefits. Emphasis is given to independence and security of supply in emergencies and war; to equipment designed to meet the special requirements of European forces; and to wider economic and social benefits in the form of employment, high technology and the balance of payments. However, these alleged benefits need to be clearly identified and supported with evidence. All too often they reflect nationalism and special pleading by interest groups seeking to protect their incomes. Nor are such benefits achieved without cost. Usually, there are alternative and often better ways of achieving these benefits. For example, more jobs might be created if defence spending were reallocated to other government current and capital expenditures (eg education, health, roads[45]). Similarly, governments can promote high technology by supporting civil R & D projects in such sectors as aerospace, electronics and pharmaceuticals. Nonetheless, proposals to re-allocate resources from defence to alternative civil spending (the peace dividend), will create major adjustment problems for some industries, firms and communities. Such groups which are likely to lose from disarmament will oppose changes which make them worse-off.

Opposition to Change

Major interest groups within the military-industrial complex will comprise defence ministries, armed forces, defence contractors, scientists, trade unions, and towns dependent on military spending. Such groups will oppose policies likely to make them worse-off. Faced with the prospects of disarmament, they will lobby governments to change their policies and to offer generous compensation to the losers (eg attractive redundancy terms or compensating work). References will be made to the "dire and catastrophic consequences" of disarmament for jobs and technology. At the same time, national defence ministries, their armed forces and contractors might find it even more attractive to offer collaborative projects as the most appropriate and efficient solution to purchasing defence equipment in an era of reduced military spending. Collaboration can be presented as offering cost savings, promoting European integration and contributing to European security. In addition, the economics of politics predicts that governments will be more attentive to producers than consumers (voters) when formulating policies; hence, public policies tend to favour producers more than consumers[46]. On this basis, collaboration will create larger producer groups more likely to influence goverment policies in their favour.

Conversion

Questions also arise as to how far collaboration will affect the opportunities for conversion. Will it make conversion more difficult or easier: why and how? Here, much depends on the industrial arrangements. If collaboration creates more specialist defence groups, it is unlikely to facilitate conversion. However, if collaboration brings together large industrial conglomerates with a range of military and civil activities, such diversified groups are more likely to survive losses of defence business. But this raises the central issue of how conversion is being defined.

Two definitions are available. First, a narrow interpretation focusing on the direct conversion of defence plants to civil work (see Chapter 9). Second, a broader interpretation focuses on the re-allocation of resources from declining defence industries to expanding sectors of the economy. Both definitions involve adjustments which can take time and might be costly. Typically, though, attention has been given to the narrow definition. What problems are likely to be encountered if defence firms seek to convert to civil markets?

Previous experience suggests that in market economies very few defence establishments will convert in the sense of making fundamentally the same product for a civilian market. There are no obvious civil markets for guided weapons, nuclear-powered submarines, strike aircraft and tanks. More likely is an attempt to use the technological expertise developed for defence production in new civilian areas. Possibilities include aerospace manufacturers converting to civil aircraft and space activities, warship builders to merchant shipbuilding and tank manufacturers to producing tractors. Evidence suggests that such proposals represent a triumph of hope over experience! These efforts at conversion will face three major difficulties. *First*, many defence companies are not used to operating in civil markets. The process of obtaining and fulfilling orders, the contract and monitoring procedures, standards, the incentives to control costs and all aspects of doing business differ between the defence and civil markets. Some defence companies have become specialists simply because of the benefits of specialisation. *Second*, identifying civilian products which can be made using the resources available is only part of the issue. As important is identifying a *profitable* market. Companies which may be expected to do best in this search for new types of business are those which have established links with businesses already operating successfully in civil markets - either as joint venture partners, members of conglomerates or groups, or through a long business association. The commercial value of such links is likely to be as important as the value of other resources available to the defence contractors. It is an advantage which can only be gained by experience: no amount of planning, or government aid to conversion can overcome a lack of basic business or entrepreneurial ability. *Third*, once potentially profitable civil markets have been identified, it has to be recognized that conversion might be costly. Plants, equipment and workforces which are highly specialized for defence production might not be the most competitive for civil work, so that conversion is likely to involve substantial "start-up" costs in redesigning plants, purchasing new tools and retraining staff. Private capital markets might signal that it is not worthwhile to incur such start-up costs.

A simple framework can be used to assess the prospects for converting industrial capacity (including collaborative organisations) from military to civil work. Two characteristics are important. *First*, a firm's dependence on defence sales with reliance on a single customer, cost-based contracts, protected markets, guaranteed profits and a culture of dependency on government rather than on entrepreneurship, risk-taking and seeking profitable market opportunities. *Second*, a firm's dependence on defence-specific resources, namely technology, production facilities and personnel. For example, some defence technologies have extensive civil applications such as radar, aircraft and avionics; others have few, if any, civil applications such as stealth, armour and nuclear weapons. Similarly, some production facilities and their human resources are highly specific to defence with little, if any, market value, in the civil sector. Figure 8.1 outlines a framework as a starting point for analysis[47]. Firms and collaborative groups in the A region are the ones where conversion is easiest and most likely. In contrast, firms and international groups in the D region, face the greatest difficulties of conversion: defence sales dominate their business; and their business depends on marketing technological resources which are specific to defence. This framework needs to be related to the facts on defence companies.

Figure 8.1: A Framework for Conversion

		Dependence on defence sales	
		Low	High
Dependence on defence-specific resources	Low	A	B
	High	C	D

Amongst the top 100 arms producing companies in the OECD in 1990, almost 50 per cent were in the USA and these were also amongst the world's largest defence companies accounting for about 60 per cent of the arms sales of the top 100 firms. Elsewhere, the top 100 included 14 British, 10 French and 8 German firms which, in total, accounted for over 25 per cent of the arms sales of the top 100 companies[48]. Differences in firm size and market shares between the top American and top European companies are an indicator of their relative competitiveness (Table 8.10). Aerospace, missile and electronics companies dominate the top 100. Defence equipment sales are highly concentrated with the 10 largest firms accounting for over 40 per cent, and the top 25 accounting for almost 65 per cent, of the arms sales of the top 100 companies, respectively[49].

In response to defence cuts, the companies most vulnerable are those wholly or largely dependent on defence sales. Only 3 European firms in the top 100 in 1990 were totally dependent on defence sales (VSEL, UK; DCN, France and Oto Melara, Italy); and, amongst the European companies, a further 13 had defence business which accounted for 70 per cent or more of their total sales (eg Dassault and GIAT, France; and CASA, Spain). Conversely, some companies were diversified, with 11 European corporations in the top 100 in 1990 where defence activities accounted for no more than 20 per cent of total sales (eg Daimler Benz, Germany; Thorn-EMI, Hawker-Siddeley and Racal in the UK).

Conversion also raises wider issues. The defence industry has often been criticized for pre-empting scarce resources, particularly of R&D and skilled manpower (Chapter 2). On this basis, successful conversion or re-allocation of resources from defence to civil work might well contribute to some improvement in the economy's performance. But for some towns and regions, this re-allocation process will not be without its difficulties and problems.

The adjustment problems associated with conversion raise questions about the appropriate role for public policy. Should governments restrict themselves to assisting a re-allocation of resources (eg via regional, manpower and training policies); or, should they intervene more directly and identify new market opportunities for defence firms? In this context, UK experience suggests that governments are not very good at "picking the winners" (eg Concorde).

Conclusion: Policy Recommendations

Collaboration is not necessarily the most efficient procurement option. Indeed efficiency-conscious EC defence ministries have every incentive to favour a liberalised competitive market for defence equipment, with the market open to the world. Alternatively, they might prefer a centralised purchasing agency buying standardised defence equipment for all EC states. However, the existing large EC defence contractors and collaborative organisations form powerful producer groups which will lobby their governments to ensure that they do not lose from any policy changes. Within a liberalised market or with an EC central purchasing regime, they will argue for "managed" rather than open competition and for work-sharing arrangements to protect jobs and technology.

Clearly, there is considerable scope for introducing competition into EC defence markets. The IEPG 1988 Action Plan aims at a stepwise approach to opening-up national armaments markets by removing obstacles to cross border competition[50]. It aims to create a European Armaments Market in which competition, joint ventures and the formation of multinational consortia can be developed. However, the Action Plan's commitment to *juste retour*, to recognising the special problems of countries with less developed defence industries and to the development of Co-operative Technology Projects suggests potential conflicts with the commitment to competition. A concern with *juste retour* is that it will interfere with an efficient allocation of resources between member states and a similar result is likely with co-operative research and development programmes. Nevertheless, there are opportunities for improving the efficiency of European collaboration.

Two basic economic principles offer guidelines for policy towards collaborative projects. First, the *principles of competition and comparative advantage* need to be applied to collaborative projects. R&D and production work need to be allocated on efficiency rather than equity criteria. This principle offers a range of possibilities from greater competition for sub-contracts to the creation of competing consortia with partners selected on commercial criteria. Second, is the *principle of compensation.* Policies designed to improve efficiency require adequate arrangements to compensate the potential losers and to assist a re-allocation of resources. Manpower and regional policies, together with income-deficiency payments to groups and individuals, would replace *juste retour.*

Endnotes

1. Pugh, P., **The Cost of Sea Power**, Conway, London, 1986.
2. HCP 169, **Defence Implications of the Future of Westland plc**, Defence Committee, London, HMSO, 1986, p. 204.
3. Lorell, M.A., **Multinational Development of Large Aircraft**, Rand Corporation, Santa Monica, 1980.
4. Hayward, K., **International Collaboration in Civil Aerospace**, Frances Pinter, London, 1986.
5. Draper, A.G., **European Defence Equipment Collaboration**, RUSI, London, 1990; Hartley, K., **The Economics of Defence Policy**, Brassey's, London, 1991.
6. Hartley, *Ibid.*
7. *Ibid.*

8. *Ibid.*

9. Hartley, K., **NATO Arms Co-operation: A Study in Economics and Politics**, George Allen and Unwin, London, 1983; Hartley, K., **Aerospace: the Political Economy of an Industry**, in de Jong, H.W. (ed.), *The Structure of European Industry*, 1988; HCP 37-II, **Defence Commitments and Resources and the Defence Estimates 1985-1986**, Defence Committee, HMSO, London, 1985.

10. Moravcsik, A., **The European Armaments Industry at the Crossroads**, *Survival*, xxxii(1), January - February 1989, pp. 65-85.

11. National Audit Office, **Ministry of Defence: Initiatives in Defence Procurement**, HMSO, London, 1991.

12. Hartley, 1991, *op. cit.*

13. National Audit Office, *op. cit.*

14. Farrar, D. and Balthazor, L., **Analysis of High Technology Collaboration**, *European Collaborative Projects*, Royal Aeronautical Society, London, 1981.

15. Hoffert, F., **The Franco-German Alpha Jet Programme**, *European Collaborative Projects*, Royal Aeronautical Society, London, 1981.

16. National Audit Office, *op. cit.*, p. 8.

17. Pugh, P., *op. cit.*, p. 357; WEU, **Armaments Co-operation Between WEU Member Countries**, Western European Union, Brussels, p. 7.

18. Hartley, 1983, *op. cit.*

19. *Ibid.*

20. National Audit Office, *op. cit.*, p. 13.

21. Farrar and Balthazor, *op. cit.*

22. Hartley, 1983, *op. cit.*

23. National Audit Office, *op. cit.*

24. *Ibid.*, p. 14.

25. Farrar and Balthazor, *op. cit.*

26. Rich, M., Stanley, W., Birkler, J. and Hesse, M., **Multinational Co-production of Military Aerospace Systems**, Rand Corporation, Santa Monica, 1981.

27. *Ibid.*

28. Taylor, T., **Defence, Technology and International Integration**, Frances Pinter, London, 1982.

29. Hartley, 1983, *op. cit.*

30. Hartley, K., **The Evaluation of Efficiency in the Arms Industry**, in Borner, S. and Taylor, A. (eds.), *Structural Change, Economic Interdependence and World Development*, Macmillan, London, 1987.

31. Martin, S., **Economic Collaboration and European Security**, in Kirby, S. and Hooper, N., *The Cost of Peace: Assessing Europe's Security Options*, Harwood, Reading, 1991.

32. Martin, S. and Hartley, K., **European Collaboration in Aerospace: Recent Trends and Future Prospects**, *European Research*, Vol. 2, No. 6, November 1991, pp. 14-19.

33. Farrar and Balthazor, *op. cit.*

34. Hartley, 1983, *op. cit.*

35. Rich *et. al.*, *op. cit.*

36. Vredling, H., **Towards a Stronger Europe**, Vol. 2, IEPG, NATO, Brussels, 1986.

37. Farrar and Balthazor, *op. cit.*

38. Martin, 1991, *op. cit.*

39. Martin and Hartley, 1991, *op. cit.*

40. *Ibid.*

41. Hartley, 1991, *op. cit.*

42. HCP 265, **Concorde, Second Report from the Industry and Trade Committee**, HMSO, London, 1981.

43. Taylor, T. and Hayward, K., **The UK Defence Industrial Base**, Brassey's, London, 1989.

44. HCP 169, *op. cit.*

45. Barker, T., Dunne, P. and Smith, R., **Measuring the Peace Dividend in the UK**, *Department of Applied Economics Working Paper*, University of Cambridge, 1990.

46. Downs, A., **An Economic Theory of Democracy**, 1957.

47. Dussage, P., **The Conversion of Military Activities**, in Schmidt, C. and Blackaby, F. (eds), *Peace, Defence and Economic Analysis*, IEA, Macmillan, London, 1987.

48. SIPRI, **Yearbook 1992**, Stockholm, Sweden, 1992.

49. *Ibid.*

50. IEPG, **Luxembourg Communique**, Luxembourg, November 1988.

Chapter 9

Defence Technology, Industrial Structure and Arms Conversion

Steven Schofield

Introduction

In the last two years interest has revived in the subject of arms conversion and diversification. From an historical perspective this is unsurprising, since academic, political and industrial interest has corresponded to the prospects (or lack of them) for disarmament and its consequences for the arms industries.

There is now no doubt that a remarkable transformation has occurred in East/West relations, even if the recent conflict in the Gulf, the instabilities in Eastern Europe and nationalism in the now disintegrating USSR serve to demonstrate that considerable international tensions still exist. Despite the uncertainties about future international relations, it seems clear that we are entering a new era with concrete disarmament agreements for both nuclear and conventional forces and sustained cuts in defence expenditure. The speed and scale of this process, coupled to the perception that this is now an irreversible trend, has led to a large increase in the literature on conversion. Compared to previous peaks of interest, the range of publications and the spread across Europe, the USA, the former USSR and China makes this one of the most active periods for conversion research.

This chapter, while welcoming the renewed study, argues that the concept of arms conversion needs a radical re-evaluation and overhaul if it is to be relevant to the conditions of the 1990s. It puts forward the case that the traditional, factory-based approach of `swords into ploughshares', most commonly associated with the concept of arms conversion and derived from the successful post-World War II experience, is no longer tenable as an effective industrial policy in response to disarmament and defence cuts.

The major focus will be a technological one, as a means of identifying the special characteristics of defence companies operating at the systems level of production. As a result, the wide range of topics addressed in the general conversion literature can only be covered in passing. Likewise, analysis of the conversion experience in China, the former Soviet Union and other countries previously in the Warsaw Pact is excluded because of their profoundly different economic and social structures in comparison to Western economies, and the over-arching problems of transition to market economic processes. The Chapter focuses on the UK, though research on other Western economies is used to provide additional information.

It is necessary to focus on the historical legacy of the post-Second World War conversion experience which is still the primary conversion model, despite the radically different industrial and technological conditions prevailing in contemporary Western industrial societies. A brief review of immediate post-war conversion identifies why the process of change was carried out relatively smoothly, and also why that experience has little significance today.

Having identified changes since 1945 and the growth of a highly specialised and technologically sophisticated defence industry, the paper focuses on theoretical models which attempt to explain its structure. Key concepts are *hierarchies of technologies and products* with major defence companies positioned at the upper levels where complex systems integration takes place. Also, the potential synergies between military and civil technologies which could facilitate the transfer from defence to civil production are identified and evaluated.

It is argued that while similar large-scale systems companies operate in the civil sector, the major defence companies are characterised by highly specialised forms of system integration on defence platforms, using dedicated technologies in very different ways from even the most complex forms of associated areas of civil production. Conversion is, therefore, a very difficult process for those systems companies at the level of industrial and technological change.

Other influences affect the potential for conversion and diversification: the level of defence dependency; the position within larger corporations of those divisions that specialise in defence work; and the culture of defence companies imbued sometimes over decades, which emphasises the importance of the relationship with the MoD.

For companies which operate at the lower levels of the product and technology hierarchy where dual-use technology is characteristic, the potential for new civil work, even in companies with a heavy existing dependency on defence work, may be greater. It has, however, to be acknowledged that our understanding of the structure of the defence supplier network is limited and unsatisfactory, so this presumption may be premature.

If correct, however, this presumption has implications for conversion policy and some concluding observations are made on the need to integrate conversion into the mainstream of industrial and regional policy. Essentially, the concept of conversion has to be broadened so that, irrespective of the fate of particular military-industrial sites, the objective of policy should be to compensate for declining defence work by increasing the overall level of civil manufacturing capacity and employment.

Post-World War Two Experience

The history of conversion is dominated by the immediate post-Second World War experience. Indeed, it would be no exaggeration to say this still constitutes the received model for arms conversion, despite the radically different industrial and technological conditions prevailing in the defence sectors of contemporary Western industrial societies.

According to Government figures, over 3.5 million people had been released from munitions industries and upwards of 4.2 million service men and women had returned to civil life by 1946. Despite the fact that many married women and those past the age of retirement simply left the workforce, there was an overall increase of 2.6 million in total civil employment.[1] Such a major disarmament programme, one of considerably larger scale than required today, was assisted by both macro and micro-economic conditions. At the macro-economic level, there was a massive backlog of demand built up during the war years and both consumers and producers accumulated considerable liquid assets. Thus, in 1946, disposable income rose by only 4.1 per cent, yet consumer expenditure increased by 21.4 per cent on 1945 levels.[2]

At the micro-economic level, conversion for the vast majority of companies simply meant a return to the pre-war situation: re-conversion by using existing plant and equipment which needed little modification from defence work. Where companies had substantially changed operations for military production, there is evidence that new skills and management expertise influenced a search for new civil products which were not manufactured prior to the war. Also significant technological breakthroughs were made during the war which undoubtedly influenced the options for peacetime work.[3]

In summary, some major industries including metals, engineering, vehicles and shipbuilding suffered a large decline in employment (that is, those industries which were most heavily dependent on war production), but the high level of savings and demand coupled to ease industrial conversion at the end of the war. Perhaps it also helps to explain a common contemporary perception that defence companies now face a straightforward process in changing to civil production.

However, the post-war environment has very little relevance today. The macro-economic advantages stemming from the release of large levels of saving are not available and, crucially, defence industries of the 1990s are significantly different from their predecessors. The long post-war period of sustained high levels of defence expenditures, unprecedented in peace-time history, has seen the emergence of specialist defence companies serving military niches within aerospace, electronics, shipbuilding and engineering with limited experience of the different demands for civil production and markets. The contrast between civil companies temporarily involved in defence work that re-converted at the end of the Second World War, and specialist defence companies now moving into civil activities in mature civil markets for the first time should be clarified.

The Defence-Industrial Context in the 1990s

If the post-war conversion experience is an inadequate framework for understanding today's circumstances, a clear theoretical approach is necessary which identifies the characteristics of defence firms and the scope for conversion in the UK.

Initially, a more formal definition is required of defence industries and conversion/diversification terminology. Inga Thorsson, in her report to the Swedish government, refers to three types of products supplied to the armed forces: *standard manufactured goods* for which the defence sector is one of many customers; *specific products*, having primarily civilian uses, but which are modified to meet military requirements; and *defence material* developed and manufactured to military specifications and for which there is normally only a military demand. For Thorsson then, the defence industry consists of:

"those industrial resources used to develop, manufacture and service material which is produced according to specific military requirements and which has no or virtually no civil applications."[4]

While one could debate the boundaries between military and civil applications, this seems a reasonable definition for our purposes.

Another way to view the defence industrial base is to concentrate, not on the final products of military requirements, but on the indigenous industrial assets which are essential for national security. This approach has been used extensively in the USA where concern has grown that in certain key strategic industries, the country has become increasingly uncompetitive in international markets and reliant on overseas suppliers:

"While most visible technologies in defense systems come from DoD and companies that contract with it, a significant part comes from the non-defense sector. ... And at the sub-component level, much also comes from the civilian side. Increasingly, these `dual-use' industries are sources of advanced technology, sources from which the DoD should be able to draw (and in some cases must draw because the technology is ahead). Moreover, `dual-use' industries are becoming increasingly internationalised, raising issues of the competitiveness of US firms in the world market and dependence on foreign suppliers in defence procurement."[5]

A defence industrial base is, therefore, much more than just the industrial assets of the defence prime contractors on which any product-based definition tends to focus, but encompasses national capabilities in key civil technologies without which a country would find itself dependent on foreign suppliers for its defence needs (see Chapter 3). Importantly, the British MoD has no policy on the need for indigenous capabilities apart from very specialist areas including cryptography, nuclear, chemical and biological technologies, and does not subscribe to the view that it has a responsibility to maintain a UK defence industrial base in the broad sense defined here.[6]

For the purposes of this study of conversion and diversification, the analysis focuses on the prime contractors to the MoD using Thorsson's definition of the defence industries. Attention is also given to the defence supplier network: that is, the subcontractors who provide a substantial element of defence work (perhaps as many as 10,000 on a major procurement programme), in turn reflecting the importance of defence work to the wider manufacturing base. However, it has to be acknowledged from the outset that our understanding of the defence supplier network is limited and unsatisfactory.

It is also important to distinguish between arms conversion and diversification. The former refers to the process by which part of the military-industrial capacity transforms completely from military to civilian activities, while diversification is more accurately defined as entry into a substantially different business field through either internal development or acquisition. Conversion, therefore, requires a complete change to civil work on the same site, while diversification implies a widening of the product base without abandoning defence work.[7]

In the UK, the MoD's equipment procurement budget is over £9 billion, of which £2.5 billion is for R&D - British industry's single biggest customer responsible for significant proportions of sectoral activity. As far as employment is concerned 480,000 workers are dependent on MoD contracts, while another 130,000 jobs are generated by defence exports. In total, approximately one in ten manufacturing jobs are defence related, (see Table 9.1).

Table 9.1: UK Employment Dependent on Defence Expenditure

Thousands

	1980-81	1981-82	1982-83	1983-84	1984-85	1985-86	1986-87	1987-88	1988-89	1989-90
Equipment Expenditure										
direct	230	240	225	215	225	200	170	175	160	150
indirect	190	190	180	160	170	160	140	150	130	130
Non-equipment expenditure										
direct	100	80	90	85	85	85	85	85	80	85
indirect	80	70	70	70	70	70	70	70	70	70
Total MOD expenditure										
direct	330	320	315	300	310	285	255	260	240	235
indirect	270	260	250	230	240	230	210	220	200	200
Exports										
direct	75	75	75	70	65	60	65	80	70	80
indirect	65	65	65	60	55	50	55	70	60	70
Totals										
direct	405	395	390	370	375	345	310	340	310	315
indirect	335	325	315	290	295	280	255	280	260	270
all	740	720	705	660	670	625	565	620	570	585

Source: Statement on the Defence Estimates, Volume II, 1991

Specialised defence divisions of some of the UK's largest manufacturing companies are heavily represented: British Aerospace (BAe), for example, Europe's largest defence company, has a military aircraft division and a division specialising in missile production; and the Marconi divisions of GEC specialise in radar and torpedo work, and the military engine division of Rolls Royce is another typical example. Defence work can represent a large or small proportion of a company's overall activities but still be very significant at the divisional level. For other companies including VSEL, defence dependency can be almost total, in this case predominantly nuclear submarine production.

The 1980s, it should be stressed, witnessed significant changes which predated the impact of disarmament (see Chapter 7), and led to considerable restructuring. These factors included increased concentration at the national level because of the influences of increased equipment costs, the need to share R&D costs, the privatisation programme and the new procurement regime which emphasised competition and the elimination of cost-plus contracting where possible.

More recently, international consortia have increased in significance partly because of the demands of defence markets, but also as part of the general internationalisation of industries in which the defence divisions operate. While the speed and scale of this process is determined largely by companies rather than government, the emergence of the IEPG and a potential role for the EC in encouraging liberalisation of what were traditionally national procurement markets may accelerate this process within the development of the Single European Market.[8]

Various forecasts have been made about the industrial and employment impact of the gathering pace of restructuring. Both in Europe and the UK, the prospect of job losses in the region of one third of total defence employment by the middle of the decade seems realistic. The major UK defence contractors have all announced considerable job losses and the intention to rationalise production by reducing the number of sites they operate.[9]

In the context of the present economic recession the loss of 40,000 to 50,000 defence jobs per annum begs the question, what is so special about defence? The issue of the relationship between conversion and wider economic and industrial policy is perennial in conversion literature, dating back to the 1960s. While some have argued that defence industries and workers should be made a special case in the event of disarmament, a major pre-occupation has been how to ensure that the objectives of conversion are seen to be equitable with wider industrial and employment objectives - an issue considered subsequently. First, a more detailed analysis is necessary of the contemporary barriers to the traditional model of conversion.

Barriers To Conversion

Many obstacles to factory-based conversion have been identified in recent studies, including organisational, cultural, and technological factors specific to defence companies, particularly in the light of a long and close relationships between the prime contractors and the MoD, which, it is argued, are not conducive to successful commercial operation. This section focuses on the technological dimension which is crucial to understanding the origins of the constraints to factory-based conversion. While other factors are significant, it will be argued that they are subordinate to the role of specialised technologies and their impact on industrial structure.

A useful way to look at defence industries at the prime-contractor level is to view them as systems manufacturers who integrate a variety of sub-systems into a complex final product. Importantly, many large-scale civil companies have similar characteristics, i.e. power generation and telecommunication. Defence companies however, also require specialist technologies and products from the component level up to sub-system level: for example, the exploitation of sound waves for under-sea detection and band-hopping radios' which have no civil equivalent. For many defence prime contractors there may be no large-scale civil alternative (e.g. in the case of nuclear submarine production), or requirements may be significantly different from the nearest civil equivalent (e.g. military and civil aircraft). Thus, while a general case can be made that large civil platforms could provide alternative work, the specialist nature of defence production still needs to be taken into account as a potential obstacle.

Two elements are thus crucial to understanding the technological dimension of defence work: first, the hierarchy of products; and second, product uniqueness and differentiation. The latter has been categorised as follows:

a) products which are unique to defence markets;
b) products which are common to defence and civilian markets but which are significantly differentiated between them;
c) products which are identical or nearly identical in military and civilian markets (eg memory chips).

As an example, Walker *et al* considered micro-chips and similar components, making the distinction between generic and specific components. Generic components have pervasive applications and play an important role in enabling technological developments in many different areas. Specific components are those without pervasive application, such as the exploitation of sound waves for under-sea detection and communications.[10]

Within the product hierarchy, therefore, a clear case can be made that technological specialisation can extend from the level of components through to upper levels. Large defence contractors dominate the production of *specific* components, sub-assemblies and sub-systems: for example GEC/Marconi's radar and sonar equipment divisions are vertically integrated, embracing component as well as systems manufacture:

"While the essential specialisation of the large firms operating in defence markets lies in their system capabilities, they also command the specifically military "tendrils" of technology which reach from the lowest levels of the product hierarchy to its higher reaches. *These tend to be the least diversifiable parts of the firm*."[11]

The final element of their taxonomy is an attempt to integrate these two previous concepts of the product hierarchy and distinct fields of technology in the definition of systems products. As a general rule, the probability that there will be a close affinity between military and civilian products diminishes as one ascends the hierarchy, but this may not apply to generic technologies. At levels 5 and 6 (Figure 9.1), the systems, although increasingly complex, are still subject to batch and series-production and there can be considerable overlap with civilian technologies. Distinct industries have emerged providing aircraft, vehicles and ships to both civilian and military markets.

Figure 9.1: A Vertical Product Hierarchy

Products			Processes	
		[8. Military strategies concepts] 7. Integrated weapons and information systems (eg. UKADGE)		
High unit value, complexity, systemic integration. Long product life.		6. Major weapons platforms and communication systems (eg. Ptarmigan) 5. Complete weapons and communications kit (eg. Stingray torpedo)	Unit production; large-scale project management; long lead-times	
Custom:		4. Sub-systems (eg gyroscpoes) 3. Sub-assemblies (eg sights, fuzes) 2. Components (eg. integrated circuits)	Batch/Series	Production
Standard	Custom:	1. Materials (eg. semi-conductors)	Standard	Custom
Low-unit value short product life	Higher-unit-shorter product life		Mass-production scale economies	Batch to series production; lesser-scale economies

Source: Walker, W., Graham, M. and Harbor, B., **From Components to Integrated Systems: Technological Diversity and Interactions between Military and Civilian Sectors.**

By constructing this taxonomy, Walker *et al* demonstrate that much of what is commonly called defence technology, particularly at the lower levels of the product hierarchy, is actually dual-use technology with no special `defence' characteristics. Also, at the upper levels of production, defence companies' expertise lies with the integration of a variety of sub-systems into an integrated final product. Many civil companies have a similar structure as systems integrators (e.g. power generation, satellites, and telecommunications).

However, within this general taxonomy, various technologies are recognised as flowing from the specialist demands of the defence systems companies (for example, at the component level, hardened chips, secure communications through band-hopping, and encryption). These military `tendrils' have an important bearing on the scope for conversion at the systems level, even though defence and civil systems companies share many characteristics.

Schofield's research on VSEL, a case study of a defence systems company, identified that given the role of specific components in military production and the extension of the military hierarchy through from component level to the level of systems manufacture, the problem of transition may be greater than Walker *et al* suggest.[12]

VSEL's expertise lies in the integration of a whole range of sub-systems within a major defence platform: the nuclear submarine, augmented by work on conventional submarines and field howitzers. The specialist requirements of nuclear submarine production include nuclear reactor safety within a moving platform, engine silencing techniques, security of communications and exact positioning and location facilities. It is the integration of these sub-systems, which in many cases have no civilian equivalent, that provide the first major obstacle. Second, and crucially, these sub-systems have to interact under extremes of conditions and performance which suggest divergences, even at the systems level, between certain kinds of highly specialised defence equipment and what might be considered as similar civil systems (in this case, merchant ships and offshore rig construction).[13]

While it is important to recognise the historical conditions and experience specific to each company in the defence sector, which have seen quite different developments in terms of manufacturing skills, equipment and technologies, similar defence systems companies can also be identified amongst the MoD's prime contractors, whether for planes, frigates or tanks. Commonality exists with nuclear submarine production to the extent that the platform has to operate in very different ways to civil counterparts (where they exist), and where the integration of sub-systems requires very specialised technological demands. For example, a civil aircraft is not designed for extremes of manoeuvrability or radar invisibility. Historically, these companies also enjoyed a sustained relationship of repeat orders with the MoD.

Consideration is necessary of the general trends in technology, particularly the dynamism of civil electronic technological development (see Chapter 7). It is argued that not only is the civil sector the technological driver in telecommunications and computing, but that, because of the long timescales required to bring new kit on stream, military equipment has become reliant on older technologies which undermines its effectiveness. As a result, defence systems should use the pool of civil technology more than is currently the case.

While acknowledging the importance of civil developments, this does not detract from the approach taken here which emphasises the special characteristics of defence systems. The expertise of defence systems companies lies in the integration of individual systems which must be inter-operable under extremes of both conditions and performance. Kaldor's depiction of the `baroque arsenal', with a combination of traditional platforms and incremental change to enhance the performance of equipment as long as it can be incorporated within these platforms, provides a key element to an understanding of the dominant pattern of military technological development.[14] As long as the emphasis remains on defence platforms and is performance driven, the incorporation of civil technologies will remain subordinate to military specifications which will require specialist systems manufacturers and military tendrils down to the lowest level of the product and technology hierarchy.

The uniqueness of nuclear submarine production, VSEL's major activity, should be apparent. Not only is this system unique in having no alternative civilian counterpart but it incorporates many specific military technologies from the component level upwards making vertical diversification difficult. But *even as a systems manufacturer*, the level of complexity involved in the incorporation of diffuse technologies and products is far in excess of what could be expected for other large-scale marine systems. Therefore, at the system's level and in relation to vertical integration, changeover to civilian production would involve considerable disruption.

Electronics

Moving away from the defence platforms, a different approach is required when analysing the electronics sector. In his study of the potential synergies between two large communication systems, Harbor illustrated how different military and civil requirements led to significant technological divergences between two systems: Ptarmigan and Systems X. As a battlefield communication system Ptarmigan had to be operationally mobile, tolerant to jamming, and have a high degree of security. Harbor pointed out that the demand for security of civil communications, and other factors such as "system redundancy" also apply in civil trunk systems. However,

"...the requirement for mobility of the trunk switch remains an exclusively military requirement. Furthermore, it is one which shapes the entire development of the system along a path that is entirely separate from that of civilian switches. This reinforces the popularization of military and civilian technological development; to all intents and purposes there is little commonality of requirements and so separate technical solutions are sought."[15]

For our purposes, Harbor made two important observations. First, the technological divergence had a major organisational impact: Plessey played a pivotal role in the development of Ptarmigan and all its military subsidiaries were grouped in Plessey Electronics Ltd; and Systems X, was organised with all telecommunication companies under Plessey Electronic Systems Ltd, or more recently, in the joint GEC-Plessey company GPT. With an existing separation of military and civil communications activities, very little contact occurred between military and civil parts of the company, even when Plessey was bidding for both Ptarmigan and Systems X development programmes. Second, as far as large communications systems are concerned it is not technical complexity that lies at the heart of the lack of synergy, but simply different military requirements which are embedded in organisational separation. The operating subsidiary will concentrate on development of any new technologies within traditional (in this case defence) markets. Company organisation, therefore, remains a barrier to the civil exploitation of defence technologies.[16]

Maddock, in an earlier study of the civil exploitation of military R&D, is also sceptical about the possibility of larger defence electronic companies making a successful transition from defence to civil work, precisely because of this organisational separation and the business culture developed as a result. For Maddock, public purchasing has an important role to play in both defence and civil fields as a promotion to new civil technology applications, whereby the `market' for high technology is encouraged to thrive.[17] Harbor comes to similar conclusions.

If the question of complexity and specificity in defence technology are not the crucial issue in telecommunications, it may be the case that conversion should concentrate here on organisational barriers, perhaps through the transfer of personnel with similar technological expertise but with experience in civil markets to defence electronic divisions. However, while the technological barriers to conversion may not be as great for defence electronics companies, one should not underestimate the challenges in terms of breaking into new and highly competitive international markets.

The Defence Supplier Network

While the emphasis in conversion literature has been on the prime contractors, recent research has focused attention on the defence subcontractor network. Estimates of total employment are difficult, but any restructuring of defence activities should take into account the possible ramifications through from the prime contractors to component producers, and the potential for new civil activities at the various levels.

Hartley and Hooper's study of the Vickers Challenger tank bid was the first concerted attempt to identify the main sub-contractors and the overall effect on employment and technology, not just for Vickers, but other companies, if the bid failed. However, while providing an estimate of the total job losses and the likely technological impact on the loss of a UK capability in heavy armour, the study could not shed any further light on the level of defence dependency at the subcontractor level and the vulnerability of particular companies.[18] Interestingly, David Brown - the manufacturer of gear systems for Challenger provided their own estimate of job losses and technological impact, arguing that without this work the company would not be in a position to develop new designs for civil sector work on new railway stock. However, this is very much the exception, and our understanding of the structure of the defence supplier network is extremely limited and unsatisfactory; a situation not helped by the practice of commercial confidentiality used by the prime contractors.[19]

A useful new contribution to this area of research has been to consider the defence supplier network at the regional level. The South West has the highest per capita level of defence equipment spending in the UK, and according to a recent survey of the region's industries:

"...a significant number of companies reported defence related business accounted for more than 50% of turnover. In some instances, defence business is in excess of 95% of turnover, with examples of 100% defence related activities not uncommon."[20]

An important point made as a result of this analysis is the need to distinguish between defence-dependent employment and defence-related employment, the latter being a correlation of employment to turnover and the former representing a broader description of the importance of defence work to the total activity of the company. Numerous examples were found of companies whose dependency on defence was greater than implied by the proportion of turnover that was defence-related, to the extent that reductions in defence contracts may lead to closure. In other words, employment dependent on defence is likely to be larger than employment related to defence. As a result, and on the basis of an estimate of a 25 per cent cut in defence expenditure by the year 2000, it is argued that defence dependent employment in the South West will fall from 200,000 to 160,000.[21]

Examples are also given of individual companies at the subcontractor level and their various responses to cuts in defence expenditure. Because of commercial confidentiality, individual firms are not identified by name. It seems clear that while civil applications are being pursued, many companies express confidence that they will succeed in defence exports and emerge as preferred suppliers to the defence prime contractors. As the report warns however, their confidence in defence exports may be misplaced because of lower demand and increasing competition.[22]

Technology and Defence Dependency

A final approach worth considering is what Dussauge described as the "strategic management of the firm" perspective.[23] Recognising that companies are split into strategic business units, some of which will be civil and others defence oriented, he offered a simple analytical framework to assess the prospects for conversion and diversification (see Figure 9.2). Two main factors need to be taken into account: first, the level of defence dependency in terms of the proportion of net sales (or profits) from defence work; and second, the significance of the technological knowledge arising from the firm's military work for its civilian activities measured in terms of these two activities.

Figure 9.2: Technology and Defence Dependency

		Defence Dependency	
		Low	High
Technological synergies between the firm's military and civilian activities	Low	1	2
	High	3	4

Source: Dussage, P., **The Conversion of Military Activities: A Strategic Management of the Firm Perspective**, in Schmidt, C. and Blackaby, F. (eds.), *Peace, Defence and Economic Analysis.*

Where firms have a low level of defence dependency and technological synergies, the reduction in defence orders should not pose great problems to the company. For companies in zones 2 and 3 the problems are greater if rather different. High defence dependency - up to 20 to 25 per cent of global activity in zone 2 - would mean any conversion programme would have a strategic impact, even if defence technologies are not connected to civil work. Even worse, according to Dussauge, is the situation for companies in zone 3 where conversion would see an end to their main source of technology. Firms in zone 4 would be most adversely affected and probably the most difficult to convert because they are both heavily dependent on defence work, and derive many of their technologies for civil activities from defence work.

Unfortunately, Dussauge fails to provide a systematic analysis of what constitutes a defence or civil technology, other than to give some examples of cases where he considers close synergies exist. Also, while concentrating on the larger defence companies, he does not give adequate consideration to their position as systems integrators. In other words, while he stresses the technological dimension in assessing whether a company can make the transition to civil work, a much more thorough appreciation of the position of leading defence companies is required, both in terms of the potential synergies to civil work and the complexity of their systems integration work.

The question of defence dependency also needs clarification. Many defence companies operate as divisions of larger corporations: their parent company might, therefore, have only a relatively small defence dependency. This would put them in either zone 1 or zone 3 using Dussauge's framework. However, the defence division in a company may be heavily dependent on defence work. Hence, it becomes problematic whether one should address the issue of dependency at the corporate level when many defence divisions are treated as separate entities which are expected to generate their own resources independently of the parent company, and who, therefore, can expect little assistance if difficulties threaten their viability. For other firms, the situation is more or less clear cut: defence work makes up a massive proportion of their total activity and they would even be without the theoretical assistance of a parent company. This is the exception rather than the rule, but VSEL in the UK and DCN and GIAT in France are over 90 per cent defence dependent.

Dussauge's framework, despite its limitations, still provides a useful indicator of the combination of factors which impinge on conversion. Dussauge is also, like Maddock, sceptical that some of the more heavily exposed defence companies can make the transition successfully, and considers that it may not be possible or cost-effective to save all the firms in this position. Government should, therefore, concentrate its assistance on firms in zone 2 and 3 through either government civil contracts or `technology pumps' to provide new sources of innovation.[24]

Gilmore and Coddington, in a study of the diversification experience of defence firms in the USA, identified a considerable level of failure in entering commercial markets and shed further light on the role that government might play:

"Where diversification involved a radical change in the market being served, as in commercial diversification, the result generally was failure or limited success. Where defense firms stayed within the same customer relationship (the defence customer) there were a number of notable successes. These experiences influenced the managements of defense firms to be wary of non-defense, non-government diversification."[25]

The government, because of the relationship that already exists with major defence contractor, is given the responsibility to provide new civil programmes in, for example, transport, environmental control, infrastructure, which most closely fit the major defence contractors needs if the diversification programme is to be successful. This argument supports the general literature on diversification which emphasises how successful change at the level of the firm is usually predicated on the building on existing expertise, rather than radical departures which put great strains on the internal organisation of the company. Indeed, it is widely acknowledged that any diversification process is very demanding, requiring a high level of management commitment over a long time-scale before any tangible benefits accrue.

The emphasis on government assistance returns us to the original concern. Walker *et al*, Dussauge, and Gilmore and Coddington all put the case for a fit between a defence companies existing production, and large-scale civil systems augmented by the relationship between defence firms and government. But this does not adequately address the issue of defence systems integration. Even for government civil contracts there would still exist what could be described as redundant complexity.

An obvious question is how efficient this exercise would be if other non-defence companies have a civil production capacity which the government could use instead of a converting firm? Clearly, even at the level of government contracts, the potential for conversion or even diversification is one which needs very critical evaluation.

Conclusion

In focusing on the technological dimension of the systems level defence company, the question of complexity has emerged as a key issue when relating production capacity and organisation to policies of conversion and diversification. While the general literature on company diversification would alert us to the organisational and cultural problems facing any firm which embarks on a radical change of product and market orientation, recent research suggests that both defence systems companies, and others producing subsystems and components at the lower levels of the product hierarchy, have the potential to make the transfer to civil work if certain criteria are satisfied.

For systems manufacturers, these stem from the existence of similar large-scale civil systems and the relationship with governments expected to provide new public sector investments to stimulate the conversion process. However, the question of the specialist requirements of defence systems integration and the organisational and cultural barriers to conversion resulting from that specialism need to be addressed. The research of Schofield and others suggests that companies, or divisions of companies, face considerable difficulties in adapting those technologies to civil work without considerable dislocation. Indeed, the process of conversion through organic change at the factory-site level is an extremely difficult one for specialised defence companies operating at the systems level of manufacturing, and in all the major sectors of defence production.

For companies in electronics and telecommunications, the question of complexity may not be so crucial and here the organisational barriers need to be addressed. The levels of defence dependency, potential civil markets, and possible government programmes are all further factors that need to be considered, but they are of secondary importance when related to the traditional model of factory-based conversion.

However, for companies operating at the lower levels, the technological barriers may not be so formidable. Much of what is produced can be described as dual-use technology with major applications in the civil field. Companies, in general, have experience in satisfying both defence and civil requirements from the same pool of technology and expertise, company organisation reflects their flexibility, recognising the normal dynamic of technological innovation that is operating particularly in electronic components and new materials. It is this technological capacity that may assist companies at the lower levels of the product hierarchy in their attempts to offset declining defence sales by finding new civil work.

While the focus of the paper has been on technology, other factors also need to be considered including management commitment, marketing and sales. At the national level, there is the general question about the overall technological capabilities and competitiveness of UK manufacturing. In this context, defence industries represent important assets of high-technology capacity and skills which the country can ill afford to be dissipated. At present though, the general pattern is for defence companies to cut back on production and employment, with only marginal efforts at diversification through organic growth and little or no evidence of conversion. As part of an overall industrial and technological policy that encouraged innovation, defence companies could be given incentives for R&D and investment in civil areas as well as expert assistance in identifying potential new markets and sales requirements.

Where closures of large military-industrial sites seems unavoidable, the UK may learn valuable lessons from the "community conversion" programmes in the USA. For a number of years, when military bases have been closed, the Office of Economic Adjustment (OEA) has assisted local communities in attracting new industries and services to the affected sites. In the UK, other staple industries have suffered rationalisation, and areas badly hit have been subject to special local development assistance from the UK government and the EEC. Similar schemes would seem appropriate in the case of defence-dependent communities.[26]

In summary, the concept of conversion needs to be broadened so that irrespective of the fate of particular military-industrial sites, a variety of mechanisms can be brought into play to maximise the potential for new civil activities. As such, conversion needs to be located in the broader framework of industrial, technological and regional policy rather than remain reliant on an isolated and inappropriate model for industrial change.

Endnotes

1. Economist Intelligent Unit (EIU), **The Economic Effects of Disarmament**, EIU, London, 1963, p. 115.

2. *Ibid.*, p 116.

3. Penrose, E., **The Theory of the Growth of the Firm**, Blackwell, Oxford, 1958, pp. 125-127.

4. Thorsson, I., **In Pursuit of Disarmament : Conversion from Military to Civilian Production in Sweden**, Liber, Stockholm, 1984, p. 90.

5. Office of Technology Assessment (OTA), **Holding the Edge**, United States Congress, Washington DC, 1989, p. 4.

6. See, for example, the takeover of Plessey by GEC and Siemens, **Financial Times**, 3/9/1989.

7. For definitions of conversion and diversification see US Arms Control and Disarmament Agency (ACDA), **Defence Industry Diversification : An Analysis with 12 Case Studies**, a report prepared by John Gilmore and Dean Coddington, ACDA, Washington D.C., 1966.

8. Science Policy Support Group (SPSG), **Future Relations Between Defence and Civil Science and Technology**, SPSG, London, 1991, P. 51.

9. IPMS, MSF & TGWU, **The New Industrial Challenge - The Need for Defence Diversification**, The Institution of Professionals, Managers and Specialists, London, 1990.

10. Walker, W, Graham, M and Harbor, B, **From Components to Integrated Systems : Technological Diversity and Interactions Between Military and Civilian Sectors**, Science Policy Research Unit, Sussex University, Brighton, 1987.

11. *Ibid*, p. 12.

12. Schofield, S, **VSEL Barrow and Arms Conversion - A Case Study of a Naval Shipyard in relation to the Theory and Practice of Arms Conversion**, School of Peace Studies, Bradford, Unpublished PhD thesis, 1990.

13. *Ibid*, pp. 290-97.

14. Kaldor, M, **The Baroque Arsenal**, Andre Deutsch, London, 1982.

15. Harbor, B, **Technological Divergence in the Development of Military and Civil Communications Systems : The Case of Ptarmigan and Systems X**, *Defense Analysis*, Vol 7, No 1, 1991, pp. 81-96.

16. *Ibid.*

17. Maddock, I, **Civil Exploitation of Defence Technology**, National Economic Development Organisation, London, 1983.

18. Hartley, K and Hooper, N, **The Economic Consequences of the UK Government Decision on a Chieftain Tank Replacement**, Centre for Defence Economics, University of York, 1990.

19. **Financial Times**, 19.11.1990.

20. Bristol Polytechnic, Research Unit in Defence Economics, **The Impact of Reduced Military Expenditure on the Economy of the South West**, Research Unit in Defence Economics, Bristol, 1991, p. 45.

21. *Ibid.*

22. *Ibid.*

23. Dussauge, P, **The Conversion of Military Activities : A Strategic Management of the Firm Perspective**, in Christian Schmidt and Frank Blackaby (eds) *Peace, Defence and Economic Analysis*, Macmillan, London, 1987.

24. *Ibid*, p. 427.

25. US Arms Control and Disarmament Agency, *op. cit.*, pp. 9-10.

26. Office of Economic Adjustment, (OEA), **Summary of Completed Base Economic Adjustment Projects 1961-1981 : 20 Years of Civilian Re-use**, Department of Defense, Washington D.C., 1981.

Index

For Product Safety Concerns and Information please contact our EU representative GPSR@taylorandfrancis.com
Taylor & Francis Verlag GmbH, Kaufingerstraße 24, 80331 München, Germany

www.ingramcontent.com/pod-product-compliance
Ingram Content Group UK Ltd.
Pitfield, Milton Keynes, MK11 3LW, UK
UKHW020159200926
475702UK00004B/531
* 9 7 8 1 0 4 1 2 5 6 0 1 4 *